The Handbook of:

Global Securities Operations

Jeremiah J. O'Connell
&
Neale Steiniger

Traders Press, Inc.®
PO Box 6206
Greenville, SC 29606

Serving Traders since 1975

Editing and Cover Design by
Teresa Darty Alligood
Editor and Graphic Designer
Traders Press, Inc. ®

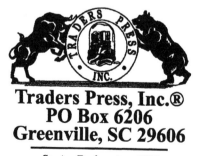

Traders Press, Inc.®
PO Box 6206
Greenville, SC 29606

Serving Traders since 1975

This book is dedicated to family and friends who
have patiently listened to us drone on about this
book for many years.

I want to thank Ellen and my children, Edward, Beth,
Mary Kate, Deven and Maggie for their
support and encouragement.

Table of Contents

Disclaimer

Because the procedures used in the marketplace are constantly evolving, our objective is to describe the processes used in global operation not the unique process used by an individual country or market. Since this book went to the publisher, there have been some notable changes referenced in this book. For example, Sungard has replaced Axion4 as the operator of GSTPA's Transaction Flow Monitor and a merger has been announced by Euroclear and CREST. To date, these changes have not affected the procedures described in the book.

Substantive changes will be addressed in future editions.

Jeremiah J. O'Connell & Neale Steiniger

Acknowledgements

When we first approached Traders Press, we agreed with Ed Dobson to send him a manuscript by the end of the year. Many deadlines passed as this book was written, re-written, updated and re-written again. For his patience and understanding we thank our publisher, Ed Dobson.

Countless people have helped make this book possible. Chuck Wiley, recuperating from major surgery and dealing with his many duties at SWIFT and axion4, readily agreed to write a forward on a subject foremost in everyone's mind. We asked associates that are experts in the industry to review each chapter. For all their generosity in giving their time and knowledge, we thank Anthony Buonocore, John Carroll, John Feeney, Christopher Gilbert, Nicole Goodnow, Cornelius Luca, Rey Mariquet, Andrew Nopper, Voilette Palion, John Robertson, Thomas Sakaris, William Salva, Charlotte Scott, Elizabeth Wilson and Clive Winton.

We also consulted with specialists at industry associations and experts within Brazil, Hong Kong and the United Kingdom markets to ensure that the chapter activities were reflected accurately. This book could not have been written without them.

Terry Allison, Association of National Numbering Agencies
Margarida Baptista, CBLC Brazil
Henri Bergstrom, European Central Securities Depositories Assoc.
Barbara Blumberg, Standard Chartered Bank
YF Cheung, Standard Chartered Bank
Trish Desouza, The International Securities Market Assoc.
Tim Dickenson, The International Securities Market Assoc.
Francine Gallet, Federation International des Bourses de Valeurs
Peter Gnepf, International Securities Market Assoc.
Stuart Goldstein, Depository Trust & Clearing Corp.
Stephen Grainger, Crestco
Stephen Letzler, Depository Trust & Clearing Corp.
Kathy Hawkes, Crestco
Dawn Hewitt, G30
Javier Jara Traub, American Central Securities Depositories Assoc.
Emily Jelich, International Swaps and Derivatives Assoc.
Jeffrey Manton, CLS Group Holdings Ltd.
Anthony Masiello, Clearstream
John Nordstrom, Euroclear
Michael O'Conor, FIX Protocol Committee
Michael Paztor, EMCC
Yolande Theis, Clearstream
Sofia Vanner, International Organization of Securities Commissions
Aviva Werner, EMTA

GLOBAL SECURITIES OPERATIONS: The Handbook of

Introduction
About This Book

As you read this, somewhere in the world an order is being placed for a security, a trade is settling, a new shareholder's name is being recorded, a dividend is being processed. The process being used is as automatic as the touch of a key or so complex it takes months to complete. This book explores the many processes used to settle global securities and the roles played by the Investors, the Brokers and the Banks in this era of ever growing international investing.

The Changing Landscape

Until the mid-80's, only a handful of Brokers were in the business of buying securities on the global exchanges. An even smaller number of Banks were able to settle the trade and hold the stock in custody for the Broker or customer. The activity was centered in a limited number of countries – mostly the United Kingdom and other large European countries and Japan, Australia, Hong Kong and Mexico. Orders were phoned to the Broker, confirmed by telex and settled when-ever (translation: whenever the stock was delivered, the trade settled). Physical delivery and manual registration were common and time consuming. The need to improve the system was not a high priority since the Investor in a foreign security was only an occasional Investor and the system worked just fine for the Brokers servicing their clients. Then the world discovered Western Mining in Australia, Telefonos de Mexico in Mexico and British Petroleum in the United Kingdom, not to mention Playmates and other growing retail companies Hong Kong – and volumes took off. Since registration into the new owners name took months, claiming a dividend became an administrative nightmare (well, maybe that hasn't changed).

Coping with Exploding volumes

Stock Exchanges, Brokers and Banks knew it was time for a change. Banks and Brokers realized that international investments could no longer be considered peripheral business – that departments had to be dedicated to clearing and settling non-domestic trades. Stock Exchanges began to investigate ways to reduce the massive paper flow required to confirm a trade or transfer ownership. The central depository, which had existed in only a few countries, became the standard for efficient settlement. Much has happened in the last fifteen years. Today, over 80 countries have regulated securities exchanges. And customers want to invest there. So Banks, Brokers and Investors have developed systems, streamlined procedures and established links to effect the efficient execution, clearance and settlement of an international security.

GLOBAL SECURITIES OPERATIONS: The Handbook of

Introduction
About This Book

This book was written for the Investor who invests in far away lands, Brokers and Banks who book, clear and settle the trade - - and yes, trace that dividend.

The book is divided into four sections: Pre settlement, settlement, post settlement and beyond settlement.
In the first section, pre-settlement, we explore the what, who and how an order is entered and processed. Investors, Brokers and marketplaces come in many forms and we will examine them all. There are two sides to every trade – a buyer and a seller. However, depending on who is on the other side of the trade, the matching process is different. The notification and agreement of the trade between the two parties is the first step toward the successful completion of the trade. The matching process for a trade executed between a Broker and their client is described in Chapter 3 – Trade Confirmation. The matching process for a trade executed between Brokers is described in Chapter 4 – Trade Comparison. Many markets have implemented procedures to protect the Brokers (and indirectly the Investors) from counter-party default. This is part of the clearance process and is described in Chapter 5.

In Part two, Settlement, we look at settlement systems and their impact on the Investor, the Broker and the Banks. Settlement, the exchange of securities and funds, sounds simple but is of great concern because of the risks involved and the processes unique to each market. If the funds are paid and the securities are not received (or if the securities are delivered and the funds are not paid), the counter-party is left exposed to potential loss. The securities industry has always relied on the premise that `my word is my bond.' This is still true today, however, exchanges have implemented changes to create a risk-less transfer of securities and funds. As improved systems are developed, many standardized procedures are evolving. However, enough differences still exist to cause confusion and errors. One of the priorities of the marketplace is to eliminate the number of trades that do not settle on time. One device for doing this is to close out (or buy-in) a trade when the security cannot be delivered. This has proved very costly for many an unwary Investor or Broker. The settlement systems used (as well as common problems) in the global marketplace are described in Chapter 6.
Since settlement cannot occur without securities, in Chapter 7 we look at where the securities are held and the role of the registrar in recording ownership of the securities. And since settlement cannot occur without funds, either on-hand or borrowed, in chapter 8 we explore how financing is achieved and managed.

Everything that happens to a security after it settles (except price increases or decreases – which are beyond the scope of this book) is the focus of Part three, the section entitled Post-Settlement. Stocks pay dividends, bonds pay interest, companies merge or change their name, stocks split, bonds are called or mature and companies issue new shares. When there is a corporate event or change in

Introduction
About This Book

the status of the securities, it is the responsibility of the entity (the Bank or Broker) holding the securities to process the event, on behalf of the owner of the securities. In the chapters on Income processing, Corporate Actions and Tax reclamation, we'll examine the processing of dividend and interest payments, stock dividends and bond redemptions, reclaiming tax paid on foreign investments and a host of other items that change the value of a security on a daily basis. The lending and borrowing of securities has evolved from an operations function, for fail avoidance, to a business to support complex investment strategies. In Chapter 12, we look at how this growing business is used to enhance revenues. Custody, the safekeeping, administration and reporting of positions, involves more than holding the securities and processing corporate action events. Other custody services are discussed in Chapter 13.

There have been advances in recent years, and many more on the drawing board. Can risk be measured? Can risk be eliminated? In the last section, Beyond Settlement, we'll take a look at the importance of risk measurement and what the industry mavens are doing to make investing in the international markets as effortless as investing in one's own market. Industry associations, CSDs and Stock Exchanges are all exploring methods to create a more efficient marketplace and reduce operational risk as they plan for the future global market. We'll take a look at who they are and what they're up to.

Comparing different procedures
Industry participants are implementing changes in the procedures used to process global securities. Changes include shorter settlement cycles, central matching facilities and expanded inclusion of a central counterparty and creation of guarantee funds to reduce settlement risk. However, not all industry participants nor markets have adopted a new procedure. As a result, one Investor or Broker might confirm a trade using a confirmation / affirmation method and another Investor uses the central matching facility. One market may clear trades against the two executing Brokers while another market may include the central counterparty. In each chapter you will find these changes addressed as each chapter explores current, evolving and proposed methods.

To compare different market procedures, most chapters contain flow charts on three markets – Brazil, Hong Kong and the United Kingdom. Contrast the comparison, clearance and settlement processes of each market. Notice the procedures used by the markets to process corporate actions and regulate securities lending.

To examine the entries and activities associated with each function, most chapters end with an example of the primary process described in the chapter.

Introduction
About This Book

The question and answer reviews at the end of each section are designed to reinforce important concepts. We hope they bring back pleasant memories of school days and help show the way through the maze of processing global securities.

Clarification of Terminology

The terms used by the industry to describe functions and participants vary by Broker, Bank and even Investors. Among Brokers the terms will vary as one Broker or Bank might refer to a function as one thing and another call it something else. The function might be called something else in another country. In this book we have attempted to use the most descriptive term for the function or participant. For example, the Broker located in the country where the order is executed is called the local Broker. The Investor's Broker is the term we use to describe the Broker in the Investor's country. However, some in the industry might describe the local Broker as the Broker in their own country. A Broker executes a trade or a deal, depending on where you work or live. The term market-side, for another example, refers to the process performed by the Brokers executing the trade (i.e., the `market'). In some countries it is called the street-side. An Agent can refer to a Settlement Agent, a Custodian Bank, a transfer or corporate actions Agent. Throughout the book we have attempted to clarify the context in which the term is used.

Finally, the book begins with a forward by Chuck Wiley. With Chuck's extensive experience in the industry and his affiliation with SWIFT and GSTPA's Axion4, he offers a unique insight into the global securities business.

Foreword
Virtual Matching Utilities (VMUs) as an Infrastructure for STP

This Foreword to *The Handbook of Global Operations* by Jerry O'Connell and Neale Steiniger was written while convalescing from a heart attack that was suffered coincidental to, but not the result of, the September 11, 2001 attacks on the World Trade Center in New York City and the Pentagon in Washington D.C.

As a frequent visitor to and traveler through the World Trade Center and its immediate surrounding area, I appreciated the landmark status that this unique complex gave to its place in Lower Manhattan. And I knew many people and companies that worked in and used these buildings. Tragically and ironically – given the focus of this Foreword, some of those friends and peers who were lost on September 11, including Arron Dack of Encompys, Scott Saber of UBS Warburg, and Hagay Shefi of Goldtier Technologies, were attending a conference on Straight Through Processing (STP) at the WTC. It is to these lost friends that I dedicate this Foreword.

I also want to thank Neale and Jerry for the opportunity to contribute to their new book. As the depth and breadth of global investment increases, all industry constituents will be forced to be more efficient in the operational processing of these investment activities. Neale's and Jerry's book should be an important aid in ensuring that the staff of these firms – who increasingly will become skilled knowledge-oriented exception processors as opposed to securities operations' traditional data entry clerks -- are properly trained and informed about global securities operations functions.

Chuck Wiley
Autumn 2001

Foreword

Operating in today's environment is difficult enough with high market volatility amidst increasingly larger average trade volumes per transaction, various regulatory initiatives and an increasingly competitive marketplace for providers of investment management, brokerage and custodian/trust services.

As such, it is often difficult to focus on the need for Straight Through Processing (STP), but it must be the fundamental consideration in preparing financial services firms for a future that will be even more volatile and volume driven than today. Particularly as settlement cycles shorten, as they will continue to do in all major markets on a global basis.

To prepare for this, a number of so-called Virtual Matching Utilities (VMUs), have been created to provide commonly-used infrastructure for comparing and matching trades as an integral part of the trade settlement process.

VMUs can exist purely on a domestic basis in certain markets, such as Japan's Jasdaq-sponsored Kessai Shogo System (also known as the PSMS (Pre-Settlement Matching System), and the trade comparison and matching infrastructures envisaged for the Singapore and Canadian markets. They also exist globally, where three entities, as of the last quarter of 2001, have announced their intent to deploy VMUs:

- **GSTP AG / axion4gstp**

    Sponsored by an association of more than 100 financial services firms in more than 40 countries, the Global Straight Through Processing Association (GSTPA) and its sister company, GSTP AG, have been created by the global securities industry to develop an industry-designed and -sponsored infrastructure to facilitate multilateral trade comparison. This infrastructure links investment managers and broker/dealers with custodians in a cooperative manner and is designed to significantly reduce the high trade failure rates and costs that characterize today's global trading environment.

    Through the dedication of its membership, over the past two years, the GSTPA has developed and subsequently registered a patent for the Transaction Flow Manager (TFM), which is the core matching engine of the GSTP solution. In order to facilitate the development of the TFM, a new Swiss-based operating company, GSTP AG, was established in 2000. GSTP AG, based in Zurich, will license the intellectual property of the TFM from the GSTPA, which will continue as an industry association engaged in research, education and other industry initiatives.

    As a result of a rigorous 3-stage, 9 month selection process that concluded in December 1999, a consortium composed of the following companies was selected to deliver the utility: SIS (SIS SEGAINTERSETTLE AG, a company of FSG Swiss Financial Services Group), TKS-Teknosoft S.A. (a software and development company working with Tata Consultancy Services, an Indian software development Consultancy) and SWIFT (a financial industry owned co-operative).

    The three companies have created axion4gstp ltd, referred to as axion4. axion4 will deliver to GSTP AG the solution, composed of the TFM (Transaction Flow Manager), the network services and the access modules. axion4 will provide all the infrastructure to support the project, e.g. implementation, customer support, education, product management, sales and marketing, standards, vendor management, finance and control, etc. The system will go into production at the beginning of 2002, following a 33-member pilot test period during the second half of 2001.

- **Omgeo**

    Omgeo is a global joint venture of the Depository Trust & Clearing Corporation (DTCC) and Thomson Financial, providing a suite of Transaction, Information and Performance services to the global securities industry.

Building on a set of products from Thomson's Electronic Settlements Group (ESG), including Oasys and Global Oasys for Investment Manager and Broker/Dealer trade comparison, and Alert, a standing settlement instructions database, and the Tradesuite products of DTCC, Omgeo will focus on moving its customer base from today's methods of trade processing to a global workflow solution for trade management.

Omgeo was created not just to improve trade processing, but to provide more comprehensive solutions that affect all points along the trade processing and settlement cycle. While all existing ESG and TradeSuite services become part of the Omgeo family and will continue to be supported by Omgeo, they are developing new evolutionary services – branded as Intelligent Trade Management, the core of which is the Central Trade Manager, which will act as the engine for Omgeo's VMU.

- **SunGard**

  In an attempt to leverage the community of 20,000 clients who use SunGard products and services, the Sungard VMU offering is an effort to help its existing clientele to reach T+1 without going to a third-party provider. SunGard expects to provide its existing clients -- broker/dealers, investment managers and custodians -- post-trade matching services, rather than seeing them communicate and match manually or go to a third party service provider and incur extra costs.

  SunGard will leverage its e-processing intelligence solution and intelliMATCH (reconciliation and automated exception-processing) engine as the core matching engine for its VMU, which will – like many other SunGard services, be run on a service bureau, or Application Service Provider (ASP), basis. The enhancement of SunGard's Transaction Network to deliver an outsourced match, in which case SunGard would function as an agent of the underlying institution, will enable SunGard to deliver confirmations back to Omgeo, GSTPA or other VMU. The SunGard Transaction Network is comprised of different object-oriented applications that are integrated using middleware from SunGard Business Integration.

Over time, it is probable that other VMUs will emerge, either in a domestic context as noted above, or on a global basis through, perhaps, a consortium of Central Securities Depositories or Stock Exchanges, or through other large vendors that operate in a global capacity.

The Future of Trade Comparison Matching

If the global securities industry is indeed facing a world of multiple VMUs, both domestically and globally, what are the implications for global securities processing world of investment managers, broker/dealers and custodian banks?

Interoperability between VMUs may be the key to ensuring that these "utilities" work in a fashion that does not further bifurcate the global trade comparison and matching process. Matching by VMUs, with or without interoperability, will centralize processes that typically take place on a decentralized, firm-by-firm basis today. However, interoperability will be easier to achieve in domestic settings, where -- as in the US -- the regulators can mandate that all VMUs interoperate as a condition of being granted the right to match trades prior to settlement.

On a cross-border basis, it will be nearly impossible to achieve a regulatory framework for global interoperability, so the promise of interoperability on a global basis between VMUs must build off of the connectivity and information exchange built to satisfy domestic requirements. This should be achievable as long as standards are properly employed, secure network connectivity is in place between the VMUs' core matching engines, and proper Service Level Agreements (SLAs) are put in place and properly monitored and managed in order to control the scope and breadth of the interoperability process.

According to the United States Securities and Exchange Commission (SEC), interoperability can be defined as interfaces between Central Matching Services (a.k.a. VMUs) that enable end-user clients or any service that represents end-user clients to gain a single point of access to other Central Matching Services. Such interfaces must link with each Central Matching Service so that an end-user client of one Central Matching Service can communicate with all end-user clients of all Central Matching Services, regardless of which Central Matching Service completes trade matching prior to settlement.

In the following diagram, the concept of interoperability would enable an investment manager of one VMU to communicate, via a bridge or processing conduit, with a broker/dealer or custodian using another VMU. Custodians could also communicate across such bridges, as could broker/dealers for market-side (broker-to-broker) trades. Such links create a network effect that can bring the critical mass that users seek in employing VMUs, without obligating all counterparties and agents to be on the same primary VMU network.

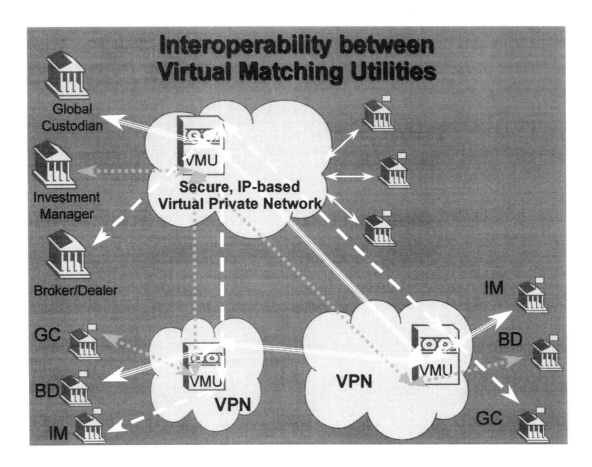

Aside from creating standardized rules for how interoperability works, as discussed below, it is also critical that each VMU communicates with other VMUs in a standardized manner that ensures consistency in the interface process. So connections between more than one VMU can be accomplished quickly assuming that an open architecture interface package is supported by all VMUs, based on an appropriate IP connectivity infrastructure, ISO15022 data elements and XML-based messaging protocols, and best market practices certification and performance management guidelines that are used to monitor and manage interactions between VMUs.

While interoperability holds out the promise that a user from any of the three constituencies shown in the diagram that will use VMUs can choose one and only one matching platform, in reality, only Investment Managers -- as drivers of the institutional investment business -- will be the only ones that can really be in such control. And even this may be true for only the largest Investment Managers who have the trading clout to dictate the choice of VMUs to their counterparties.

Broker/Dealers will most likely end up having to subscribe to and support multiple VMUs, as their Investment Manager customers may make VMU support a condition of trading. Similarly, Custodian Banks will have to support multiple VMUs since the Investment Managers will use this as a means of handing over the settlement process, and will force the Banks to accompany them in the process as a means of lowering their risk. The size of the Investment Manager, in many cases, will be the biggest determinant of how the Broker/Dealers and Custodian Banks support the VMU chosen by the fund manager.

Interoperability, again, holds out the hope that such redundant VMU support can be avoided by Broker/Dealers and Custodian Banks. Above and beyond the agreement regarding message standards and network connectivity, however, the following issues must be addressed for interoperability to bring the same type of flexibility and user benefits that a phone customer of, for instance, Verizon, has in communicating with a Sprint user:

- Where, How and When does matching take place? Where is the trade matched - by the VMU hosting the buying Investment Manager or the VMU supporting the selling Broker/Dealer)? How is the match process conducted – under tolerance constraints imposed by both counterparties or via standardized market practice guidelines? When does matching have to take place according to Best Market Practices expectations and how will matching performance statistics be shared between the VMUs?

- How is the matching process priced to users? Will interoperability impose a higher charge than if all constituents are directly connected to the same VMU during a specific trade match process? If so, will this impede market activity to the detriment of all VMU usage?

- How involved is the custodian bank in the matching process and what mechanism is used to populate standing settlement instructions (SSIs) – the custodian's and broker/dealers' internal databases (via a just-in-time enrichment process) or enrichment via a centralized SSI database? If there are more than one central SSI database, whose data prevails and how can the VMUs ensure that the data contained in these repositories is up-to-date and synchronized?

- What regulatory or self-regulating body or bodies will have jurisdiction over the interoperability process between VMUs and what mechanism(s) will they have to ensure that the Service Level Agreements are developed, maintained and monitored to ensure compliance? Again, this question has both domestic and global implications.

International telephone pricing mechanisms and regulatory frameworks may provide a potential foundation for concepts that would be applicable in the world of interoperable VMUs; however, the timeframe for organizing and administrating such a mechanism – particularly without the economies of scale afforded by the global telephone marketplace – may undermine movement toward VMU interoperability.

In the end, the industry may decide that interoperability is too difficult to put into place and the resulting pressure on VMUs may force them to merge or combine in some manner that eliminates the need for interoperability. In such a situation, the competitive pressures than may help lead to lower transaction costs and greater functionality from the VMU providers may be eliminated, thereby undermining one of the benefits of VMUs to the securities industry.

Nevertheless, VMUs do -- even without interoperability -- provide significant solutions to today's trade comparison and settlement process, and a host of concomitant benefits for each of the primary user constituents. These are outlined in Appendix ? of this book, are summarized below:

industry	broker/dealers	investment managers
• common standards • risk reduction • single channel communications • multi-lateral connectivity • utilise investments made for other services • model supports T+1	• fewer trade fails • reduced operating and financing costs • scalability and automation	• allows more focus on business • significant reduction of involvement in settlement process • reduced operational costs • MIS/SLA tracking • realize outsourcing strategies

global custodians

- earlier involvement in settlement process
- reduced operating and financing costs
- fewer trade fails
- realize insourcing opportunities

Recommendations

Many institutions may assume that choosing a VMU is conditional only upon the imposition of shorter settlement cycles, but in fact, VMUs have value that are significant and independent of a regulatory mandate for shorter settlement.

As such, financial firms involved in the institutional trade business, should seriously address the implementation of a VMU even under today's longer settlement cycles. This will enable these firms to fully integrate the VMU into their operations so that when settlement cycles do shorten, they will be prepared for the changes in a way that will have a less disruptive impact than if the VMU was introduced in the same timeframe as the reduction in the settlement cycle.

Other things that financial institutions should consider, or take account of, as part of the introduction of a VMU include:

- **Implement a formal, data-dictionary approach to messaging standardization**

  In this type of solution, there is a separation between the business elements contained in a message and their syntax (or formatting) representations. When a message-based instruction has to be produced, an application program queries the database and creates a temporary buffer containing relevant information. This buffer, which has a proprietary format, is kept as the technical representation of the business information and passed to the central message-processing hub.

  Using a central data dictionary hub for syntactical representation of the data implies that the same business element may be represented in an XML, FIX, GSTP, SWIFT or other format and the same data can be (re)used on multiple networks such as those connecting Central Securities Depositories, International Central Securities Depositories, local clearing firms, stock exchanges, etc.

ISO 15022 business elements and rules have been selected as the way forward by the global securities industry to enable all players to communicate in a standardized way across the entire chain of a security's life cycle. ISO 15022 enables financial institutions, through business analysis and modelling, to take advantage of all the new features and values for which the messages can accommodate, from trading, through confirmation, settlement, reconciliation, corporate actions and collateral management. In the medium and long term, ISO 15022 implementation within a data dictionary framework will decrease operational costs as software update and maintenance costs will be reduced since it is not necessary to rework all the development and system integration efforts each time a new ISO 15022-based message is created.

- **Improve the support of referential data**

Referential data such as security master details, securities and organizational identifiers and cross-reference information, and standing settlement details, etc. provides much of the 'static' information that complements trade-specific transactional details as part of the trade comparison, matching and settlement processes.

According to a report by the Tower Group, Reuters and Capital Markets Company, as much as 30 per cent of failed trades are caused as a direct result of poor data management. The chief cause of the fails is attributed to the inaccurate identification of settlement counterparties.

Moreover, over one third of the industry does not have a reference data strategy, despite the fact that 10 percent of organizations employ over 200 staff to re-key information, with as much as a third of the industry facing a situation where 90 per cent of their data is updated manually. Less than 5 per cent of the industry has automated maintenance for over 90 per cent of their reference data.

Clearly, as settlement cycles shorten and the industry moves to a more centralized model for trade comparison, (via one or more VMUs), the need to exchange referential data that is of high quality and therefore, can be relied upon by the VMUs and the various parties using this data, will increase dramatically.

- **Adhere to industry best market practices**

Message standards provide a mechanism, or syntax, for formalizing the communication of information between two counterparties that helps to remove any ambiguities in the process. However, because of the nature of standards, the message process involves the use of both mandatory and optional fields, and typically, allows firms flexibility in the way that the message content is communicated.

Such flexibility is both a blessing and a curse – it provides a means of encoding certain information that may be important to either the sender or the receiver, but it also limits the standardization of the communication process because what may be important to one set of correspondents, may be irrelevant to another set.

Market practices within a user community exchanging standardized messages provide a means by which the group defines and enforces a level of consistency regarding the scope and format of the message contents. In this way, the market practice becomes the 'rulebook' that helps determine what should and should not be included, how this content should be constituted within the context of the message standard, and the conditions under which the message contents can or should be changed and/or altered to suit the communication requirements associated with the underlying transaction.

Without the use and enforcement of market practices, standardization can be compromised as noted above, but more importantly, ancillary processes -- such as operational alerts/warnings and performance benchmarking that are tied to how and when the standards are employed for communication -- can also be undermined. Market Practice guidelines need to be utilized at the group or user community level to ensure that communication becomes appropriate to the needs of the transaction and so that external STP can be put into place. However, unless Market Practices are adhered to at the individual firm level, such community-level utilization will not be possible.

Safe automotive driving conditions depend on each and every driver adhering to the 'rules of the road' – in the same way, if one market practitioner disobeys the agreed-upon Market Practice conditions, all users will suffer and the underlying rules – or in this case the Standards – will be undermined, with the concomitant negative impact on external STP, communication costs and counterparty risk.

- **Treat STP as an end-to-end, rather than a purely internal operational process**

  Too many financial firms focus their attention on an internal, as opposed to a fully end-to-end, STP process.

  This often leads to situations where communication within the firm is fully 'STP-able' in terms of the integration between the firm's various front-, middle-, and back-office systems, but breaks down once it leaves the firm – either because it goes out as a completely un-automatable facsimile, or because the electronic standards employed in communicating with the external party don't adhere to accepted Market Practice guidelines and therefore can't be processed by the recipient in an automated fashion. In either case, this forces the recipient to re-key or correct the information, and therefore, impedes their own STP rates.

  For STP to become the foundation for operational efficiency and cost/risk reduction that the financial industry anticipates, it must not be treated as a process that occurs in a vacuum bounded by the walls of the firm Instead, it has to be seen as an end-to-end process that benefits not only the firm sending the message in an automated manner, but the firm receiving the message in a way that allows them to fully automate its associated processing.

  VMUs provide a greater opportunity than in a more traditional point-to-point connectivity model to rigidly enforce adherence to message standards and the associated market practice guidelines, because the VMU service provider can be given the authority to validate message contents at a much more rigorous level to ensure proper functioning of the matching model. However, if the users of the VMU don't ensure that their messages accommodate the agreed-upon standards and market practice requirements, the whole matching process can be severely compromised. Hence, the golden rule for VMU users must be to treat other users as one would like to be treated – meaning that messages must be structured and populated to ensure full end-to-end STP for both the sender and the receiver.

Part I

Pre-Settlement

Chapter 1
Setting the Stage

Part 1: PRE-SETTLEMENT
Chapter 1
Setting the Stage

This chapter sets the stage for processing foreign securities. The main cast of participants in executing an order is the Investor, the Broker, the Custodian Banks, the Marketplace and Settlement facilities. Exhibit 1-1 lists the participants in a typical overseas trade. You will notice there are more participants when executing an overseas trade than when investing in one's own country. To invest in an overseas security, the Investor must have access to that overseas marketplace and settlement facility. As a result, there may be two Brokers (one in the Investor's country and one in the country of investment) and two Banks (again, one in each country).

In this chapter we will examine the
- Participants involved in execution, clearance and settlement of a trade
- Products traded in the global marketplace and their characteristics

Who are the participants when dealing overseas?

The Investor is the person or institution placing an order to buy or sell a security in the market - their own or an overseas market. Because some exchanges have regulations about the type of Investor, let's examine the different types of Investors. Investors are grouped into two broad categories - retail and institutional Investors.

Retail Investors are individuals who buy stocks for their own investment or retirement account. Typically, they invest smaller amounts of money at any one time and leave their securities in their account with their Broker. Some exchanges (for example India) do not permit individual Investors to buy on their exchanges. They require an Investor be an institution with a minimum amount of assets.

Institutional Investors are companies that invest on behalf of other groups or individuals. Examples of institutional Investors include mutual funds, retirement funds or unit trusts. Institutional Investors are sometimes referred to as Foreign Institutional Investors (FIIs) Qualified Foreign Institutional Investors (QFIIs) Accredited Investors (AIs), Qualified Institutional Buyers (QIBs), etc. Typically, they invest larger amounts of money at any one time and request delivery of their securities to their Agent or Custodian Bank.

Part 1: PRE-SETTLEMENT
Chapter 1
Setting the Stage

Exhibit 1-1

Participants in an overseas trade

- The Investor
    The Retail Investor
    The Institutional Investor
- The Brokers
    The Investor's Broker (IB)
    The Local or Overseas Broker (LB)
- The Marketplace (Exchange, Over the Counter, ATS or ECN)
- The Agent or Custodian Banks
    The Global Custodian Bank (GCB)
    The Sub-(or local) Custodian Bank (SCB)
- The Foreign Exchange Bank
- The Clearance Agency
- The Central Securities Depository (CSD) or Settlement Facility

---

The Broker is the participant who will execute the order. In many cases, two Brokers will be involved in executing the trade - - one is the Broker from the country of the Investor (we call this Broker the Investor's Broker - IB). The other is the Broker who is a member of the exchange where the trade will be executed. The Broker who is a member of the exchange or executes orders in the overseas market is called the Local Broker (LB). When will two Brokers be involved in executing a trade? When an Investor buys a stock listed on their own local exchange, they enter the order through a Broker who is a member of the stock exchange as well as a member of the clearing agency and depository. That same Broker may or may not be a member of another country's exchange (sometimes it's not cost effective, nor in some cases, permissible for foreign Brokers to be direct members). As a result, the Investor will place the order through a Broker in their own country, who forwards the order to a Broker in the other county.

> The Investor's Broker (IB) is the Broker in the Investor's own country. If they are a member of the exchange where the Investor wants to deal, they can execute the trade directly on their Investor's behalf. If the IB is not a member they will forward the order to a Broker who is a member of the exchange. Brokers execute orders for retail Investors, for institutional Investors, for themselves or for other Brokers. The Broker executes orders as a market-maker or as an agent. A Broker executing a trade as a market-maker, executes the trade versus their trading account (the trade is called a proprietary trade or a principal trade). A Broker executing the

trade as an agent, executes the trade versus another Broker, a client or on the exchange.

The Local Broker is a Broker who is a member of the exchange where the Investor wants to invest.

The Marketplace is where the order can be executed. Orders in stocks, bonds and derivatives are executed on the country's listed exchange, in the over-the-counter (OTC) market, through an alternative trading system or a matching system. The Marketplace is composed of the following types of entities:

- Main Exchange
  - o Listing requirements for the Main Exchange include a minimum number of years of financial statements (usually 3 years), a minimum number of years of profitability (usually 2 or 3) and a minimum number of shareholders. Typically, it's the larger, established companies that meet these requirements and trade on this exchange.
- Over the Counter (OTC), New or Emerging Exchanges
  - o Most countries have an OTC or a Emerging Market Exchange for new and developing companies which do not yet meet the requirements of the Main Exchange
- Electronic Communication Networks (ECN) execute orders received from their participants. The order execution is continuous, i.e., orders that can be matched are executed as received
- Alternative Trading Systems (ATS) also execute orders received from their participants. However, unlike an ECN, an ATS matches buy and sell orders during set crossing sessions. These systems are also known as matching systems or Private Trading Systems (PTS).

Before deciding to invest in a foreign security, Investors and IBs must first determine the rules of the Marketplace. For example, does the marketplace require that the Investor receive approval from the country's regulatory agency? Are there restrictions on who may invest in a market? Are there restrictions on the number of shares that can be purchased? Does the marketplace permit short sales? What is the settlement period? Other useful information includes the market hours, the products that trade in the market and how an order will be executed.

The Custodian Bank or Agent is the Investor's and/or IB's agent or representative. When dealing in an overseas market, the Bank or Agent plays a crucial role as the institutional Investor's and Broker's representative in the country where the trade is taking place. The Bank or Agent provides information

Part 1: PRE-SETTLEMENT
Chapter 1
Setting the Stage

on the overseas marketplace, settles the trade and holds the securities in custody.

To facilitate the process of finding a Bank in each country, many Investors and Brokers select a Bank (or agent) in their own country (called the Global Custodian Bank) who contracts with local Banks to act as their agent in the overseas market (the local Bank is called the Sub or local Custodian Bank). The Global Custodian Bank (GCB) develops a network of banks - either a local Bank or one of their own branches with whom they contract to settle trades in the local market. The Investor or Broker authorizes the GCB to settle a trade; the GCB forwards this information to their local or Sub Custodian Bank (SCB). Examples of GCB's include J. P. Morgan Chase Bank, Citibank, Credit Suisse, Deutsche Bank, Paribas and State Street Bank. Some Brokers, who have overseas branch offices or affiliations with local Brokers or Banks, will utilize that branch as their execution and settlement agent in that country rather than use a GCB.

The Foreign Exchange (F/X) Bank is the Bank used by the Brokers or the Investor to buy (or sell) the currency needed for (or resulting from) the trade. Most Banks and many Brokers trade currency through their F/X trading desk. An institutional Investor determines the amount of foreign currency they need to settle their trades and executes the F/X through a Bank that trades currencies – this might be their own GCB or another Bank of their choosing. Banks that trade a wide variety of currencies include Hong Kong Bank (HSBC), Credit Suisse and Citibank.

The Clearance agency is the entity that facilitates settlement by obtaining the trade information, matching the details of the buyer's and seller's trade and reporting the results of the match to the executing Brokers (and, in some cases, to the CSD). With this information, the buyer will arrange to pay for the securities and the seller will arrange to deliver the securities (i.e., settle the trade). The clearance process may also include netting the trades between counter-parties and protecting investors against Broker default by implementing and managing a guarantee fund. The clearance process is performed by different entities depending on many factors - - some markets do not have a separate clearing agency and the process is performed by the stock exchange system or the CSD; some securities are not listed on the exchange and are cleared through an industry clearing system or directly between the counter-parties.

The Central Securities Depository (CSD) or Settlement System is the entity responsible for delivering the securities, receiving or paying funds and processing securities resulting from corporate actions. Depending on the system used in the country, settlement may involve a physical transfer of the certificate

Part 1: PRE-SETTLEMENT
Chapter 1
Setting the Stage

between the buyer and seller or it may be a computerized book-entry transfer between the buyer and seller's accounts at a depository.

The Products

Let's examine some of the products that are traded in the marketplace and how their characteristics effect trading and settlement. Exhibit 1-2 lists examples of the types of securities that trade in the international markets.

Equity Products

Ordinary shares are the most common type of equity securities issued. Ordinary shares typically are issued with voting and dividend rights. Many countries limit the amount of voting rights that may be held by any single investor or cumulatively, the number that may be held by all foreign investors. For example, when some ordinary shares are issued, they are issued as Series A and some as Series B shares. The Series A shares may be owned by the local investor and Series B by the foreign investor. Sweden, Denmark, Finland and Norway are examples of countries that have issued both Series of shares but have since removed the foreign investor restriction (i.e., both may be owned by anyone). China and the Philippines are examples of countries that still have both Series and limit ownership by foreign investors to the Series B shares.

On other exchanges, you will find only one class of ordinary shares but the percentage of shares that can be owned by the foreign investor is regulated. The percentage may vary by country, security and industry and change as countries reduce (or increase) the restrictions on foreign ownership. These shares trade as one security until the maximum number of shares permitted are owned by foreign investors (called reaching their foreign cap). When investing in shares that have a foreign ownership ceiling, investors should be aware of the following effects of ownership:

1) The premium price of a foreign registered shares
2) The diligence needed at settlement to ensure delivery of the correct type of share
3) The effect of buying local registered shares
4) The method used to track foreign investor holdings

The Premium Price
When the cap is reached, the foreign owned shares may begin to trade at a premium price over the local owned shares. The exchange will quote two prices, one for local shares and one for foreign (also called alien) shares. For example, assume Thailand's Siam Cement Ordinary shares are limited to 20% foreign ownership. When 20% of the shares are registered to foreign

shareholders, and more foreigners' want to buy the stock, the foreign registered shares may trade at a price higher than the local registered shares.

Ensuring correct delivery
When processing the trade, care should be taken to book the correct description of the shares - - either `foreign' or `local' shares. If the investor purchased foreign registered shares (especially if they paid a higher price for the shares) their custodian Bank will ensure that the shares received at settlement are foreign registered shares. If local registered shares are inadvertently accepted, registration of the shares may not be possible if the foreign cap (or limit) has been reached.

Effect of Owning Local Registered Shares
Most countries that have local and foreign shares permit local registered shares to be purchased (and sold) by foreign investors. However, if the foreign cap has been reached, these shares cannot be registered until such time as a foreign investor sells their shares or the percentage of shares available for foreign investment is increased.
Positions in local registered shares should be monitored for:
   a) Registration - - shares will remain local until they can be registered as foreign. Before selling, check the status. To avoid an error, the shares should be sold as local shares if the shares are still in local form. Remember that local and foreign registered shares often trade at different prices.
   b) Entitlements - - in many countries, it is the registered holder who is entitled to dividends, votes, etc. Shares pending registration are not entitled to these benefits.

Tracking Ownership Limits
Monitoring the quantity of shares owned by foreign investors is normally the responsibility of the company's or the exchange's registrar. In most countries, the registrar announces that the foreign ownership limit is near (called the caution limit) or that the limit has been reached and no additional shares can be registered to a foreign investor. Some exchanges track the ownership limit at the exchange (instead of by the registrar at the time of settlement). For example, the Mak-Trade execution system of the Philippine stock exchange tracks the Foreign Investor limit. When the limit is reached, additional buy orders from foreign investors will not be executed.

Part 1: PRE-SETTLEMENT
Chapter 1
Setting the Stage

Exhibit 1-2

Examples of the Most Frequently Traded Products

Equity Products
Ordinary Shares
Series A and B
Foreign and Local

Preferred Shares
Cumulative Preferred
Preferred Investment Certificates

Equity related Products
Depositary Receipts
Subscription Rights, nil-paid shares
Partly Paid Shares
Warrants

Non Voting Equity Products
Investment Certificate
Voting Certificate
Dividend-right Certificate

Debt Products
Corporate
Government
Foreign Bonds
Eurobonds
Global Bonds
Brady Bonds

Form of debt products
Straight or Convertible
Fixed or Floating
Par or Discount
With Warrants, call or put options

Futures and Options
Equity Options
Index Futures
Government Bond Futures
Currency Futures

Part 1: PRE-SETTLEMENT
Chapter 1
Setting the Stage

Equity Related Products

Depositary Receipts, subscription rights and partly paid shares are the most frequently traded products of equity related instruments.

- *Depositary Receipts* (DR) are receipts (or sometimes shares) that are issued and traded in a country other than where the shares were issued and represent the underlying shares traded on the overseas exchange. The most common are Global Depositary Receipts (GDRs) and American Depositary Receipts (ADRs). Both are typically issued by a DR Bank - the most active DR Banks are Bank of New York, Citibank, Deutsche Bank and J.P. Morgan Chase. DR's are created by purchasing the underlying shares and delivering them to the DR Bank responsible for issuing the receipts. The receipts are delivered by the DR Bank to the account of the purchaser either at Euroclear (where most GDRs are held) or the Depository Trust Corp. (where most ADRs are held).

- *Subscription rights* are issued to existing shareholders in proportion to their holdings. For example, if H.K. & China Gas were to issue new shares, they may offer their existing shareholders the right to purchase these additional shares through a rights offering. Investors frequently face problems with rights issues for two reasons: The first reason is the time the issue is outstanding - - the typical rights issue exists for only about two weeks and notification of the offering (from the issuer, to the SCB, to the GCB, to the investor) is time consuming and quite often frantic. The second reason is the restrictions that may be placed on shareholders to subscribe or sell their rights. These restrictions may be at the issuer's option or the regulations governing new issues in the country of the shareholder. The issue's Prospectus will contain details on any restrictions.

- *Partly paid shares* are new shares issued in installment or partly paid form. The investor is asked to pay only part of the total price as the initial payment and subsequent payments are required at a later date. Tracking these shares and collecting the periodic payments can be a logistical nightmare for the Brokers and custodian Banks that are holding shares in custody.

Debt Products

Debt products (also known as bonds) are issued in the international market place by many types of issuers, in many forms and in all currencies. They are issued in either a specific country and traded on that country's exchange or OTC market or

Part 1: PRE-SETTLEMENT
Chapter 1
Setting the Stage

are issued in the international marketplace where they are traded by market-makers in many markets including London, Zurich, Frankfurt and New York, Tokyo.

- The local debt market of a country is made up of bonds issued by corporations and local governments; denominated in the local currency or another country's currency; they may pay interest in the same currency in which the bonds are denominated in or another currency - - e.g., dual currency bonds offer investors a choice of currency in which to receive their interest payments.

    The types of bonds include:
    - Convertible Bonds
        - Bonds that are exchangeable into another asset (usually stock). They are converted at a price at parity with the other asset. The parity price is the equivalent price, i.e., upon conversion, the value of the bonds to be converted and the acquired shares will be of equal market value.
    - Bonds issued with warrants or options attached.
        - The warrant gives the investor the opportunity to exchange the warrant for another asset (e.g., shares or cash payments triggered by the price of oil).
        - A bond with a put option gives the investor the right to sell back the bond to the issuer at a set price during a stipulated period of time.

- In addition to bonds that are issued in a specific country, there are bonds issued in the international marketplace. Most of these are Eurobonds (also called International Bonds) that are issued in almost all currencies (most in USD, EUR and JPY). Eurobonds are traded in more than one market (unlike bonds that are listed on one specific exchange) and most settle through Clearstream or Euroclear. Another type of bond that has been widely issued are the Brady Bonds. These bonds are issued as a result of restructuring debt, they are denominated in many currencies –including USD, EUR, JPY, and GBP.

Futures and Options

As shown in Exhibit 1-2, futures and options are created on many standard products. The characteristics of derivative contracts vary by country and contract. When dealing in options in a particular market, the features to look for include the terms of contract and exchange regulations, which will specify:
- The underlying asset
- The number of shares the contract represents
- When the contract will expire
- When the contract may be exercised.

Part 1: PRE-SETTLEMENT
Chapter 1
Setting the Stage

For example, in the U.K., a Glaxo Smithkline 110 Sept call option gives the owner the right to buy 1,000 Glaxo Smithkline shares at 110 and will expire on the Third Wednesday in September. The option may be exercised any time before the September expiration date. Options that that may be exercised at any time are called American style options (vs. options that can only be exercised on the expiration date which are called European style options).

Now that we've seen the products that are traded and who the players are, in the next chapter we will examine their role in the execution of an order.

BRAZIL TRADE LIFE CYCLE

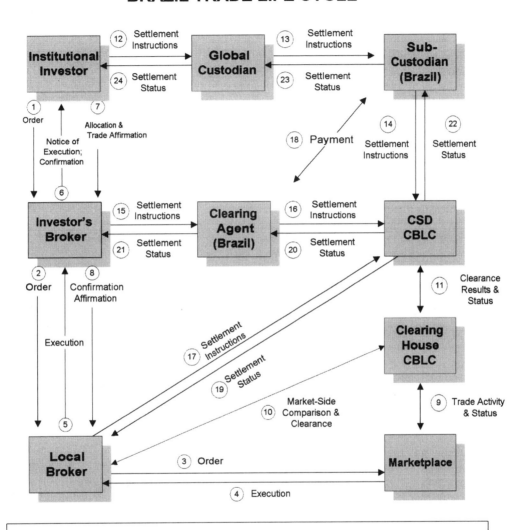

Footnotes:
Bovespa: Bolsa de Valores (Stock Exchange) de Sao Paulo
CBLC: Companhia Brasileira de Liquidacao e Custodia (Brazilian Clearing House and Depository)
BACEN: Banco Central do Brasil (Central Bank of Brazil)
CETIP: Central de Custodia e Liquidacao Financiera de Titulos (Payment Netting system)
SELIC: Sistema Especial de Liquidacao e Cuatrodia (Book entry system for government bonds maintained by BACEN)

HONG KONG TRADE LIFE CYCLE

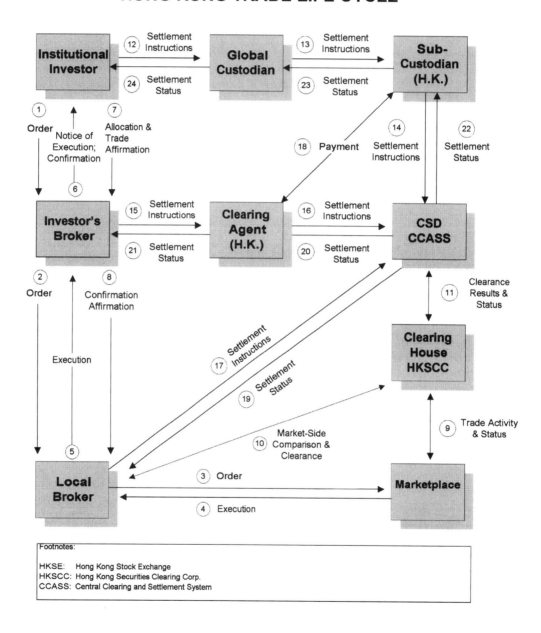

Footnotes:

HKSE: Hong Kong Stock Exchange
HKSCC: Hong Kong Securities Clearing Corp.
CCASS: Central Clearing and Settlement System

UNITED KINGDOM TRADE LIFE CYCLE

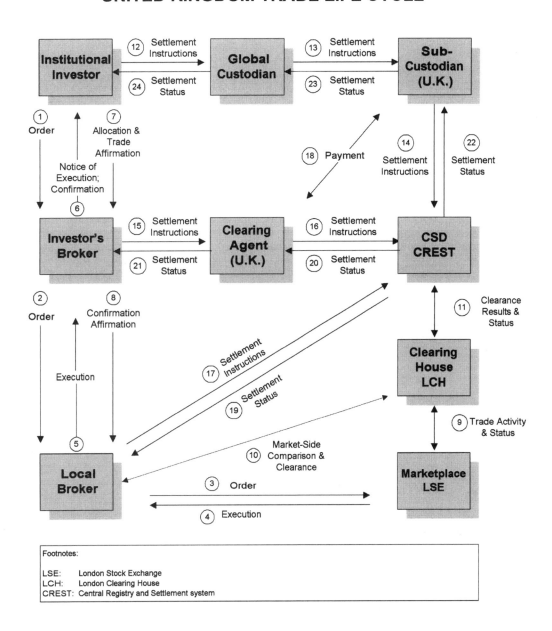

Footnotes:

LSE: London Stock Exchange
LCH: London Clearing House
CREST: Central Registry and Settlement system

Part I

Pre-Settlement

Chapter 2
The Order Flow

Part I: PRE-SETTLEMENT
Chapter 2
The Order Flow

We are all familiar with how an order is executed in our own country. We even know the regulations in our marketplace. For example, we know how an order can be entered, the hours the market is open, the number of shares in a round lot and when the trade will settle. But every market has their own practices and regulations. Before dealing in an overseas market, investors should familiarize themselves with the regulations, execution and settlement requirements that apply to the foreign investor.

As you read this chapter, contrast an order placed in your own market with an order placed in an overseas market. When investors trade in their local market, there are very few restrictions on the securities they can buy and they typically deal with a Broker who has direct access to the execution and settlement facilities. But, as we saw in the previous chapter, the Broker we use in our own country may not be a member of an overseas exchange.

In this chapter, we will examine:
- Execution methods
- Market regulations and practices
- Steps in the trade flow
- The order flow for an order placed by a typical retail investor
- The order flow for an Institutional Investor's order

Execution Practices in the International Marketplace

How is an order executed? The rules of a marketplace tell us when and how an order will be executed. These procedures have a direct impact on the price of execution and the trade's clearance and settlement. Before investing in a market, a investor should determine:
- The market hours
- The types of securities traded and their unit of trading
- The types of orders
- The foreign ownership restrictions
- Trading procedures including the method/s of execution
- The settlement period

Every market has their own unique characteristics. When a trade may be executed varies by market. Where a type of security trades also varies - - some markets trade equities, bonds and derivatives on the floor of their exchange, while other markets have separate markets for each instrument. What securities can be owned is another variable - - the foreign ownership restrictions range from protecting only sensitive industries to wide ranging restrictions on the quantity of shares in general.

Part I: PRE-SETTLEMENT
Chapter 2
The Order Flow

Trading procedures and regulations include the method of execution (order or price-driven, floor or screen based, continuously traded or limited price fixings), the time and price of an odd-lot execution (in some markets there is no distinction; in other markets odd lots trade at a set time of day) and the types of orders accepted (including the ability to sell short). Many securities trade in more than one market. Although their primary listing is in their home market, the security may trade on other exchanges or OTC markets as well as through the Alternative Trading Systems (ATS) or Matching Systems. Securities frequently are listed or trade in their home market as well as on other exchanges.

To contrast the characteristics of investing in the global markets, let's compare three exchanges -- Exhibit 2-1 shows the trading rules and regulations of the Sao Paulo Stock Exchange (Bovespa) in Brazil, the Hong Kong Stock Exchange (HKSE), and the London Stock Exchange (LSE) in the U.K.

The Market Hours
The hours the market is open determines when an order can be executed. Knowing the market hours becomes important the first time you hear news that may have an impact on the price of a security that you own. In an effort to buy (or sell) before the market closes, you place an order – but (you ask) when does the market close? Perhaps the market doesn't close. Some countries have execution systems that accept orders 24/7. The London market officially closes at 5:00 but, as with many exchanges, after-hours trading is available. Notice the Bovespa officially closes at 5:30 but trading in international issues continues until 10:00 p.m. Some markets have both a floor market and an electronic market. The hours may be different for trading on the floor and trading in the computerized system.

The Types of Securities traded and their unit of trading
The unit of trading (or round lot) varies with each market and each security. The unit of trading in Hong Kong securities is either 1,000 or 2,000; in Brazil it depends on the Market Value. Odd-lots (a quantity less than the unit of trading) are difficult to execute in most markets and purchasing an odd-lot is discouraged.
Note: When purchasing a round lot that is to be split among numerous accounts (the allocation process described later in this Chapter and in Chapter 3 – Client Confirmation), the quantities allocated to each account should also equal a round lot. For example, if a purchase of 10,000 shares of HK & China Gas were allocated to 4 accounts - each account would receive 2,500 shares. If the unit of trading for H.K. & China Gas is 1,000 shares, this leaves each account with an odd-lot (500 shares). It is not possible to transfer 500 shares and thus very difficult to sell.

The Types of Orders
The most common types of orders permitted around the world are market, limit and sell short orders. All markets accept orders to execute 'at market' (the best price at

Part I: PRE-SETTLEMENT
Chapter 2
The Order Flow

the time) and 'limit' orders (to buy or sell at a specified limit price). Markets that permit sell short orders, allow them under certain conditions. These conditions vary by market but most markets require 1) reporting the trade as a short sale to the exchange, 2) selling on a price increase or up-tick (this rule requires that the short sale be executed at a price either equal to the previous up tick or above the previously traded price) and 3) the ability to borrow. Since selling short is selling securities that are not owned, unless the securities can be borrowed, the settlement of the trade will fail. For this reason, the short sale order is contingent on the availability of the stock to be borrowed. In many markets borrowing is difficult which makes sell short orders permissible but not practical. And finally, some markets permit short sales only in designated securities.

Some markets accept qualifiers on the orders. The most common qualifiers are contingent, at opening or close, at discretion and fill or kill. A 'contingent' or conditional order is an order to buy or sell, subject to an event, e.g., executing a buy order only if a sell order is executed. Only a few markets accept 'at opening' or 'at close' (executing at the opening or closing market price) or 'at discretion' orders (orders to be executed at the Broker's discretion) or 'fill or kill' orders (orders to be executed immediately or cancelled).

The most common durations (i.e., the amount of time an order is in force) are good for the day (a Day order), good until the order is cancelled (GTC) or good for the week or month. All exchanges accept Day orders. Most accept GTC orders. However, to enter an order for a week or month, the Broker either enters a Day order and re-enters it each day or enters a GTC order and cancels it after the week or month.

Part I: PRE-SETTLEMENT
Chapter 2
The Order Flow

Exhibit 2-1 Trading Regulations

STOCK EXCHANGES:	BRAZIL	HONG KONG	THE U.K.
Market hours:	10:00 - 5:30 6:00 – 10:00	10:00 - 12:30 2:30 - 4:00	8:00 - 5:00

Method of Execution:
  Order-driven (OD)
  Price-driven (PD)
	OD and PD	OD	OD and PD

Round Lot / Unit of Trading:	most 100	1,000 or 2,000	500 / 1000
Types of Orders:	Market, Limit	Market, Limit	Market, Limit, Fill or Kill Conditional
Sell Short:	permitted with approval	permitted in designated Securities on 0/+ tick	permitted
Restrictions:	Specific Sectors	Broadcasting shares	National Declaration Shares
Settlement Period:	T+3	T+2	T+3

Foreign Ownership Restrictions
Foreign ownership restrictions on Hong Kong and the U. K. exchanges are few. The broadcasting industry is protected in Hong Kong (as in most countries) and the percentage of foreign ownership is controlled. The U.K. designates some securities as National Declaration shares and limits their foreign ownership. In Brazil, the percentage of Ordinary shares (with voting rights) that may be owned by Foreign Investors is restricted in Finance, Petroleum, Transportation and Telecommunications. (Restrictions on equity issues are addressed in Chapter 1)

Executing the order
After we've determined when the market is open, the round lot quantity and the restrictions that might impact our investment decision, the next question is - - How will this order be executed?

Orders are executed either by an order-driven system or a price-driven system. Some markets offer a combination of both.
- In an order-driven system, two orders (a buy order and a sell order) are entered and matched (either manually or electronically) by the electronic / computer system. In this system, the highest bidder buys the stock. For this reason, it is also known as an auction system. Exhibit 2-2 shows orders that have been entered into the London Stock Exchange Electronic Trading Service (Sets), an order-driven system. To execute an order in an order-

driven system, a buy (or sell) order is entered by a Broker on behalf of an investor, and waits until an order on the opposite side is entered. The orders are then matched with each other. If no match is entered, the order will not be executed. To find a match, many Brokers contact their customers or other Brokers to solicit orders. Upon finding a match, the Broker/s enters both orders in the system.

Exhibit 2-2 The U. K.'s Sets: Example of an Order-driven Execution System

GLXO.L ①		GLAXO SMITHKLINE PLC ②			PRV 1933-1935 ③
SET 1 GBp ④					
LAST ⑤	1944	1945	1947	1944	1947
1 ⑨	3620 ⑥	1944⑦	1948 ⑧	2250	1 ⑩
3	6826	1943	1949	8564	1
1	11000	1942	1950	10000	1
1	2000	1941	1955	5000	1
2	34450	1940	1958	25000	1

This screen tells us the following information on orders that have been placed in Glaxo Smithkline PLC:
1) The symbol for Glaxo Smithkline PLC
2) The full name of the security
3) The Previous Close: the closing bid was 1933 and offered price was 1935
4) The currency in which Glaxo is quoted (Great British Pounds)
5) The last five (5) prices traded: the last price was 1944 pence or 19 pounds and 44 pence
6) The quantity bid for: an order was placed to buy 3,620 shares at 1944p
7) The bid price: 19 pounds 44 pence
8) The offered price: 19 pounds 48 pence (or 1948p)
9) The number of orders represented in the bid: 1 order has been entered to buy 3,620 shares at 1944p. Notice the next line - three orders have been entered to total 6,826 shares.
10) The number of orders represented in the offer: one order has been entered to sell 2,250 at 1948p

NOTE: In a price-driven system, sometimes called quote-driven, Brokers advertise the price at which they will buy (called the bid) or sell (the ask or offer).
- The Brokers are called dealers or market-makers
- The bid and ask is referred to as the 'quote.'
- The difference in price between the bid and the ask is called the 'spread.'

GLOBAL SECURITIES OPERATIONS: The Handbook of

Part I: PRE-SETTLEMENT
Chapter 2
The Order Flow

- A bid wanted or Offer wanted is called a 'one sided quote' (this occurs when a Broker is looking to buy (or sell) but is unable to sell (or buy) themselves

To place an order, the investor contacts one of the Brokers advertising their quote and either negotiates a price with the Broker or trades at the price the Broker is quoting. Exhibit 2-3 shows the London Stock Exchange's Automated Quote system (SEAQ), London's price-driven system.

Exhibit 2-3 The U. K.'s SEAQ: Example of a Price-driven Execution System

```
SEAQ                                           371784        16:12
GLX    GLAXO SMITHKLINE PLC PLC Ord 25p     Currency GBX
NMS    50,000                                 CLOSE      1933-1950
PREV 5 TRADES    1944  1945  1947  1944  1947
VOLUME   9,729,000
①  GSCO KLWT 1945 - 1950  CSFS  WDR.

②  AITK   1944-1954 ③    25x25 ④   KLWT  1945-1955    50x50
    MLSB   1944-1955      50x50     CSFS  1940-1950    50x50
    MOST   1944-1955      50x50     DMG.  1943-1953    50x50
    GSCO   1945-1955      50x50     WDR.  1940-1950    50x50
```

Note: Glaxo Smithkline PLC is no longer quoted in SEAQ – Glaxo orders are executed in Sets. But to contrast the two systems, this SEAQ screen is simulated to show the market-makers' Glaxo prices.

As above in the Sets screen, the security symbol and title is shown as well as the currency (Great British Pounds – GBX), the closing price and previous 5 trades. Also shown is the Normal Market Size (NMS), which is the typical quantity traded. Additionally, the screen shows:

1) The Broker and best bid and offer: GSCO and KLWT with the best bid (1945p), and CSFS and WDR are offering to sell at the lowest price (1950p)
2) The Brokers who make a market in Glaxo
3) The bid and offer price of each Broker
4) The maximum quantity that they will buy or sell at that price. e.g., AITK will buy 25,000 shares at 1944p and sell 25,000 at 1955p.

Most exchanges are order-driven markets, but price-driven systems are increasing (although a small percentage of the overall global marketplace). Traditionally, larger equity securities were traded by market makers while smaller issues were executed in order-driven systems. However, since finding a matching order in a smaller issue can sometimes be a problem, market makers are increasing quoting smaller issues. Bonds that are listed on an exchange, trade under that exchange's system (order or price-driven) while the bonds that trade in the Over the Counter (OTC) marketplace are traded by market-makers. Since most bonds are traded by market-makers, the bond market is primarily a price-driven market.

And finally, the larger issues are typically traded in more than one market. Called Dual Listed Securities, these issues trade in their home market as well as other markets, including Frankfurt, London, New York, Tokyo and Zurich.

Exchanges are constantly evaluating the merits of the two systems. Both systems have their advantages and disadvantages.

According to industry experts, the price-driven systems offer better liquidity. Since a market-maker continuously quotes a bid and ask (or offer) price, an investor will always be able to buy or sell stock.

In an order-driven system, an order to buy will be executed only if there is a sell order for the quantity and at the price wanted. This system gives the investor direct access to the market (vs. through a market maker) and, from a processing point of view, the order-driven system can offer greater efficiency.

When an order is entered into an order-driven system, the order is matched and processed. The quantity, description, price and counter party will match, because the execution and matching are results of the same booking. This is called a locked-in trade (more on locked-in trades in Chapter 4). On the other hand, many orders executed in a price-driven system are negotiated over the phone, electronic mail or proprietary system and booked into the system after the trade has been agreed upon and executed. Frequently, counter-parties misunderstand the price or the quantity that is reported or just plain book it wrong.

The Liquidity Factor
The two examples in this chapter - Glaxo Smithkline and HK & China Gas are both large companies, are heavily traded (liquid) and held by thousands of shareholders. These issues will easily trade on or off their exchanges. On most days, a buyer can easily find a seller at the exchange or in an automated matching system. However, on most international exchanges an investor will find that many securities are smaller companies, not heavily traded and require patience and careful handling to acquire or sell. Since the process used to execute an order has a direct impact on the execution price, clearance and settlement of a trade, let's look at how an order in an illiquid security is executed.

Typically, when an investor calls their Broker with an order to buy an illiquid stock, the Broker has three choices. 1) The Broker will try to find another investor who is a seller of the stock, or 2) the Broker will enter part of the order in the marketplace (disclosing a large order in an illiquid stock may have an adverse effect on the stock's price before the order can be completed). By entering only part of the order, small quantities are purchased until the entire order is completed. In this way, the

Part I: PRE-SETTLEMENT
Chapter 2
The Order Flow

Broker has executed the order without disturbing the price of the stock. However, this order may take days to complete. As a result, the order that started as one order will clear and settle as many orders - - each requiring instructions to the custodian bank, a purchase (or sale) of foreign currency and settlement. 3) This choice is the most likely way this type of order will be executed. The third choice is for the Broker to use all the resources available – executing the amount available in the marketplace, utilizing a market-maker and crossing stock with another customer.

Over the years, especially with the growth of large pension and mutual funds, the size (and of course, the quantity) of orders has increased. Investors have sought better, cost-effective ways to execute these orders. Automated matching systems have developed which allow institutions to trade with each other. Exchanges, too, have sought ways to increase the ability of investors to execute orders on the exchange. On many exchanges, an investor will find a combination of electronic and manual execution. For example, in Germany, an order can be simultaneously worked by Brokers on the floor (e.g., in Frankfurt), in the exchange's Xetra screen-based system, and by market-makers in the Broker's offices. As Brokers work to execute an investor's order, their market-makers may sell stock to the investor, they may buy stock offered on the Stock Exchange floor as well as any stock offered in Xetra. By utilizing all three mechanisms, the trader hopes to complete the order to the satisfaction of the investor.

The Steps in a Trade Flow

There are fourteen (14) steps in a trade flow. However, within each step there, a trade will flow differently depending on the method of execution and the type of investor. The Method of execution varies because an order can be entered to either a market-maker or to a Broker who will execute the order as agent (perhaps forwarding it to the exchange or, if not an exchange member, to a LB who is a member of the exchange). The method used to execute the order is usually transparent to the investor (except in markets that require the method to be disclosed to the investor - -especially if the Broker is a market-maker in the stock).

Exhibit 2-4 lists the steps in the trade flow of an order. Not every order will include all the steps. Retail investor orders typically start with the receipt of the order (step 2) and, after execution (steps 3,4 and 5) the order will be processed, confirmed and settled (steps 7, 8 and 13). The other steps involve institutional orders who may first request or respond to an indication of interest in a security before placing an order and split (or allocate) a notice of execution (NOE) between various accounts. In this chapter we will examine steps 1 through 5; the rest are covered in later chapters.

Part I: PRE-SETTLEMENT
Chapter 2
The Order Flow

Executing an order for a retail investor

A retail investor typically trades through their local Broker, in their own currency and, with a few exceptions, leaves the securities in their account with their Broker. Let's examine the steps for an order for a retail investor.
Note: Since the steps for retail investors do not include the first step, the numbers below do not correspond to the step numbers in Exhibit 2-4.

1) Order receipt and validation
After receiving an order from a retail investor, the Broker will first validate the account. This process includes checking both internal requirements and the market's regulations. Internal procedures, for many Brokers, require that the account information is on file and that the investor is authorized to make such an investment. In addition, steps are taken to determine if there are local market restrictions limiting foreign ownership of securities.

2) Order routing
Next, the order will be routed to the place of execution. This can be to the Broker's trading desk or the agency desk, the market-making trading desk or proprietary trading desk, directly to an exchange, to another Broker or to an ATS or ECN

3) Order Execution
If the executing Broker is a market-maker, the Broker may sell the security from their trading account to the account of the investor. Depending on the size of the order, this may be an automated process. Many market-maker's systems automatically execute an order for under 1,000 shares. If the order was forwarded to another party for execution, that party - the exchange, another Broker, an ATS or ECN - executes the trade and sends a report of the trade. In this case, the Broker has acted as an agent.

Also, in this case, the Broker may need to execute a foreign exchange deal. A F/X deal is necessary if the party executing the trade settles in a currency other than the investor's currency. On the other hand, if the trade was executed by a market-maker, a F/X deal is typically not required - - the market-maker's currency and the investor's currency is usually the same.

4) Notice of execution
After executing the trade, the Broker will advise the investor of the details of the trade (quantity, price, amount due, etc.) If the order was received through an on-line system, the investor may receive an on-line Notice of Execution.

Part I: PRE-SETTLEMENT
Chapter 2
The Order Flow

5) Trade Processing
If executed as a market-maker, the Broker will book a trade from the trading account to the investor's account. If executed as agent, the trade will be booked from the marketplace to the investor. If the Broker also purchased the currency necessary to settle the trade (as is the case in most trades for retail investors), the Broker processes the following trades: a) a purchase of the security in overseas currency, b) a purchase of the foreign currency (needed to pay for the security), c) a sale to the investor's account of the security in investor's currency (which reflects both the security and F/X trade).

Following the steps listed above, let's look at an example of an order executed for a retail investor.

Ms. or Mr. Retail Investor, who want to buy 100 shares of Glaxo Smithkline PLC, checks the price at which Glaxo Smithkline PLC is trading. This investor is from the U. S. and wants to pay for the stock in U. S. Dollars. He sees that the quote is $29 to $29.25 (orders are in the marketplace to buy at 29 and sell at 29.25). He places an order to buy 100 Glaxo Smithkline PLC at the market. His Broker will send this order to the place of execution, execute the order and report back to the investor that he purchased 100 shares at 29.25. It looks pretty simple to execute this order (and it is) but a lot went on behind the scenes to execute this order.

First, when the Broker received the order, the account was checked for account information and possible market restrictions. Before routing the order, the Broker determined where the stock could be purchased at the best price. Glaxo Smithkline PLC is a popular U. K. stock that trades in many countries and in a variety of execution systems.   The order could have been executed in an ECN; it could have been executed by the Broker who may be a market-maker in the stock; or it could have been forwarded to one of the exchanges in London.

If the Broker is a market maker in the stock, the Broker will execute the trade versus their trading account. The market-maker advertises the bid and ask price of the security in an electronic quote system (examples include the UK's SEAQ system, the US's NASDAQ system). Upon receipt of this order, the Broker sells the investor 100 shares at 29.25.
If the Broker is not a market-maker, the Broker will forward the order to the place where the stock is listed or to an order execution system. Let's assume the Broker forwards the order to the London Stock Exchange (LSE).
The order will be handled differently, depending on whether or not they are a LSE-member.
   a) If they are a member of the LSE, they will purchase the shares directly on the LSE. In London, the shares are quoted 1944 – 1948 (see Exhibit 2-3). The Broker buys 100 shares at 1948p and books the trade to the investor.

Part I: PRE-SETTLEMENT
Chapter 2
The Order Flow

>   The Broker then buys GBP 1,948.00 (100 shares multiplied by GBP19.48)
>   plus commission and charges; then books a trade to the investor for 100
>   shares vs. $2,930.00 ($2922.00 plus commission, assuming an exchange
>   rate of 1.5).
>
>   b) If they are not a member of the LSE, they will send the order to a LSE
>   Broker. In this case, the investor's Broker buys the stock from the LSE
>   Broker (as above) and sells the stock to the investor.

Finally, the Broker reports to the investor that they now own 100 shares of Glaxo
Smithkline PLC.

Execution of an Institutional Investor's order

How is an Institutional Investor's trade different from a retail investor's trade? In just
about every way. Differences occur in the way an order is given and how an order is
executed (the currency in which the trade will settle, the confirmation and settlement
process is also different, but they are discussed in later chapters). An Institutional
Investor may trade through their Broker, through a local Broker or directly with
another Institution. They may want the Broker to arrange the foreign currency as
part of the execution or they may choose to do that themselves. As most institutions
require delivery (or receipt – called Delivery Versus Payment or DVP) of the
securities via their Custodian bank, their Custodian bank's account information is
needed at the time of execution or shortly thereafter. Keeping in mind that the order
flow will be different according to the circumstances just mentioned, let's examine
the steps in a typical institutional order.

Exhibit 2-4

Steps in the International Trade Flow
1. Indication of Interest (IOI)
2. Order receipt and validation
3. Order routing
4. Order execution
5. Notice of execution (NOE)
6. Trade Allocation (TA)
7. Trade processing / booking
8. Client confirmation
9. Notification of settlement instructions
10. Exchange comparison
11. Arrangement of financing
12. Pre-match of instructions to deliver or receive securities and/or funds
13. Settlement of securities and funds
14. Registration of securities

Part I: PRE-SETTLEMENT
Chapter 2
The Order Flow

1) Indication of Interest (called the IOI)
To find a seller of a security that an institution is interested in buying (or to find a buyer of shares to be sold), an institution could make numerous phone calls or look at a screen that shows what other institutions or Brokers are dealing in that day. Indications of Interest are posted via e-mail, a Broker's proprietary systems or industry systems designed for this purpose. Brokers and institutions make daily lists of securities they want to deal in that day. The Autex system is an example of a system used by the industry to advertise and look up buyers and sellers of a particular security. The Financial Information Exchange (FIX) Protocol is an example of a standard message protocol that is used by Broker's and Investor's to electronically advertise indications of interest. (The Financial Information Exchange is discussed in Chapter 15). After checking a screen or receiving a message that a Broker or another investor is indicating that they are a seller of a security the investor wants to buy, the investor will enter an order.

2) Order receipt and validation
Most Institutional Investors enter orders electronically to an ATS, ECN, an exchange or Broker. As with a retail order, the Broker will validate the account requirements before an order is executed. Both internal compliance and overseas regulations must be verified when an order is received (or shortly thereafter). Steps to validate internal compliance include checking the credit limit of the investor, whether the account is permitted to invest in a particular country and in the particular security. Overseas regulations may require the investor be pre-registered and approved for investing in the market.

3) Order routing
An institutional order may be routed to the Broker in their own country, the local Broker, an ATS, a PTS, an ECN or traded directly between institutions.

4) Order execution
If executed through a Broker, the order may be executed internally versus the trading account, externally via an exchange or another market-maker or Broker. A trade execution by a Broker through their trading account may occur in different ways. By checking the IOI (in step 1), they may see a potential seller of the same stock they just received an order to buy. In this case, they buy from the seller and sell to the buyer. If no seller can be found, they might sell directly from their trading account or execute the order on the exchange (either directly or, if not a member of the exchange, through a local Broker). An order sent to a local Broker may also be executed via their trading account or executed by them on the exchange.
And finally, an order may also be executed versus another institution directly or through an automated trading system (ATS). An order may also be executed partially by all of the above. An institution may have entered an indication of interest

Part I: PRE-SETTLEMENT
Chapter 2
The Order Flow

(IOI) through an ATS, purchased some from Brokers and completed their order by buying from an institution that responded to their IOI in the ATS.

If a Broker executes multiple trades to complete the Investor's order, the Broker might combine the executions and report one trade to the Investor. This is called an average price trade. The Broker books all the trades executed for the investor in a particular stock, computes an average price for the trades and reports to the Investor one trade at the average price of the trades. Instead of having several trades to book, the investor now has only one.

Finally, after the execution is completed, a decision about the currency must be made. Does the institution have the currency needed for the trade, do they have a credit line or must the currency be purchased? If it must be purchased, who will execute the foreign exchange (F/X) deal? Will the institution purchase the required currency through their own bank? Would they prefer it be purchased by their Broker? Only when both the security is purchased (or sold) and required currency arranged is the trade completely executed.

5) Notice of Execution (called the NOE)
After the trade is executed, the investor will receive a notification that the trade has been executed. How is this notice received? In some cases it may be a phone call, more likely it is an e-mail, an electronic notification system or a notice via the ATS where the execution took place. If this order was executed for one account, the next step is to book or process the trade. If however, the trade was executed for multiple accounts, the institution must advise the Broker the breakdown of the accounts. This step is called the trade allocation and discussed in Chapter 3.

Following these steps, let's look at an example of an order placed by an institutional investor. Unlike the retail investor (whose main tasks are to place the order and pay for it), an Institutional Investor is involved in every step of the process – beginning with determining where their order can be executed at the best price.

A U. K. Institutional Investor plans an investment in Hong Kong & China Gas. They check the IOI system to see if anyone is advertising as a seller. They also contact market-makers for their quote in the stock. They'll check the price in Hong Kong and if Hong Kong has closed for the day, they'll check London or New York. Finally, they decide to place the order with a Broker to buy 100,000 shares at HKD9.00 on the Hong Kong Stock Exchange (HKSE), settlement in Hong Kong dollars (HKD).
If the Investor's Broker (IB) is not a member of the exchange, the IB routes the order to a Local Broker (LB) in Hong Kong on behalf of the investor.
The LB buys the shares, confirms the purchase to the IB who sends a Notice of Execution (NOE) to the investor.

It is at this point that the differences between a retail and institutional order are greatest. The differences occur because institutional investors typically
- a) Allocate the shares to multiple accounts
- b) Take delivery of the security - - because of short settlement cycles, the investor and broker must arrange for settlement as soon as possible. To facilitate settlement, many exchanges are requiring custodian bank information at the time of execution. If the investor allocated the trade to various accounts, the names of each of the account's Sub-custodian Banks are required by the stock exchange on the day of execution, e.g., Spain and Taiwan.
- c) Arrange payment for the trade

A look at the Currency Execution

How does the Institutional Investor pay for this trade? The Institutional Investor may have sufficient Hong Kong Dollars (HKD) on deposit in H.K.; they may have an arranged credit line; they may choose to ask their Broker or authorize their custodian bank to buy the currency; or they may choose to buy it themselves through a F/X Dealer. The various ways of financing this and other overseas investments are further discussed in Chapter 8. At this point, let's take a look at one of the ways this institutional investor could finance this purchase.

In our example, the Institutional Investor is a U. K. Institution and they decide to buy the needed HKD and sell Great British Pounds (GBP) trough a F/X dealer.
1) First, they determine how many H.K. Dollars they need and when they need it. In this example, they will need HKD 905,576.50 (100,000 shares @ 9.00 plus commission and charges) and they need it two days from today (the same day the shares are due to settle).
2) They check their Bloomberg or Reuters screen (or whatever system they have) for the best HKD/GBP rate available, and enter the order to the bank that is quoting the best rate and with whom they have an account.
3) To enter the F/X order, they might subscribe to a F/X Dealing System or they'll pick up a phone and call the trading desk. Let's assume the bank they selected was Hong Kong Shanghai Bank (HSBC). The trader at HSBC tells them they will sell HKD vs, GBP at a rate of 13.25. The Institutional Investor buys HKD 905,576.50 at 13.25 - - total cost in GBP 68,345.40

Part I: PRE-SETTLEMENT
Chapter 2
The Order Flow

After execution
After a trade has been executed, the report of this trade is generated to all parties involved in the trade - - to the exchange members if executed on the exchange and to the investor for whom it was executed. The next two chapters examine the confirmation of the trade to the investor and to the exchange Brokers. Regardless of where a trade was executed, both parties to the trade must compare the details of the trade as the first step toward settlement.

BRAZIL EXECUTION PROCESS

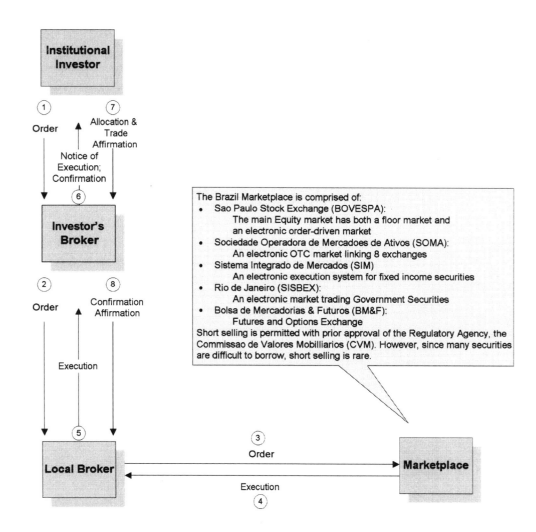

The Brazil Marketplace is comprised of:
- Sao Paulo Stock Exchange (BOVESPA):
  The main Equity market has both a floor market and an electronic order-driven market
- Sociedade Operadora de Mercadoes de Ativos (SOMA):
  An electronic OTC market linking 8 exchanges
- Sistema Integrado de Mercados (SIM)
  An electronic execution system for fixed income securities
- Rio de Janeiro (SISBEX):
  An electronic market trading Government Securities
- Bolsa de Mercadorias & Futuros (BM&F):
  Futures and Options Exchange

Short selling is permitted with prior approval of the Regulatory Agency, the Commissao de Valores Mobilliarios (CVM). However, since many securities are difficult to borrow, short selling is rare.

HONG KONG EXECUTION PROCESS

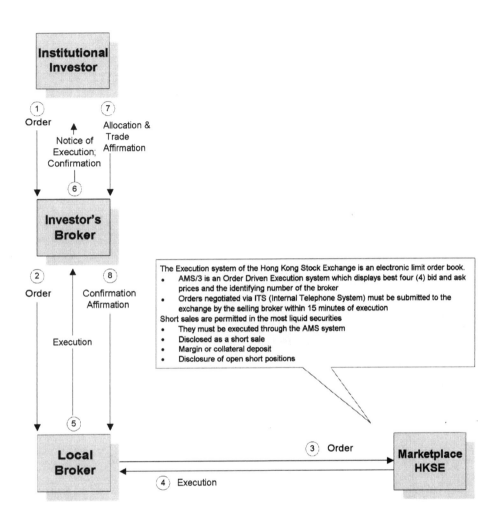

UNITED KINGDOM EXECUTION PROCESS

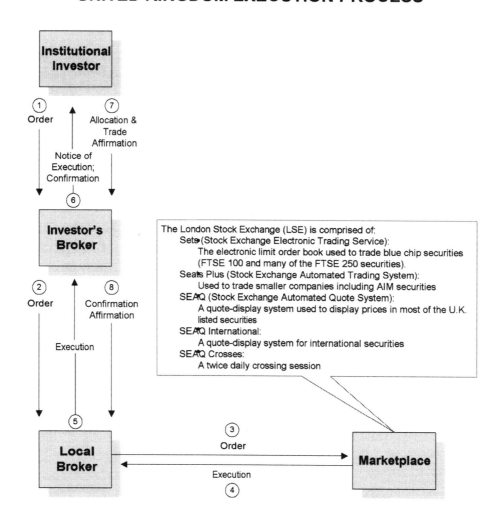

The London Stock Exchange (LSE) is comprised of:
- Sets (Stock Exchange Electronic Trading Service):
  The electronic limit order book used to trade blue chip securities (FTSE 100 and many of the FTSE 250 securities).
- Seats Plus (Stock Exchange Automated Trading System):
  Used to trade smaller companies including AIM securities
- SEAQ (Stock Exchange Automated Quote System):
  A quote-display system used to display prices in most of the U.K. listed securities
- SEAQ International:
  A quote-display system for international securities
- SEAQ Crosses:
  A twice daily crossing session

Part I: PRE-SETTLEMENT
Chapter 2
The Order Flow

CHAPTER PROCESS FLOW

The following reflects the flow of internal and external activities required to process a trade execution.

On March 19, 2002
an Institutional Investor enters an order to purchase
100,00 Hong Kong and China Gas (HKCG) @ HKD 9.00
on the Hong Kong Stock Exchange (HKSE)

As a result, the following activities occur:
- The Institutional Investor (II) transmits the order to the Investor's Broker (IB)
- The IB transmits the order to a Local Broker (LB) on the HKSE
- The LB transmits the order to the HKSE

On March 19,
upon receipt of the order forwarded by the IB, the LB executes, on the HKSE,
an order to Buy 100,000 HKCG @ HKD 9.00,
Trade Date March 19, Settlement Date March 21

The LB buys 100,000 HKCG
@ HKD 900,000.00
vs. the HKSE (Contra-Broker)

The HKSE (contra-broker) sells
100,000 HKCG @ HKD 900,000.00
vs. the LB

On Trade Date March 19,
the LB books the sale vs. the IB of 100,000 shares @ HKD 9.00 plus commission
and charges for Settlement Date March 21.
The IB books a buy of the shares vs. the LB

The IB buys 100,000 HKCG
@ HKD 904,451.15
vs. the LB

The LB sells 100,000 HKCG
100,000 HKCG @ HKD 904,451.15
vs. the IB

> *On Trade Date March 19,*
> *the IB reports the trade execution by sending a Notice of Execution (NOE) to the Investor. Pending the account breakdown from the II, the IB books the trade to the Fund Manager's (general) account.*

- Upon notification of the execution from the LB, the IB transmits a NOE of 100,000 shares @ HKD 9.00 to the II
- Pending notification of the trade allocation, the IB books the following trade:

Fund Manager account	**IB account**
Buy of 100,000 HKCG	**Sale of 100,000 HKCG**
@ HKD 905,576.50	**@ HKD 905,576.50**
vs. the IB account	**vs. the Fund Manager account**

> *On March 19,*
> *The Investor books a purchase of 50,000 shares to A/c #1 and 50,000 shares to A/c #2 and transmits the allocation to the IB.*
> *The IB, upon receipt of the Investor's trade allocation,*
> *cancels (CXL) the trade booked to the Fund Manager Account and rebooks the trade to the Investor's individual accounts.*

- The II transmits to the IB the trade allocation of 50,000 shares to Account #1 and 50,000 shares to Account #2
- The IB cancels the trade booked to the Fund Manager Account and rebooks the trade per the II's trade allocation.

Fund Manager account	**IB account**
CXL Buy of 100,000 HKCG	**CXL Sale of 100,000 HKCG**
@ HKD 905,576.50	**@ HKD 905,576.50**
vs. the IB account	**vs. the Fund Manager account**
The II / Account #1 buys	**The IB sells 50,000 HKCG**
50,000 of HKCG @ HKD 452,788.25	**@ HKD 452,788.25**
HKCG vs. the IB	**vs. the II / Account #1**

Part I: PRE-SETTLEMENT
Chapter 2
The Order Flow

The II / Account #2 buys 50,000 of HKCG @ HKD 452,788.25 vs. the IB account	The IB sells 50,000 HKCG @ HKD 452,788.25 vs. the II / Account #2

Part I

Pre-Settlement

Chapter 3
The Confirmation Process

Part I: PRE-SETTLEMENT
Chapter 3
The Client Confirmation and Trade Matching Process

The confirmation is the notification received by the Investor detailing the trade that has taken place. The confirmation process, however, involves more than simply notifying the Investor of the trade. The process, which is a result of booking the trade, includes the allocation of the trade and an acknowledgment by the parties that they agree with the terms of the trade. Also during the confirmation process, the parties exchange any information required for settlement.

The systems and procedures used in the confirmation process are undergoing monumental changes. At the current time, there is a mix of electronic and manual processing - - Brokers and most institutions use Electronic Trade Confirmation (ETC) systems while some, especially institutional investors with low volume of international business, receive confirmations by fax. In this chapter, we will contrast the ETC systems and discuss the central matching facility – a process that will streamline many of the time consuming, error-prone steps in the confirmation process.

In this chapter we will examine the entire confirmation process:
- The information contained in the confirmation
- How the information contained in the confirmation is used by the parties
- The methods used to transmit the confirmation
- New systems impacting this process

What is a Confirmation?
The confirmation (also called a contract note) is the official notification to the Investor of the details of the trade. After the Investor enters the order with their Broker, the Broker executes the trade and informs the Investor that the order has been executed (this is called the notice of execution or NOE). If the Investor is an institutional Investor, they respond to the NOE by giving their Broker the account breakdown (called the Trade Allocation). The Broker then responds with a trade confirmation for each account. These communications between Broker and institutional Investor are typically via an electronic confirmation system, but may initially be by phone, fax or e-mail. The initial communication, if by phone, is followed by an official notification - - either in electronic or written form.

Although the confirmation generated by the Broker may vary in form, it will contain, at a minimum, the following information:
1. Name of the Broker
2. Security description
3. Security identifier
4. Buy or sell
5. Quantity bought or sold
6. Unit Price or price per security
7. Consideration or principal amount
8. Commission and other charges

Part I: PRE-SETTLEMENT
Chapter 3
The Client Confirmation and Trade Matching Process

9. Total amount (due on purchase or proceeds of a sale)
10. Trade date and settlement date

Additionally, the exchange rate and custodian bank details may also be included. The exchange rate is reported if total cost or proceeds is not in the currency of execution. The Foreign Exchange (F/X) confirmation is sometimes sent separately and in other cases combined with the confirmation of the security trade. Some Brokers add the custodian bank details to verify where the institutional Investor receives purchased securities or where they will deliver sold securities.

For example, when the Broker purchased 100,000 HK & China Gas at HKD 9.00 for the Investor, the Investor responded with instructions to the Broker to allocate the trade to two accounts (50,000 shares to each account). The Broker then sent the Investor two confirmations – one for each account. Exhibit 3-1 shows one of the confirmations sent to the Investor.

Exhibit 3-1 Trade Confirmation

① **ABC Securities Ltd.**	
Contract Note	
Confirmation of Bought Trade for the Account of:	
Account:	Investor Account #1
	1 Royal Lane
	London, U.K.
Account No.	9876543

④ **Bought**	② **Security**	Hong Kong & China Gas Ord
	③ **ISIN**	HK0003000038
	⑤ **Quantity**	50,000
	⑥ **Price**	9.00
	⑦ **Consideration**	450,000.00
	⑧ **Charges**	
	Brokerage	2,250.00
	Stamp Duty	506.25
	Transaction Levy	22.50
	Transfer Fee	9.00
	Trading Levy	0.50
	⑨ **Total Cost**	452,788.25
	⑩ **Trade Date**	3/19/02
	Settlement Date	3/21/02

Notes to Exhibit 3-1

Exhibit 3-1 shows the following:
1) The Broker who sold the shares
2) The name of the shares
3) The security's identifier. Most countries have their own internal security numbering system (in Hong Kong it's the AMS or Teletext number, in the U.K. it is the Sedol number, in the U.S. the Cusip number). Many countries are adopting the international numbering system, called the ISIN Code. The Association of National Numbering Agencies (ANNA) is the agency charged with overseeing the implementation of the ISIN code and is discussed in Chapter 15.
4) The trade is a purchase
5) The quantity purchased
6) The price paid per share; this price may be the actual price of the shares executed on the exchange or an average price of the trades executed.
For example, if the Broker purchased 50,000 shares at HKD 8.90 and 50,000 at HKD 9.10, the Broker might report to the client one trade of 100,000 at the average price of HKD 9.00. This simplifies the booking and settlement for the Investor. Since, even though the Broker must book and settle two trades (the trade at HKD 8.90 and the trade at HKD 9.10) with the exchange, the Investor has only one trade to book and settle. If the Investor is allocating the trade to multiple accounts, an average price trade simplifies things even more. Consider the result if the Broker did not report one trade at the average price -- In our example, the Investor would have to book four trades (25,000 at HKD 8.90 and 25,000 at HKD 9.10 for one account and the same for the other account). By averaging, the Investor only has to book one trade to each account.
7) The amount paid before charges.
8) The amount of charges to be paid - these will vary depending on the exchange, type of security and how the trade was executed.
Here are three examples of how the charges will vary:
- In Hong Kong the charges include Stamp Duty (0.1125% of the consideration), Transaction Levy (0.005%) Trading Levy (HKD0.50 per ticket) and Transfer Fee (0.002%/maximum HKD 100 if settled through the depository and HKD 1.50 per board lot if certificates will be physically delivered). Fees charged by exchanges vary and may range from as few as no charges to as many as 5 or 6 different fees.
- The type of security also determines the type of charges. If the type of security is a bond, and interest has accrued, the amount of accrued interest is calculated and included as one of the charges.
- Orders can be executed either on a `gross' basis or a `net' basis. Gross basis trades are reported at the price per share plus/or minus commission and fees. The trade of HK China Gas is an example of a trade executed at a gross price. The price paid for the shares is HKD 9 plus commission and

fees. Net trades are reported at a price which includes commission or charges or both commission and charges. If this trade had been executed at HKD 9 net of all charges, the amount due on the trade would be HKD 450,000.00 (50,000 x 9). If the trade had been executed at HKD 9 net of commission (but not net of charges), the amount due on the trade would be HKD 450,538.25 (50,000 x 9 plus all fees except commission). One of the reasons for problem trades is the discrepancy in the amount of final money on the trade. Both parties must agree on the total amount of the trade – the amount of accrued interest and if fees, taxes and commission are included in the execution price or not.

9) The total amount charged on this purchase (if this was a sale, the amount would reflect the total proceeds from the sale). The total amount, 452,788.25, is in Hong Kong Dollars because the Investor requested the trade be executed in HK Dollars (HKD). If, however, the Investor had requested the Broker to buy the required HKD and produce a confirmation in the Investor's currency, the rate and amount due in the requested currency would also appear on the confirmation. For example, assume the Investor is a U.K. Fund who requested an execution in Great British Pounds (GBP). The Broker purchases HKD 452,788.25 versus GBP at a rate of 13.25. The total amount due is now GBP 34,172.70. The confirmation will show either the final GBP amount, or it will itemize the amounts in HKD, the rate and the GBP amount, or a separate confirmation for the F/X trade will be sent - - depending on the Broker's procedures or the Investor's instructions.

10) The date the trade was executed and the date the trade should settle.

Who receives the confirmation and how is it used?
Every Investor who has purchased or sold securities must receive a notification of the executed trade. As the trade is booked into the Broker's system, a confirmation of the trade is generated. Many systems are designed to produce a hard copy confirmation that will be mailed that day or on the following day. With shorter settlement periods, this mailed confirmation has very little practical purpose. The shares sold, or the funds due, will be required long before the confirmation is received. Since most countries require a written trade report, this mailed confirmation fulfills a legal requirement. In many countries, this regulation has been amended to permit an electronic transmission to replace the paper confirmation. As a result, depending on the requirements of the market and the Investor, the confirmation will be sent in different ways. First, let's look at the requirements of the Retail Investor.

The Retail Investor and their use of the Confirmation
The Retail Investor typically receives their confirmation via the mail (hard copy or via e-mail). For them, the confirmation is a legal notification that a trade was transacted in their account. Unlike the institutional Investor, they do not have to

GLOBAL SECURITIES OPERATIONS: The Handbook of

Part I: PRE-SETTLEMENT
Chapter 3
The Client Confirmation and Trade Matching Process

do anything with the confirmation. Of course, if they disagree with the information in the confirmation (e.g., they did not enter an order to sell the security mentioned in the confirmation), they will notify their Broker. But if the information is correct, no action is required by them. Typically, they have an account with their Broker that holds their securities and, very often, their cash. In some markets, the Retail Investor has an account at the depository and a cash account at the authorized bank (see Asian Model in Chapter 7). In either case, the Retail Investor's account will be debited (cash for a purchase, securities if a sale) and credited (securities if a purchase, cash if a sale) on the settlement date by either their Broker or the stock exchange / depository. On the other hand, an institutional Investor needs the confirmation as soon as possible and must take action if the trade is to settle.

The Institutional Investor and their use of the Confirmation
The Institutional Investor receives their confirmation via an electronic trade confirmation (ETC) system (see examples in this chapter under ETC Service Providers), an electronic message service (e.g. SWIFT), e-mail or fax. The mailed confirmation (sent in markets where regulations still require it) is not used by the Investor. It is the information received on trade date that is used for any (or all) of the following reasons:
- To affirm agreement to the trade details
- To advise settlement instructions
- To notify their Investor of a transaction
- To arrange financing and/or currency exchange
- To notify their custodian bank

Affirming agreement to the trade details
When an Investor receives a trade confirmation on trade date and responds, either by agreeing to or rejecting the trade if they disagree, a trade correction can be made quickly. When both parties know they have a good trade, the risk of a costly error is greatly reduced. When the parties are unaware that they have an error, the chances of incurring a loss increase each day. When the incorrect trade is unwound (i.e., reversed - - an incorrectly purchased security is sold at the current market price) and the correct trade is executed, it is likely that the price of the security will have changed. The sooner an error is discovered, the greater the chances that the price of the stock will not have moved and the loss on the error can be minimized
Investors agree to the details of a trade in one of two ways:
1) Positive Reply - this method requires a response from the Investor. When an e-mail or fax is used to send the confirmation, some Brokers may request the Investor to respond by agreeing to or rejecting the trade. But this is not common practice. The positive reply is used with a confirmation / affirmation (ETC) system. The Broker transmits the

59

confirmation and the Investor responds with an affirmation of the trade (if they agree) or a rejection (if they disagree).

The confirmation / affirmation method is being replaced by matching systems. Instead of affirming the information from the Broker, both parties enter the trade details as they know them; the matching system then reports to each party either a match (if the details agree within tolerances set by the parties) or an un-match (if the details do not agree).

2) Negative reply – this method is used when an Investor receives their confirmation via e-mail or fax. The Broker assumes the trade is correct unless the Investor informs them of an error.

These systems are further discussed in the next section – ETC Service Providers.

Advising Settlement Instructions

As previously mentioned, institutional Investors do not leave the securities with the Broker who executed the trade. Instead, they instruct their Broker to settle the trade with their Global Custodian Bank (see the section on Participants in Chapter 1). Both the Broker and the Global Custodian Bank (GCB) have an agent in the country where the trade was executed. The Investor tells their Broker the information on their GCB's sub-custodian bank (SCB); and the Broker tells the Investor the information on their GCB or local clearing agent.

The settlement information that the Investor (called the Standard Settlement Instructions or SSI) and the Broker (called the Broker Delivery Instructions or BDI) send to each other, includes the following:

- The Investor's account name and Tax ID Number
- The Global Custodian Bank's address and BIC Code (the BIC Code is the SWIFT Bank Identification Code)
- The Sub Custodian Bank or Clearing Agent and the address and BIC Code
- Security Account Number
- Cash Account Number
- Security Type (many Investors use one agent for Equities and another one for Debt instruments)

How do the Investor and Broker obtain this information? And how do they tell each other of the information? The Investor receives their GCB and SCB information from their GCB. The Broker receives their settlement information from their Clearing Agent. Typically, the Investor and Broker obtain this information when they start investing in the country. Updates are then received as changes (e.g., a switch of SCB or Clearing Agent bank, a new account number, etc.) are made. When the Broker opens an account with an Investor, they receive the Investor's settlement information (i.e., the GCB's sub-custodian accounts) and the Broker sends their information (i.e., their GCB's sub-custodian accounts or Clearing Agent banks) to the Investor. The information can be available either electronically or manual.

Electronic Settlement Information

Due to the increase in volume and the decrease in settlement periods, exchanging and confirming settlement instructions has become an onerous task. To alleviate this problem, vendors have developed electronic settlement databases. An example is Omgeo ALERT®, the global database for the communication of settlement and account instructions. It is a product of Omgeo, the joint venture between the Depository Trust and Clearing Corporation (DTCC) and Thomson Financial. **Exhibit 3-2** is an example of Omgeo ALERT® settlement instruction screen. The Investor and Broker's settlement instructions are maintained in the system. Notice that in addition to the Custodian (GCB) and Sub Agent (SCB) information, the screen information reflects the name of the country where the trade will settle, the security type and the SWIFT BIC Code (Bank Identification code).

During the account opening process, the Investor and Broker exchange the access code that allows each other to access the information when needed.
The Broker retrieves the Investors SSI and forwards the information to their clearing agent or the Broker's agent retrieves the information directly. The Investor or their custodian, at the same time, is retrieving the Broker's information.

The most important aspect of these databases (*if* the details are updated as agent information changes) is that they provide updated settlement information on all parties that can be accessed by the parties involved in the trade. Some firms create an internal settlement instruction database utilizing the information in Omgeo ALERT®. Other firms, especially the larger banks and brokers, access the information from ALERT when they need it eliminating the maintenance function. As the industry moves to a shorter settlement period, knowing the correct settlement instructions, as soon as possible, becomes crucial to a timely and successful settlement.

Part I: PRE-SETTLEMENT
Chapter 3
The Client Confirmation and Trade Matching Process

Exhibit 3-2   Omgeo ALERT® Settlement Instruction

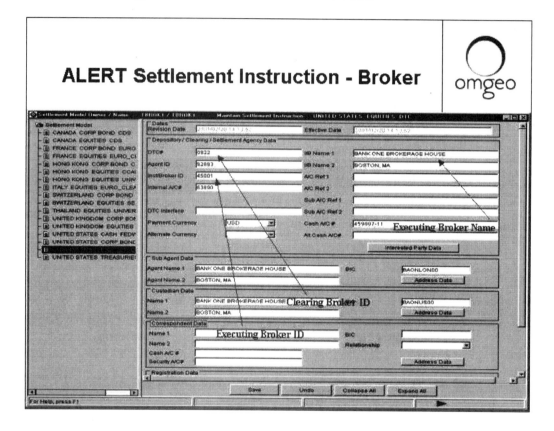

Part I: PRE-SETTLEMENT
Chapter 3
The Client Confirmation and Trade Matching Process

Manual Settlement Information
Sending the information manually means sending a fax. Although not the method of choice, this is still the way the information is exchanged by some Investors in some countries. When the accounts are set up with the Broker and Investor, the parties fax each other the information listed above. Each party verifies the accuracy of the information every time a trade is executed.

To notify the Investor of a transaction
Often, the Investor entering an order is buying or selling on behalf of another party. Brokers frequently enter orders, not for themselves, but on behalf of their customers. Investment Managers invest for pension or mutual funds. After executing a trade, they notify their client of the transaction. Upon receipt of the confirmation, with the exact description, money and settlement date details, they forward this information to their client.

To arrange financing and/or currency exchange
With a confirmation in hand, the Investor knows exactly how much currency they need and the date when they will need it. This process is discussed in Chapters 2 - Order Flow and 8 - Financing and Cash Management.

To notify their custodian bank or agent
By the end of trade date the Investor sends the trade information to their GCB; the Broker to their GCB or Clearing Agent. Investors typically send a SWIFT message or fax the details to their bank; Most Brokers transmit this information via SWIFT. Both the GCB and/or the Broker's Clearing Agent should receive this instruction as soon as possible for three reasons: to execute the F/X deal if requested, pre-match the instructions with the counter-party's local agent and instruct the settlement facility to settle the trade.
1) Buying or selling the foreign currency if requested
   The Investor may request their GCB to buy or sell the currency resulting from the trade. Upon receipt of the Broker's confirmation, the Investor sends the instructions to their GCB who will buy or sell the required currency. This process is discussed in Chapters 2 and Chapter 8.
2) Pre-matching the trade details
   To settle the trade, both the Broker's SCB or local Clearing Agent and the Investor's SCB must know and match the details of the trade. This process, part of settlement, is explained in Chapter 6.
3) Sending settlement instructions to the settlement facility. The Broker's SCB or local Clearing Agent and the Investor's SCB forwards the

instructions to the CSD or other settlement facility. (Note: In some markets, presently in the U.S. and in the near future the U.K., Omgeo links directly to the depository – further streamlining the transmission of the settlement information.) This process, the settlement of the trade, is also discussed in Chapter 6.

Following our example, let's examine how our trade would progress through these steps.

- First, the Broker books the purchase of the H.K. and China Gas shares generating a confirmation (Exhibit 3.1). The Investor (or their automated matching system) affirm (or match) the trade.
- Next, both parties verify that they have Hong Kong settlement instructions for each other, either on file or via Omgeo ALERT®.
- If the Investor's policy is to buy or sell the currency as needed, they will contact a F/X dealer and buy the required HKD.
- Finally, the Investor forwards the instructions (the trade confirmation and settlement instructions) to their GCB and the Broker to their GCB or local Clearing Agent.

The Methods used to transmit the Confirmation
If this trade is going to settle, the information sent to the GCB (and forwarded to the SCB) and the Broker's local agent must agree. The SCB and the Broker's agent will match if the matching trade details, resulting from the confirmation / affirmation or matching process, are electronically forwarded to them. If the trade was matched manually (and re-entered into a system that forwarded the trade details to the local agents), there is no guarantee that the trade details are the same. When a person re-keys the trade information into another system, they might incorrectly enter the cost, proceeds, security identifier or any of the other trade data. As a result, the matched trade between the Broker and Investor will not match when it reaches their local agents. To eliminate this problem, the industry has adopted the use of Electronic Trade Confirmation (ETC) messages or, as an alternative, the SWIFT message format or have connectivity vendors generate and read a SWIFT message from an internal system. (For information on SWIFT, see Transmitting Messages later in this chapter.)

Confirmation and Affirmation by ETC
Electronic Trade Confirmation (ETC) systems provide reliable and timely trade information. Automated systems, used by Brokers and Investors, are either trade matching systems or trade confirmation/affirmation systems.

- Trade matching systems require both parties to enter the trade, as they know it. The system then reports to each party either a trade match or an

un-match. If the trade details do not match, both parties research their internal records to determine why the trade did not match.
- ETC trade confirmation/affirmation systems require one party to enter the trade details and the counterparty to respond - - by agreeing (the affirmation) or disagreeing with the trade details.
- Note: As we write this, the industry is adopting the use of *central* trade matching facilities that receive and process electronic confirmations (see next section – Central Trade Matching Facilities).

Because ETC systems have revolutionized the confirmation process, let's examine what an ETC system does.
The steps in a typical trade confirmation/affirmation system are:
1) The transmission of a notification of the execution.
   The Broker sends their Investor a report of the execution. This is called the block trade or Notice of Execution (NOE).
2) The response from the Investor.
   The Investor responds in one of two ways: 1) agreeing and allocating the trade to one account or multiple accounts, 2) rejecting the terms of the trade.
   - Using the allocation feature, the Investor transmits the account number/s for the execution. When the investor sends the order to be executed, they typically do not disclose the account for which the trade is being executed. After they receive the NOE from the broker, the investor sends to the broker the account name and/or number and the quantity of shares to be allocated to each account (this is called the breakdown or Allocation).
3) The Trade Confirmation. The Broker sends the Investor a confirmation detailing the terms of the trade. If the trade has been allocated to more than one account, a confirmation will be sent for each trade (allocation).
4) The Investor Affirmation.
   In this step the Investor transmits their agreement (called the affirmation) to the terms of the trade/trades or rejects the trade/trades. If the Investor does not agree with the details as reported by the Broker, they discuss the differences with the Broker. One party (or both) amends the trade until there is agreement between the parties.
1) Settlement Instructions (the SSIs) are captured from an electronic data base (discussed in previous section)

Trade Matching systems are slightly different than Confirmation / affirmation systems. Trade Matching systems match information entered by both parties. The steps in a typical trade matching system are:
1) The first step is the same as in a confirmation /affirmation system. The Broker sends the Investor a report of the executed trade.

Part I: PRE-SETTLEMENT
Chapter 3
The Client Confirmation and Trade Matching Process

2) This step is also the same. If in agreement, the Investor sends the Trade Allocations to the Broker.
3) The Broker sends a trade confirmation.
4) This is where the systems differ. The matching system compares the information in the trade allocation with the Broker's trade Confirmation. The system then reports either a match or an un-match. This allows for exception processing only, saving time and money for both parties.
5) Settlement instructions are appended to the trade instructions.

ETC Service Providers
There are many systems available that process Electronic Trade Confirmations (ETC) – too numerous to mention here. Some of them require both parties to subscribe to the system; others send the information though a matching facility. Most systems begin with the block trade report followed by the allocation, confirmation and finally the affirmation.
An example of an ETC provider is Omgeo, a joint venture owned equally by the Depository Trust and Clearing Corporation (DTCC) and Thomson Financial

Omgeo OASYS Global – An Electronic Trade Allocation and Confirmation Service
OASYS Global is a product of Omgeo. Omgeo ALERT is a standard settlement instruction database. After a Broker sends a trade execution via OASYS Global, the settlement instructions (SSI) may be enriched from the ALERT system. If the trade is to be split between multiple accounts, the Investor sends the allocations (again accessing SSI via ALERT) which the Broker can accept or reject. Exhibit 3-3 displays Omgeo OASYS Global^{SM},Bargain Entry Screen. Notice the screen shows the account information, the security code and description, the transaction price and the amount of the trade.   After receiving the confirmation, the Investor affirms or rejects the confirmation. Copies of the confirmation may be sent to another party (for example, the Global Custodian Bank) with authorization of the Investor.

Exhibit 3-3 Omgeo OASYS Global^{SM}, Bargain Entry Screen

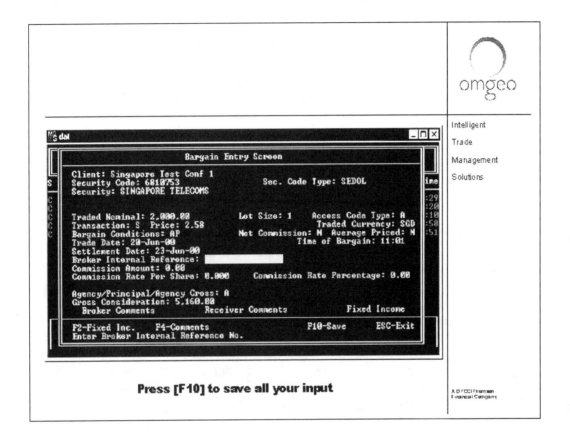

Part I: PRE-SETTLEMENT
Chapter 3
The Client Confirmation and Trade Matching Process

Transmitting Messages to an ETC Provider
SWIFT (the Society for Worldwide Interbank Financial Telecommunications) is an industry organization that has developed both a system to transmit messages and standardized messages that can be transmitted via the SWIFT system or over other systems. (SWIFT is discussed further in Chapter 15.) The SWIFT formatted messages are used with the SWIFT system or other ETC systems. One of the SWIFT messages is the MT 541 - - a message to instruct the Global Custodian Bank used by an institutional money manager to settle a trade by receiving securities in exchange for cash (receive vs payment). The MT541 is designed to be used after a typical trade comparison process, including potentially the exchange of Notice of Execution (MT513), Allocation (MT514), Confirmation (MT515) and Affirmation (MT517) messages between the Investor and its Broker.

SWIFT's MT 541 - - the client instruction
Exhibit 3-4 shows an excerpt from the MT 541, the Receive Against Payment instruction used by an Institutional Investor, a Broker or Global Custodian Bank. The message is divided into 6 parts (or sequences). Excerpts from Sequence A, B, C and E are shown in Exhibit 3-4. (For the purposes of this book, Sequences D and F have not been included.)
- Sequence A shows the general information about this trade, i.e., the trade reference number, and type of message (new, cancel or pre-advice) etc. Each line contains a Tag number (16R, 20C etc.) and an M for Mandatory (required) or O for Optional information. Tag 20C is Mandatory and requires the Senders Reference number; 23G describes the Function of the Message (a NEW message) 22F asks if this transaction is linked to another SWIFT message.
- Sequence B confirms the Confirmation Details. Tag 98A shows the settlement date, 90B the settlement amount and 35B the Security Identification Code.
- Sequence E details the settlement instructions. The information input into Tag 22F shows the condition of settlement as physical (PHYS) and tag 95Q shows the Delivering Party (either the Agent, Custodian or the Seller).

Although this is the data included on SWIFT messages, operators using SWIFT will probably not see a screen that looks like Exhibit 3-4. System developers usually format `user friendly' screens that most of us can understand. The system then generates a SWIFT message.

Part I: PRE-SETTLEMENT
Chapter 3
The Client Confirmation and Trade Matching Process

Exhibit 3-4 SWIFT MT541N Message

```
Sequence A - General Information
:16R:GENL                          M  Start of Block
:20C::SEME//01424                  M  Senders Reference
:23G:NEWM/A2C4                      M  Function of the Message
:98C::PREP//19991231232359         O  Date / Time
:99B::SETT//123                    O  Current Instruction # /Count
:16R:LINK
:22F::LINK/A2C4E6G8/A2C4            O  Linkage Type Indicator
:13A::LINK//513                    O  Type of Transaction Linked
:20C::PREV//x                      M  Reference
:16S:LINK

Sequence B Trade Details
:16S:GENL
:16R:TRADDET
:94B::TRAD/8C/A2C4/30x              O  Place where traded (e.g.,
Exchange)
:98B::SETT/A2C4E6G8/A2C4            M  Settlement Date
:98B::TRAD/A2C4E6G8/A2C4            O  Currency Code and Price
:90B::DEAL//A2C4/USD1,3456789012345 O Deal Price
:99A::DAAC//N123                   O  # of days used to calculate acc
int
:35B:ISIN A2C4E6G8I0K2             M  Security Identification
:16S:TRADDET

Sequence C - Instrument
:16R:FIAC
:36B::SETT//A2C4/12345678901234,   M  Quantity of Security to be
                                      settled
:19A::SETT//USD300000000000,50     O  Settlement Amount
:70D::DENC//x                      O  Narrative
:13B::CERT/A2C4E6G8/x              O  Certificate Number
:97A::SAFE//x                      M  Safekeeping Account
:97A::CASH//x                      O  Cash Account
:16S:FIAC

Sequence E - Settlement Details
:16R:SETDET
:22F::STCO/A2C4E6G8/PHYS           O  Settlement Transaction Condition
:22F::SETR/A2C4E6G8/A2C4           M  Type of Settlement Transaction
:16R:SETPRTY
:95Q::DEAG//x                      M  Delivering Agent
:95Q::DECU//x                      or Deliver's Custodian
:95Q::SELL//x                      or Seller
:16S:SETPRTY
:16R:CSHPRTY
:95Q::ACCW//x                      M  Party to which payment is to be
made
:95S::ALTE/A2C4E6G8/A2C4/US/x      or Identity of alternate party
:97A::CASH//x                      O  Account of party in this sequence
:16S:CSHPRTY
```

Part I: PRE-SETTLEMENT
Chapter 3
The Client Confirmation and Trade Matching Process

Benefits of an Electronic Trade Confirmation
Must a confirmation be sent over an ETC system? No, but it sure cuts down on a lot of problems. Since the confirmation is used for purposes other than just a legal record of the trade, the trade information must be received promptly and accurately. A trade that has been reported electronically, amended for allocations in the same system and confirmed electronically and forwarded to the custodian bank without being re-booked or re-keyed eliminates many errors. A trade that has been reported by fax must be booked by the Investor to their internal booking system. The trade could be booked as the wrong security at the wrong price or for different money. The same could happen when the instructions for the custodian bank are being prepared. By booking the trade once, at the point of execution, and forwarding that same information electronically, the likelihood of the trade pre-matching (and settling) between the Broker and the Investor's custodian bank are greatly enhanced.

New Systems Impacting the Process
With T+1 fast approaching, there is a need to expedite trade matching, settlement instructions retrieval and SCB and local Clearing Agent notification. Central matching facilities are in development to accelerate the process of sending and matching instructions. The Global Straight through Processing Association's axion4, Omgeo and Sunguard have, or are developing, central trade matching facilities.
The GSTP AG has developed the Transaction Flow Manger (TFM). Omgeo has developed the Omgeo Central Trade Manager^{SM}. To solve the problem of Investors and Brokers each using a separate central trade matching system, the U. S. market has stipulated that the developers must provide interoperability of their systems. Global marketplace regulators may require the same. Interoperability enables each system to accept each other's instructions, match the instructions and speed them on their way. Of course, this means that all parties must be using an electronic confirmation system.

Let's look at the processing steps using the TFM:
1) The Broker sends the NOE, using systems that have developed an interface with the TFM.
2) The Investor also enters the block trade details (again, using any trade order management or ETC system that has developed an interface with the TFM). The Investors trade entry is called the Block Order Notification (BON); it is the block trade information prior to allocating the trade.
3) The TFM matches the NOE and BON and notifies both parties of the matching results and the Trade ID#.
4) The Investor enters the Trade Allocations; the TFM forwards the allocations to the Broker and the Investor's GCB

Part I: PRE-SETTLEMENT
Chapter 3
The Client Confirmation and Trade Matching Process

5) The Investor and Broker book the trades by exchanging net proceeds for each allocation and the TFM reports, to each party, a result of each match. This match includes the security description, quantity, price and net amount including the commission, fees and taxes. (The net amount is matched based on tolerance levels set by each party - - i.e., if the parties agree to a $0.25 difference in amounts, the TFM will match amounts with a money difference of $0.25 or less)

6) Having received the account breakdown (in Step 4) the GCB sends settlement instructions to the TFM. The Broker also provides settlement Instructions to the TFM. The TFM compares the receipt of settlement instructions from both parties to ensure that they are compatible (e.g., that both parties expect to settle at the same CSD or settlement facility).

As with the TFM, use of Omgeo Central Trade Manager^{SM} (CTM) has major advantages over the current use of ETC systems.

- Central matching is not sequential (the Broker and the Institutional Investor do not have to wait for the other to enter data as in the ETC process). Either party may begin the process and matching will occur as the data is available or entered.
- The Investor's GCB is notified of the trade immediately after it is allocated. Using an ETC system, the GCB was notified after the Broker and Investor agreed the trade, which was much later in the process. This should minimize problems in markets that require the GCB's special handling since the GCB will be aware of these trades earlier in the processing cycle.
- The GCB provides the Investor's settlement instructions (SSI). With an ETC system, the Investor provided the information, which they obtained from the GCB. Using the CTM, it is not necessary for the Investor to obtain the information – it is provided by the GCB.
- And finally, the SCB and the Broker's Clearing Agent have access to the information. The CTM will create SWIFT messages that are sent to CSDs, Clearing Brokers and Sub Custodians.

The Next Step
As the trade is being booked and confirmed by the Broker and the Investor, the exchange is also booking the trades executed on their exchange. The steps taken by the exchange (and related facilities) are the subject of the next chapter.

GLOBAL SECURITIES OPERATIONS: The Handbook of

Part I: PRE-SETTLEMENT
Chapter 3
The Client Confirmation and Trade Matching Process

CHAPTER PROCESS FLOW

The following reflects the flow of internal and external activities required to process the confirmation and affirmation of the trade data between the Investor and their Broker. We refer to Investor, Broker and Custodian without specifying which broker or custodian is responsible. This way we hope to reflect the process rather than confuse our readers with 'who' is doing 'what,' 'when.'

Note: As we know, confirmation / affirmation systems will be replaced by central matching systems. As of this writing, central matching systems are not yet the primary process for verifying trade data. Therefore, this example examines the flow using the confirmation / affirmation process.

On March 19, 2002
An Institutional Investor (II) verifies the accuracy
of the trade confirmation for their purchase of
50,000 Hong Kong and China Gas (HKCG) vs. HKD 452,788.25.
Note: This trade is a result of the trade allocation exampled in Chapter 2.

Broker's Clearing / Settlement Agent:
ABC Securities Ltd., H.K. (Securities) and HSBC (Funds)
Investor's Settlement Agent:
GCB: Deutsche Bank A.G., SCB: Deutsche Bank, H. K.

As a result, the following activities occur:
- Both the Investor and Broker subscribe to a confirmation / affirmation (C/A) system.
    - Many C/A systems auto-affirm trade data that match within a specified tolerance amount, the parties are alerted to only the un-matched trades. In other C/A systems, the affirmation is a manual function.
    - Some Investor's have arranged for their Custodian Bank to affirm trades; in other cases, the Investor affirms their own trades.
    - In this example, the C/A system requires a manual affirmation and the function is performed by the Investor.
- Both the Investor and Broker subscribe to and maintain their settlement instructions in Alert.
- Both the Investor and Broker transmit their trade instructions to their Agent/Custodian Bank via SWIFT.

Part I: PRE-SETTLEMENT
Chapter 3
The Client Confirmation and Trade Matching Process

On March 19,
the investor compares the confirmation received from the Broker against
their internal booking and affirms a matched trade.

- The Investor verifies the following information:
    - Quantity: 50,0000
    - Trade Date: March 19, 2002
    - Settlement Date: March 21, 2002
    - Transaction Type: Buy
    - Security ID: HK0003000038
    - Price: 9.00
    - Commission: 2792.75
    - Total Net Amount: 452,788.25
    - Account Number: II / Account #1
- If the trade details do not agree, the II researches the reasons for the difference. (Tolerance levels are set to accept minimal differences in some fields – notably the commission/charges amount.)
- If the trade details agree, the II transmits the affirmation.

By close of business on March 19,
the investor and the broker send trade instructions to their
Clearing Agent / Custodian Bank.

- The Investor sends Trade Instructions to their Custodian Bank, Deutsche Bank.
    - The Information on the Trade Instruction includes:
        - The information contained in the confirmation
        - Broker's Delivery Instructions (BDI)
    - The Investor accesses the BDI information, maintained in Alert, and forwards the information to their Custodian Bank. The BDI information includes:
        - Delivering Agent: ABC Securities Ltd., H. K.
        - Payment Recipient: HSBC, a/c ABC Securities Ltd., H. K.
    - The Investor transmits their Trade Instructions via the SWIFT MT 541 (receive Against Payment) Instruction.

Part I: PRE-SETTLEMENT
Chapter 3
The Client Confirmation and Trade Matching Process

- The broker sends Trade Instructions to their Clearing Agent, ABC Securities Ltd., H. K.
    - The information on the Trade instruction includes:
        - The information contained in the confirmation
        - The Investor Standard Settlement Instructions (SSI).
    - The Broker accesses the SSI information, maintained in Alert, and forwards the information to their Clearing Agent. The SSI information includes:
        - Receiving Custodian: Deutsche Bank, H. K.
    - The broker transmits their Trade Instructions via SWIFT.
- Depending on the level of automation of the systems used by the Investor and Broker, the Trade Instructions are transmitted to the Clearing Agent or Custodian Bank:
    - Automatically, requiring no action by the Investor or Broker, on all matched trades
    - Automatically, in response to a release by the Investor or Broker, on all matched trades
    - Manually, by the Investor or Broker

Part I: PRE-SETTLEMENT
Chapter 3
The Client Confirmation and Trade Matching Process

- The broker sends Trade Instructions to their Clearing Agent, ABC Securities Ltd., H. K.
  - The information on the Trade instruction includes:
    - The information contained in the confirmation
    - The Investor Standard Settlement Instructions (SSI).
  - The Broker accesses the SSI information, maintained in Alert, and forwards the information to their Clearing Agent. The SSI information includes:
    - Receiving Custodian: Deutsche Bank, H. K.
  - The broker transmits their Trade Instructions via SWIFT.
- Depending on the level of automation of the systems used by the Investor and Broker, the Trade Instructions are transmitted to the Clearing Agent or Custodian Bank:
  - Automatically, requiring no action by the Investor or Broker, on all matched trades
  - Automatically, in response to a release by the Investor or Broker, on all matched trades
  - Manually, by the Investor or Broker

Part I

Pre-Settlement

Chapter 4
The Market-side

Part I: PRE-SETTLEMENT
Chapter 4
Market Side Comparison

At this stage of the transaction the Investor has given an order to their broker, the Investor's Broker validates the order and transmits it to the Local Broker (LB) for execution. The LB, usually a member of the local marketplace, executes the order usually as an agent. The result of an execution is a trade. There are at least two sides of each trade, one satisfying the client order ("client side") and the other the contra-side (street side) of the client order.

This chapter describes the market side activities occurring after the trade has been executed and includes:
* Locked-in trades
* Two sided comparison
* One sided comparison

After an order has been executed the street side trade details must be compared with the counter-party's trade details. The comparison process is the matching of the selling counter-party trade details of the buying conter-party trade details. This process occurs between the Local Brokers representing the selling and buying investors.

For example, when a client sells 100 HK China Gas ordinary shares another investor(s) purchases 100 HK China Gas ordinary shares. This is known as the counter-party trade. The source of the counter-party trade can originate from 3 three situations: 1) another client of the LB who wants to purchase the security, 2) the LB purchases the security for their inventory or 3) another LB purchases the security for their client or their own account (true "market side").

The client portion of the trade is processed through a Confirmation/Affirmation (C/A) system, which is illustrated in Chapter 3. In the first situation cited in the previous paragraph, the process occurs between the LB and the buying client and the selling client within a C/A system. In the second example the LB, in addition to the C/A system, would reconcile the trade with their Dealer trading area.

The third example is the area of focus for this chapter. These are the trades that take place between LBs. Since the trades are among the LBs they are known as a "market side" activity (opposite of client side). It is an important function and is the first step in the post trade process insuring timely and accurate settlement. This is an opportunity for both LB counter-parties to review their trade details and ensure that they meet the client or their own order requirements.

Part I: PRE-SETTLEMENT
Chapter 4
Market Side Comparison

It is important that comparison take place as close to the time of execution as possible and that both LBs actively partake in the process. The sooner each LB confirms that the trade satisfies their order requirements, the more certain that the trade will settle properly. After that, each LB prepares for the remaining activities leading to settlement. The remainder of this chapter will illustrate various forms of comparison, presenting the ideal environment first and then others.

Types of Comparison Environments

Locked In

A Locked In trade is the ideal environment because it eliminates the need for comparison, but satisfies the requirement for LBs to be obligated to settle a trade. A Locked In trade begins with a specific type of trading environment. An automated system, that insulates the LB from mistakes or errors caused by an external participant, usually provides a Locked In trade environment. An external participant can be another LB, a market maker or a specialist.

Locked In trades are executed via an automated trading system with no manual intervention other than the LB processing an order. In this way there is no possibility of an error beyond one caused by the originating LB. These types of errors may be data entry mistakes such as a wrong security, quantity or a buy instead of a sell order.

The transaction flow begins with the LB receiving the order from the Investor's broker and transmitting the order to an automated execution system (AES). The AES satisfies the order by completing the transaction versus the market maker (MM), Specialist (S) or Central Limit Order Book (CLOB). The order is executed at the stipulated or prevailing price offered by the MM/S or the local broker at the time the order is received. The submitting LB is advised of the trade details immediately upon execution and at that time is automatically obligated to the conditions of the trade. Since the order was not manually processed or modified before execution, the trade was created based upon the specific conditions outlined at the point of order entry by the LB. The trade represents the requirements outlined by the LB and no further review or comparison is required. Thus the trade is locked in.

The greatest benefit of this environment is the elimination of the comparison process. Another benefit is the ability to use a Straight Through Processing (STP) approach and it also minimizes execution costs. STP is the approach to processing client instructions, such as trades or security/cash transfers or other

Part I: PRE-SETTLEMENT
Chapter 4
Market Side Comparison

types, without reentry into the LB's or Industry Service Organization's (ISO) system.

This approach reduces errors caused by reentry of transaction between participants or phases of each process. This in turn reduces related expenses thereby reducing client costs. In addition, the marketplace offering Locked In trading usually assesses lower costs to Locked In trades versus manually assisted trades. Markets that support this type of trading/comparison system are usually established, sophisticated environments that experience heavy volumes.

This type of system permits large number of trades to be executed, in a highly automated manner, facilitating a high rate of timely settlement. Locked in trades are automatically marked as compared and don't require additional processing before the next step, which is Clearance.

Two Sided

Another environment is the Two Sided comparison. This is the process for trades executed between LBs on an exchange, marketplace or in an over the counter (OTC) environment. Because the trade was executed between LBs, in a centralized marketplace, there is a need to compare the details of each to insure accuracy and timely settlement.

Two-sided comparison is usually provided by an ISO. This can be the exchange, marketplace or a Clearing Corporation (CC). CCs are usually industry owned and operated as a service bureau for the benefit of its members. As you will see, the comparison service provided is of mutual benefit to the LB participants. The two-sided comparison process can begin immediately after execution or might start at the end of the trade date. Obviously, the earlier that comparison is performed the better it is for the LBs involved since they will be assured that the trade was executed as the client wanted. If there is a problem there is still time to research and resolve the issue.

Part I: PRE-SETTLEMENT
Chapter 4
Market Side Comparison

Two Sided

The process, whether done immediately after execution or the next day is the same. It begins with the submission of trade details to the ISO. In some cases the trade record maybe reported directly to the exchange, but for illustrative purposes we will assume that each LB is required to submit their trade record. Both LBs submit their own trade to the ISO. It is imperative that both LBs submit trade details or the match <u>will be unsuccessful</u>. The following information is submitted:

- Trade Date
- Buy/Sell
- Security
- Execution Price
- Trade Conditions
- Executing Broker
- Settlement (Pay) Currency

- Settlement Date
- Quantity
- ISIN or Common Code
- ICSD Counterparty Number
- Settlement Instructions
- Clearing Broker

The ISO performs a match of the information submitted by each LB. There are three results from this match:

1. Matched
2. Unmatched
3. Advisory

This information can be provided in various forms: transmission of electronic media or paper based reports. The results of the match will drive various processes at the LB. The trade is matched when each side of a trade has agreeing trade details. The LB will update their internal records to reflect the Matched status. At this point the comparison process is complete. There is another possible impact on this trade that is addressed later in this chapter in the section titled *Advanced ISO Comparison Services*.

The other two results of the match performed by the ISO are processed together. Unmatched trades, the second result, are trades that one LB (#1) submitted to the ISO but there was no other trade submitted by a counter-party LB that matched the trade details, resulting in an unmatched trade. Advisory trades, the third result, are trades submitted by a #2 LB that did not match trades submitted by #1 LB. As a result, each outcome is reported to each LB, for example the ISO advises #1 LB that trades were submitted, identifying it as the counter-party, and requests a corresponding trade. These situations must be addressed immediately to insure the timely settlement of the client side of the trade.

Part I: PRE-SETTLEMENT
Chapter 4
Market Side Comparison

Two Sided

Often times the same trade appears on both unmatched and advisory files/reports with one or more of the trade details not matching. This is the cause of the unmatched/advisory status. For example #1 LB may report a buy of 1000 shares of HK China Gas at HKD100 while the counter-party #2 LB reports a sell of 100 HK China Gas at HKD10. Though all other trade details match, this trade will be not match due to the quantity and price differences. This can be true of any and all of the data submitted by LBs to the ISO and may result in more than one data comparison difference. Other reasons for trades to appear on one report or the other is failure of one counter-party LB to submit trade activity to the ISO or misidentification of a LB by another LB. In any case it is important that each LB react to the information submitted by the ISO, and resolve any differences in a timely and efficient manner.

The first comparison differences reviewed are trades on the unmatched and advisory report with one or more details differing. The first step by each LB is to review the internal records to determine if the trade was submitted accurately. LBs review the source of the trade information. Which usually originates from a trade ticket, voice entry, or electronic feed. Voice entry is still evolving and is not in common use. Electronic feeds usually are not the cause unless the message is reentered into the system. Trade tickets are the common source document referenced for this process. Analysis is performed to insure that the original trade submitted matched the trade ticket details. A common cause of errors at this stage of processing is handwriting transcription or voice recognition errors. In either case, once a LB identifies the cause of an unmatched or advisory trade, they endeavor to correct and resolve the problem.

The normal process is to notify the counter-party LB of the problem and advise that corrective action will be taken with the ISO. The next step is to process trade adjustment entries to reflect the proper trade details. This activity affects the LBs internal records by canceling the incorrect trade detail and reestablishing the correct trade details. At the same time it will also pass along this activity to the ISO, in the proper format, advising of the cancellation of the erroneous trade and advising of the correct trade. The ISO will delete the unmatched trade. The correct trade will now match the original trade submitted by the counter-party LB and eliminates the advisory trade.

Part I: PRE-SETTLEMENT
Chapter 4
Market Side Comparison

Two Sided

For trades not submitted by LBs, or misidentified, appropriate corrective processing is required. In the first situation, the non-responsive LB is contacted; the situation reviewed and as a result proper adjustment trades will be submitted to the ISO. Misidentified LBs are recognized, through the unmatched and advisory reports, and adjusting entries are submitted to the ISO.

Two-sided comparison is the ideal process in the absence of an automated trading system that provides the ability to lock in trades. It is the minimal level of service that must be provided to consider the country or marketplace reasonable from various perspectives; assurance that trades will settle, risk controls and mandated procedures.

The International Securities Market Association (ISMA) formerly the International Association of Bond Dealers (IABD) launched TRAX in January 1989. TRAX is an example of a two-sided comparison system. Designed by ISMA members, TRAX is primarily used to match the details of bond trades although the instruments that can be matched in the system include derivatives, equities, warrants as well as domestic and international bonds. The system also has links to various regulatory authorities and will report trade details (with the permission of the subscriber) to country regulators. TRAX also interfaces with Euroclear and Clearstream (two international clearing agencies discussed in Chapter 15) and will forward settlement instructions to the clearinghouses eliminating the need for the participants to re-key and re-transmit trade information to the clearing agencies for settlement.

The functions provided by the ISO are important to the success of two-sided comparison. The basic service is the trade matching that permits the LBs to submit their trades for matching and results in three forms. These forms, Matched, Unmatched and Advisory allow the LBs to use the concept of exception processing. Exception processing identifies and separates the trades that matched from the trades that require further manual processing. This will ensure timely and accurate settlement. The ISO also serves as a catalyst in identifying and motivating LBs to actively participate in the Comparison process. The final function provided will be addressed at the conclusion of this section in the section titled *Advanced ISO Comparison Services*.

Part I: PRE-SETTLEMENT
Chapter 4
Market Side Comparison

One Sided

The final type of comparison found in the global marketplace is One-sided comparison. This manual process usually does not involve an ISO and may not be a formal procedure within a marketplace. It is the basic form of comparison and relies on the active participation of the LBs involved in trading. Since no ISO is required to conduct this process, it lacks many of the services and resulting benefits that an ISO provides. Often there is no requirement for LBs to actively participate in the process.

The flow of the process is not consistent across markets but we will discuss a typical process. It usually begins with the selling LB advising the buying LB of the trade details. This advice is provided in paper form in a standard or variable format. It is the responsibility of the buying LB to review and advise on the accuracy of the information provided by the selling LB.

The buying LB's method of review is to visually compare the selling LB advice of trade details to their own contra side records. This process involves a field-by-field review of the data from each LB's record. Trades that match are signed to signify agreement and a copy is returned to the selling LB. A copy of the same advice is attached to the buying LB's records as proof of matching trades. This may be needed in the future to resolve settlement differences.

Discrepancies identified in trade details must be resolved between the LBs. The buying LB will advise the selling LB of the difference and seek to resolve the difference in an equitable manner. The weakness of one-sided comparison is that it relies on a visual review of trade details, which exposes the LBs to errors. Because there is no ISO acting as an intermediary, the process is driven by one half of the transaction.

The One Sided comparison system is found in emerging markets with low volumes and a small number of counter-party LBs. It is not the type of system that supports large or expanding trading volumes. The infrastructure may be in development that will provide an ISO in the form of a clearing agency or a depository to provide this service in the future.

Part I: PRE-SETTLEMENT
Chapter 4
Market Side Comparison

Advanced ISO Comparison Services

There is another process that occurs when a trade is executed in a Locked In system or when a successful match is achieved via a two-sided comparison. It is the process where the ISO interposes itself between the selling and buying LB to become the counter-party to each. The ISO reassigns each LB from selling/buying from each other to itself, thereby becoming the Central Counterparty (CCP) to each LB. The effect of this process is that each counter-party now owes or is due the shares or monies from the CCP instead of the original LB. There are a number of benefits to this process. One is that it transfers the credit risk on each LB's books from the original counter-party LB to the ISO, reducing credit exposure. Another benefit is that the ISO acts as an advocate for each LB by performing risk management and oversight functions.

The CCP must be strong, independent and have the legal right to reassign obligations in the particular country for this process to work. Markets that have this function enjoy a higher degree of completed transactions, at reduced cost, than those of markets without this function. This concept of a CCP is gaining more interest and acceptance by the European and Asian markets.

Importance of the Comparison Process

Comparison is the first step, after execution, leading to settlement. As such it is a vital process that when realized supports timely and accurate settlement and insures clients' investment objectives for the acquisition or disposal of a security. Each marketplace must provide a comprehensive comparison process between LBs.

Markets that have no formal system, or have a one sided process, provide no or minimal support and assurance to LBs and in turn to investors in their securities. This may be sufficient for local investors and LBs, but it is unsuitable and does not allow the market to compete on a global scale and will not attract investors from other markets.

In some markets the results of the comparison process are linked to the clearance, and or settlement systems. A comparison system that is part of the preparation for and settlement process is preferable as it provides seamless handoffs with less processing interruptions. The system for Preparation and the Settlement process should encourage membership and active participation by all appropriate market participants. A strong services company with oversight of market participants should manage this process.

Part I: PRE-SETTLEMENT
Chapter 4
Market Side Comparison

Requirements For An Effective Comparison System

Basic requirements of an effective comparison system affect two areas of transaction processing. When looking at the locked in trades, the major requirements are in the order execution process. A system providing automated executions with no manual processing beyond the LB order entry is required. In addition, an exchange or other ISO is needed to enforce the rules and regulations associated with a locked in trade environment. This system must protect investors by providing good and fair executions to be successful.

In a marketplace supporting two sided matching the need is for an automated match system that will process trade input from all member LBs and report the results to each. The ISO providing this service must be unbiased and independent from undue influence in executing its responsibility. This service should be accessible from various sources including direct input, file transfer, intranet and Internet with rigorous access requirements.

Another requirement, in markets with locked in or two side matching systems is the ability for the ISO to interpose itself as the offset to each side of the trade This important process minimizes counter-party risk by substituting the CCP in place of the original LB.

The CCP requires the legal right to reassign trades from one LB counter-party to itself. Of course, this occurs for Compared trades only. Uncompared trades are not eligible since there has been no agreement between LBs on the trade and its details.

By reassigning compared trades to it, the CCP is minimizing risk by separating LBs. This permits the CCP to supervise LB members and to insure that members comply with the regulations of the marketplace.

Part I: PRE-SETTLEMENT
Chapter 4
Market Side Comparison

Evolution of Comparison in Emerging & Established Markets

Markets that have no formal comparison system will often implement steps toward the ultimate environment. Initial requirements call for the creation of an ISO. This may be a clearing company that is dedicated to activities between trade and settlement dates or a depository that provides the comparison process. The clearing company that evolves is usually dependent on the markets' business practices, customs and legal issues.

Once an ISO is in place, with the cooperation and assistance of the member LBs, the ISO can establish the criteria for a matching system and the interfaces that will be supported. The interfaces are based upon the LB members' needs and abilities. The next step is to offer the match process in stages, perhaps in series of letters (securities beginning with letters A through F, and so on) allowing member LBs to use the service incrementally. This approach allows contained yet steady growth.

After the match process has been implemented and is processing a significant portion of the markets volumes for LBs, the ISO will begin to interpose itself, as a CCP, between LBs on compared trades. This is also done on an incremental basis to permit the marketplace an evolutionary rather than revolutionary phase-in process. Another approach is for the exchange or trading marketplace to begin to offer an automated trading system that locks in executed trades. The impetus for this can come from various directions: the market regulator may mandate this type of system to permit access to different types of investors or the marketplace may pursue this type of trading system for competitive or volume enhancing purposes. Regardless of why the trading system was introduced, the effect on the comparison system will be realized by the LBs. Access to the system will be implemented in phases to permit members to use the system prudently.

Today many global markets are pursing this type of system. The motivations for this approach range from competition, continued and expanding use of technology and market efficiency. Eastern European markets, which were reestablished in the late 1980's and 90's, employed this market infrastructure because of the ease of establishment and relatively low operating costs.

BRAZIL COMPARISON PROCESS

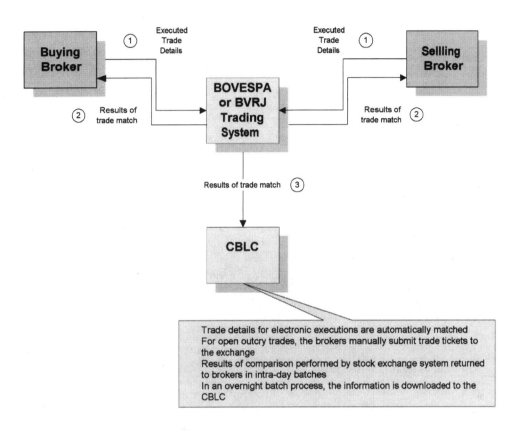

Trade details for electronic executions are automatically matched
For open outcry trades, the brokers manually submit trade tickets to the exchange
Results of comparison performed by stock exchange system returned to brokers in intra-day batches
In an overnight batch process, the information is downloaded to the CBLC

Footnotes	
BOVESPA	Bolsa de Valores (Stock Exchange) de Sao Paulo
BVRJ	Bolsa de Valores (Stock Exchange) de Rlo de Janeiro
CBLC	Companhia Brasileira de Liquidacao e Custodia (Clearing House)

HONG KONG COMPARISON PROCESS

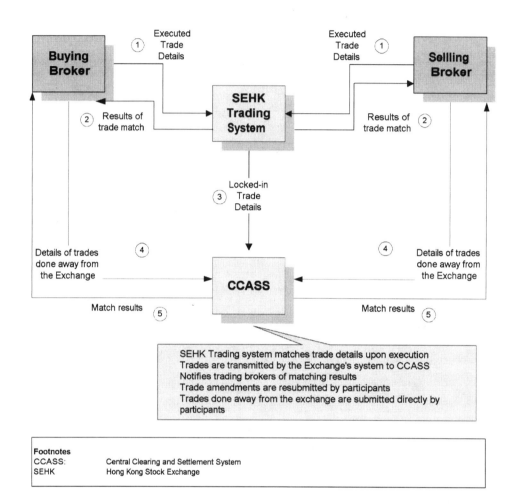

SEHK Trading system matches trade details upon execution
Trades are transmitted by the Exchange's system to CCASS
Notifies trading brokers of matching results
Trade amendments are resubmitted by participants
Trades done away from the exchange are submitted directly by participants

Footnotes
CCASS: Central Clearing and Settlement System
SEHK   Hong Kong Stock Exchange

UNITED KINGDOM COMPARISON
PROCESS

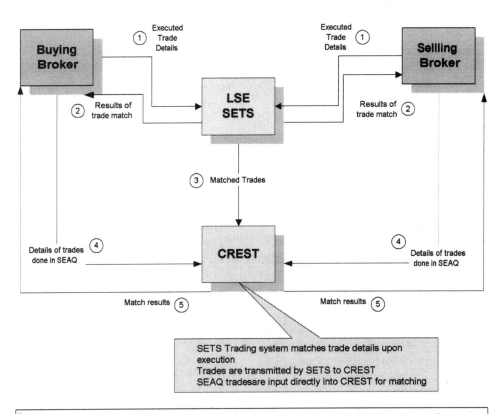

SETS Trading system matches trade details upon execution
Trades are transmitted by SETS to CREST
SEAQ tradesare input directly into CREST for matching

Footnotes	
LSE	London Stock Exchange
SETS	Stock Exchange Trading Service
SEAQ	Stock Exchange Automated Quotations
CREST	Depository for the LSE
LCH	London Clearing House

Part I: PRE-SETTLEMENT
Chapter 4
Market Side Comparison

CHAPTER PROCESS FLOW

The Comparison function takes place in a manual or automated via an Industry Service Organization such as a Clearing Corporation. Most of the activity that occurs does not result in an entry unless a trade was recorded incorrectly. This objective of this function is to ensure that the involved counterparties agree on the details of the trade. We refer to Brokers and Clearinghouse without specifying which broker or custodian is responsible. This way, we hope to reflect the process rather than confuse our readers with 'who' is doing 'what', 'when.'

A trade is executed on the Bovespa in Brazil,
between two Brokers, for 250,000 Brazilian Telephones @ 640Real,
Trade Date April 1, 2002, Settlement Date April 4, 2002

- Each broker submits trade deal specific data to Bovespa for comparison
  - This data may be submitted during the trading day by the brokers or by an exchange
  - Data is submitted no later than 12am on April 2, 2002

- CBLC processes the trades to ensure that the required data is received
  - Incomplete trade data is not processed and is returned to the Broker
  - Complete trade data is processed
  - This occurs before 6am on April 2, 2002

- The results of the Comparison are distributed to the brokers

- Upon receipt, Brokers review the output data received from the CBLC
  - Trades that do not compare are forwarded to an operations unit for resolution
  - For example if the trade in our example, 250,000 Brazilian Telephone did not compare due to a price difference between the buying and selling brokers
    - The brokers would discuss the difference and identify the cause and resolution
    - Correcting entries would be processed at the appropriate broker and the trade is resubmitted to CBLC
    - At that time our example, 250, 000 Brazilian Telephone @ 640Real would be compared
- Compared trades update the Brokers system reflecting this status

- Compared trades advance to the Clearance of Settlement process

Part I

Pre-Settlement

Chapter 5
The Clearance
Process

Part I: PRE-SETTLEMENT
Chapter 5
Clearance Process

There are two parts of the clearance process. Both occur after an order is executed and the resultant trades are generated. Simply, a clearing entity, acting as a central counterparty, provides trade guarantees through a 'Clearance Fund' and reduces settlement activity through netting and novation. The clearing entity can be a separate organization within the local industry infrastructure. Or the Central Securities Depository (CSD) can provide clearing services. The clearance processes take place between the buying and selling brokers, the street-side of the trade, and the clearing entity, which we will refer to in this chapter as the Central Counterparty (CCP) even though in some markets the role is performed by a clearinghouse. Institutional and retail investors do not currently participate in the activities described in this chapter.

This chapter describes the following street side activities, occurring after the trade has been executed, associated with the clearance function:

- Trade Guarantee
- Central Counterparty
- Multilateral Netting
- Continuous Net Settlement

The purpose of a CCP entity is to protect the participating brokers and indirectly the investors. We will present the full spectrum of how these services can be provided and identify areas of strength and weakness associated with each activity.

GUARANTEE FUND

The guarantee fund protects the buyer from the seller's default and the seller from the buyer's default. Of course you would not enter into a transaction with a counterparty that you believe was not willing and able to fulfill their obligation of the trade. But many events can occur to interrupt timely settlement and a guarantee fund is a key component to insure the completion of settlement.

Examples of incidents that would prevent or interrupt settlement include failure of the buying or selling brokerage firm, either brokers inability to complete their side of the trade due to their investor client's failure to complete their purchase or sale. The greater the interval between trade and settlement date the greater the need for a guarantee fund. For example there is greater exposure in a market with T+3 settlement than there would be in a market with T+2 settlement with all other conditions equal.

Some markets address this requirement by establishing an escrow account, with a pre-established cash balance, to be used as a guarantee fund. While other markets establish a cash deposit requirement for each broker based upon their volume, which is contributed to the guarantee fund. Other markets address this requirement outside the infrastructure of the settlement system. For example, the regulator may require brokers to make a contribution to a fund that investors can claim when a broker fails.

Part I: PRE-SETTLEMENT
Chapter 5
Clearance Process

In any case, it is vital to the safety of the processing system to provide some guarantee or insurance type system to protect brokers and in turn their investor clients against a participant's failure to meet their trade obligations. It is important to be aware of the different types of system and how each is funded as well as how and when the fund will be exhausted. The following are various methods of providing trade guarantees.

Trade Guarantee via Fixed Fund

Markets with this type of fund usually are based upon a the daily or weekly trading volumes and value. Another influence is a broker's ability to contribute. These amounts are usually fixed for a period of time. Once the broker makes their contribution the fund is static until the next review when increases or decreases are announced and funded.

This type of fund is found in markets where the business volumes and the participating brokers are stable and not subject to dramatic and sudden changes. Once established, the exchange or CCP maintains the fund. An important aspect of this type of fund is the frequency of the review of proper funding. The fund must be a sufficient amount to meet the demand of the current volumes. Without a timely review the fund may not sufficiently meet the needs of the brokers and in turn their investor clients in event of a broker's failure.

Trade Guarantee via brokers Current Volume

In these markets the CCP tracks brokers trading volume and collects an amount from each based upon the total cash value of locked-in or compared trades. In this type of fund the CCP is the focal point between the exchange and the executing brokers. The flow starts with the exchange recording executions and transmitting the trade details to the CCP.

Trades executed in a locked-in trade environment will be processed. Trades executed in a non-locked-in environment or executed away from the exchange will require successful comparison between the counterparties. This is the process addressed in Chapter 3 in the Two Sided Comparison process. At the end of the day the CCP will total the cash amount buys and sells from the locked-in and compared trades and then subtracts the smaller amount from the larger amount. This results in a net amount of a counterparties trading activity.

The net amount is then assessed a fee that is collected from the counterparty by the CCP. The assessment fee is based upon the type of security and the history of price volatility. It is subject to change by the clearinghouse. The fees collected are held in a bank account by the CCP and used in the event of the failure of a counterparty to fulfil their part of the trade. Each market, based upon their laws and regulations, has defined procedures to address the broker's failure.

This type of trade guarantee is found in markets with large trading volumes and with numerous brokers. This permits trading counterparties to centralize, or outsource, a portion of their risk management to the CCP. The CCP serves as a risk manager between trade and settlement dates assuring timely and accurate settlement as well as a "safety net" in the event of a counterparty's failure.

No Trade Guarantee

Some markets have not instituted a trade guarantee mechanism. There are a number of reasons for this situation. Often, the primary reason is that there is no clearinghouse or CCP in place to act as the intermediary between counterparties. Without an entity such as a clearinghouse to collect the fees and monitor each counterparty's activity and compliance.

Another reason for the lack of an industry sponsored trade guarantee is that the market may address this need through another mechanism. This is usually provided through an investor insurance fund that is supervised by the securities regulator. In these markets investor accounts, held by brokers, are insured against losses.

Summary of Trade Guarantees

From a trading and processing perspective market safety is vital to investor confidence. As such a trade guarantee is an important piece of the infrastructure of a market. As we have shown there are various ways that this service can be provided. The characteristics and demands of the market dictate the mechanism that is appropriate for the market.

A trade guarantee provides the assurance to brokers, directly and investors indirectly, that once a trade has been compared by counterparties, settlement will take place as expected. Without this there is failure risk between trade and settlement date. It is this time, between trade and settlement date, that the broker and investor is exposed to market losses if the counterparty fails to meet their obligation.

For this process to be effective, each market needs to have a CCP that is empowered to act independently of the brokers to protect investors and other market participants such as custodians. The CCP will need to be able to secure lines of credit and cash when a broker fails. The participating community must have confidence in the CCP and trust their judgement.

Part I: PRE-SETTLEMENT
Chapter 5
Clearance Process

NETTING

The netting process assists the local market in protecting themselves from volume volatitlies. For example, when a market is prepared, via processing systems and staff, to process 400-500 trades per day, business proceeds and is subject to little or no interruption or processing problems. If the same market experienced an rapid increase in volume of 700-800 trades per day there would be an opportunity for problems to arise. These problems would be evident in various steps between trade and settlement date such as trade comparison, the related cash & inventory movements and actual settlement of the trades. For a brief period the market participants, brokers, clearinghouse, banks and custodians would manage the increased volumes.

But after a while the resources of these organizations would be exhausted and problems would start to develop. These would evident in a number of areas; uncompared trades, inventory position differences, fails and market exposure.
This situation would get worse the longer the increased volume was sustained. There are a number of examples of this cause and result in global markets. Two that come to mind were in the United States in the late 60s and India in 1995. Increased volumes, in markets with little or no infrastructure designated to reducing settlement volumes, caused both situations.

There are a number of netting systems that reduce exposure to volume volatility. One may be more appropriate to certain markets while another may address the needs of other markets. The important issue is to understand is why a facility is needed and then based upon the environment, which type of system is appropriate. The following illustrates the various netting systems.

Trade for Trade

Trade for trade is the basic form of settlement and involves no formal netting. In markets that employ this process there is no clearinghouse or CCP to provide netting. As a result each trade is settled individually between buying and selling brokers.

The impact of this is that successful completion of trades requires that the selling broker have the securities on settlement date and is able to deliver these securities to the buying broker. And that the buying broker has the cash to pay for the securities when they are received. If either side is not prepared settlement will occur and a fail results.

Markets employing this process usually are small, low volume environments. Many may not have a clearinghouse to facilitate netting.

Part I: PRE-SETTLEMENT
Chapter 5
Clearance Process

Bi-lateral Netting

Also known as "Pair Off" netting, in this environment an intermediary will net Broker A's trades in one security against trades executed with Broker B. To be eligible for netting both brokers must have successfully compared their trades or the trades must have been executed in a 'locked-in' environment. To be effective Broker A must have bought and sold the same security with Broker B as the counterparty for each trade for the same settlement date. Ideally it may be the same quantity of the security at different prices. The process that a clearinghouse would follow would be to "net out" the share portion of the trade. As a result of this process Broker A and Broker B would not be required to exchange any shares since at the end of any exchange they would have the same amount of shares they had before the exchange. This avoids share movement and the associated costs of processing and expense related to effecting securities movement.

Cash settlement usually occurs as a separate transaction. In the above example there would be one cash settlement transaction instead of one payment and one receipt. Only the broker that sold the security for a greater amount than they bought it would receive payment. The difference in the share price multiplied by the number of shares would represent the payment received. Advice of this would be received the day before settlement. The brokers prepare to execute settlement on settlement date. Each broker must make the appropriate entries in their internal system reflecting settlement, even though only the cash payment or receipt was actually exchanged between the brokers. The activity processed on settlement dates will be illustrated in the Settlement, Chapter 6.

This system is often utilized in markets with light trading activity and low settlement volumes. Bi-lateral netting requires that two brokers have counter trades for the same security, on the same settlement date. As a result there is little reduction in number of trades to be settled.

Part I: PRE-SETTLEMENT
Chapter 5
Clearance Process

Multi-lateral Netting

This is an evolutionary step from bi-lateral netting. Here a broker's buy and sell activity is netted against the CCP without regard to the original counterparty broker. This is possible, as at this point in the process in many markets the CCP has replaced the original counterparty in the locked-in or compared trade. This process is addressed in Chapter 3: Comparison.

Similar to B-lateral netting, these trades must be compared to be eligible for netting. The process flows as follows' the day before settlement the CCP nets each participating brokers buy and sells for a security for the following days settlement. In each security a broker will be the net buyer or seller for that security for which they will owe to the CCP for settlement the next day. The results will be advised to each broker. Each broker will verify this information to assure accuracy. After that they will process entries designating that certain trades will not be settled externally. At the same time the broker will establish a new trade reflecting the number of shares owed to the CCP as a result of multi-lateral netting.

For example, Broker A may have five trades in Glaxo Smithkline for settlement on March 17th. Two are buy trades for 200 and 300 shares respectively. The three sell trades are for 200, 300 and 400 shares. Each of these trades was executed with a different counterparty participant. As a result Broker A has 5 trades settling on March 17th for Glaxo Smithkline shares.

Multilateral netting will "net" the 2 buy trades for a total of 500 shares against the 3 sell trades for 900 shares resulting in 1 sell trade for 400 shares. This is the only trade that Broker A will settle for Glaxo Smithkline. On settlement date the broker that owes a security will deliver it to the CCP versus payment. The clearinghouse, in turn, will deliver the securities to the broker or brokers that are due the securities versus payment. This method minimizes the movement of securities and cash providing a great benefit to the participating brokers.

In addition multi-lateral netting provides the industry with the ability to be insensitive to trading volumes. As a broker can be a net seller, or buyer, in a security for one settlement date. If a broker's trade volume in Hong Kong Cement leaps from 50 trades per day to 200 trades there will be no increase in the settlement of Hong Kong Cement as the CCP will reduce the 200 trades to one net buy or sell amount which is the same result of the 50 trade day volume. The cash side of each trade settles on the scheduled settlement date. But these are processed as cash only and also results in a net settlement amount based upon a broker buy and sell volume. None of our countries employ this type of clearance but it can be found in Mexico, Japan and Singapore.

Part I: PRE-SETTLEMENT
Chapter 5
Clearance Process

Continuous Net Settlement

This is the ultimate netting environment. It is also known as CNS. It operates the same way as multi-lateral netting with a few differences. The first is that only certain securities are eligible for CNS. These are the very liquid, commonly traded companies in a market. Securities in companies that are illiquid or lightly traded are usually not eligible for CNS. Trades must be compared for CNS eligibility.

The major difference is in the case of failed settlements. Usually fails are processed and resolved outside the settlement process. In the CNS environment failed trades are recycled into the next day's settlement and reconsidered for resolution in that day's netting cycle. For example if broker D owes the CCP 200 shares of Hong Kong Cement; and is not able to deliver it on settlement date of June 16th the 200 shares is recycled into June 17ths netting activity. This will continue to recycle until the trade is actually settled (value is exchanged). The cash component is processed the same way as multi-lateral netting.

The appeal of CNS is that if you fail to deliver a security today, it's likely that you will be purchasing the same security within the next few days and one will offset the other. In this way the infrastructure remains viable and fails are reduced. There are 3 markets that utilize this method. We will illustrate the Hong Kong process, in addition the U.S. and Canada, in the section following.

Conclusion

Netting and novation is vital to growing, dynamic and liquid markets. It minimizes the external exchange of securities and cash. Through this the expenses related to security and cash movement, and the related failure and problems generated, are reduced. Another major benefit of netting is that the market will realize a reduction in failed trades. The reduction of trades to be settled externally permits brokers to concentrate on the remaining trades assuring timely settlement.

It doesn't matter if the market is physical, depository or book entry. There is an expense incurred for each instruction processed internally, externally and the related reconciliation of activity. Netting permits much of this activity and expense to be eliminated.

The infrastructure required is a strong, independent clearinghouse and participants that support the CCP.

BRAZIL CLEARANCE PROCESS

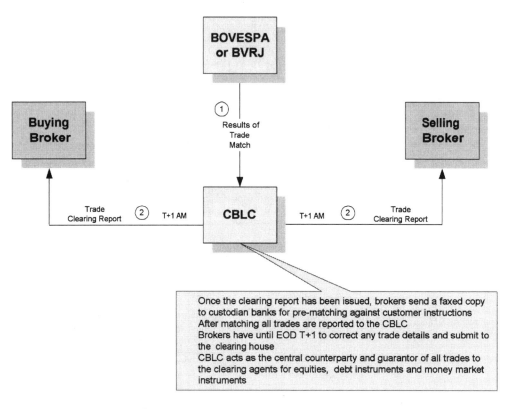

Once the clearing report has been issued, brokers send a faxed copy to custodian banks for pre-matching against customer instructions
After matching all trades are reported to the CBLC
Brokers have until EOD T+1 to correct any trade details and submit to the clearing house
CBLC acts as the central counterparty and guarantor of all trades to the clearing agents for equities, debt instruments and money market instruments

Footnotes	
BOVESPA	Bolsa de Valores (Stock Exchange) de Sao Paulo
BVRJ	Bolsa de Valores (Stock Exchange) de Rio de Janeiro
CBLC	Companhia Brasileira de Liquidacao e Custodia (Clearing House)
NOTE: Multilateral netting to be introduced 2002	

HONG KONG CLEARANCE PROCESS

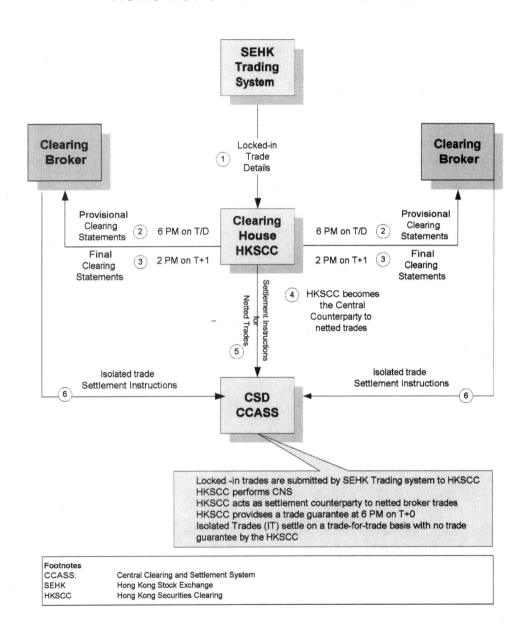

Locked -in trades are submitted by SEHK Trading system to HKSCC
HKSCC performs CNS
HKSCC acts as settlement counterparty to netted broker trades
HKSCC providses a trade guarantee at 6 PM on T+0
Isolated Trades (IT) settle on a trade-for-trade basis with no trade guarantee by the HKSCC

Footnotes	
CCASS:	Central Clearing and Settlement System
SEHK	Hong Kong Stock Exchange
HKSCC	Hong Kong Securities Clearing

UNITED KINGDOM CLEARANCE PROCESS

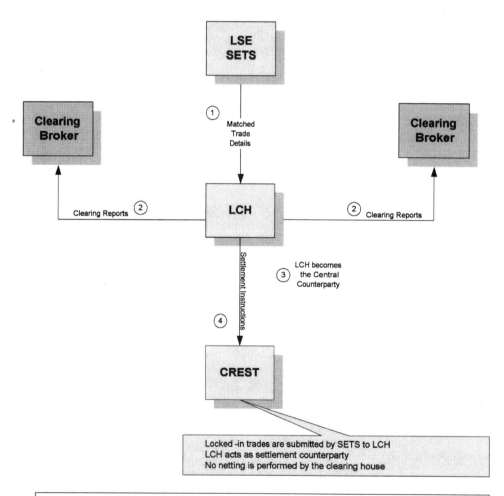

Locked -in trades are submitted by SETS to LCH
LCH acts as settlement counterparty
No netting is performed by the clearing house

Footnotes

LSE	London Stock Exchange
SETS	Stock Exchange Trading Service
SEAQ	Stock Exchange Automated Quotations
CREST	Depository for the LSE
LCH	London Clearing HouseCCASS:

Part I: PRE-SETTLEMENT
Chapter 5
Clearance Process

CHAPTER PROCESS FLOW

The following reflects the flow of internal and external activities required to process the Clearance function and maintain accurate records regarding the status of trades pending settlement. We refer to Broker and Clearinghouse without specifying which broker s responsible. This way, we hope to reflect the process rather than confuse our readers with 'who' is doing 'what', 'when'

---

*Flemings, a broker-member of the HKSE & HKSCC,
has executed the following trades in H.K. & China Gas
with various other members,
on April 1, 2002 with Settlement on April 3, 2002*

Buys
10,000 @ 56 HKD from Broker M
30,000 @ 55 HKD from Broker L
8,000 @ 57 HKD from Broker K
11,000 @ 36 HKD from Broker J

Sells
20,000 @ 58 HKD to Broker Z
12,000 @ 56 HKD to Broker Y
42,000 @ 54 HKD to Broker X
50,000 @ 52 HKD to Broker W

- The H.K. & China Gas trades were executed in the, AMS, they are 'locked–in' trades and will be transmitted to the HKSCC which then performs the following activities
  - The HKSCC, as the Central CounterParty, will legally alter each Brokers role in the trade
    - For example in the first example, Flemings buy of 10,000 @ 56 from Broker M Flemings will now receive those shares from HKSCC
    - Broker M will deliver the shares to HKSCC instead of Flemings
  - This activity occurs on April 1, 2002

---

*HKSCC will also multi-lateral net these trades on April 2, 2002,
reducing the number of settlements that Flemings will physically settle for
H.K. & China Gas as follows*

- HKSCC nets the total buys executed by Flemings on the AMS versus the total sales executed by Flemings on April 1, 2002.
  - This represents 59,000 shares bought and 124,000
- The number of shares remaining from the netting process is 65,000 shares sold by Flemings
  - The 42,000 bought 'nets' against 42,000 of the 124,000 sold on April 1, 2002

HKSCC will advise Flemings of the results of the multi-lateral netting process
for the H.K & China Gas trades and
other trades for securities traded by Flemings on April 1, 2002.
Flemings will process the following entries
reflecting the status of the H.K. & China Gas trades

Sell trades, representing 124,000, shares reduced (debited) from pending settlement status	**Buy trades, representing 42,000 shares reduced (credited) from settlement status**
	Sell trade set-up (credited) reflecting the Delivery 0f 65,000 H.K. & China to HKSCC

- This does not cancel or affect the original trades. They each occurred and will 'settle' internally and will not require an external exchange of the securities
  o The 65,000 shares will be the only external exchange of securities
- The cash portion of the netted trades are not netted, they will settle as Cash Only activity on Settlement Date
- This action occurs on April 1, 2002

Questions

1) Of the following countries, which requires that a foreign investor to be an institution to buy securities on their exchange?
   a) Argentina
   b) Chile
   c) Finland
   d) Hong Kong

2) When would an Investor's Broker execute an order through a local or overseas broker?
   a) If they are not a member of the clearing house
   b) If they are not a member of the settlement facility
   c) If they are not a member of the exchange
   d) If they do not speak the language

3) Investors should verify regulations of the overseas exchange in which they plan to invest. Regulations include all of the following except:
   a) Quality of the shares owned by institutional investors
   b) Requirements for approval of a new account
   c) Maximum number of shares that may be purchased by a foreign investor
   d) Rules for short sales

4) All of the following describe a price-driven (or quote-driven) execution system except:
   a) Brokers advertise their bid and ask price
   b) The investor negotiates the execution price with their broker
   c) An order to buy 1000 shares at 5 is executed versus another client order
   d) A large order received from the investor is worked by the market-maker

5) An Investor enters an order to buy 10,000 Raffles Center Ltd. The broker executes the order by selling the stock from their trading account. What is this type of execution called?
   a) Stock Exchange execution
   b) Market-maker execution
   c) Agency execution
   d) Order-driven execution

6) Upon receipt of the report of the purchase of 10,000 Raffles Center Ltd, the Investor disagrees with the details of the trade. Of the following, what action does the Investor take?
   a) The Investor rejects the confirmation
   b) The Investor rejects the affirmation
   c) The Investor rejects the settlement instructions
   d) The Investor rejects the prize

7) After receiving a notice of execution of a purchase of 10,000 of British Airways, the Institutional Investor advises their broker that they wish to book the trade as 5,000 to Account #1 and 5,000 to Account #2. What is this process called?
   a) The confirmation process
   b) The trade allocation process
   c) The affirmation process
   d) The matching process

8) The Board Lot / Round Lot for China Southern Airlines Co., Ltd, is 2000 shares. An Institutional Investor is allocating a purchase of 10,000 shares to four (4) accounts. What is the quantity of shares that should be allocated to each account?
   a) 2,500 shares to each account
   b) 2000, 2000, 3000, 3000
   c) 2000, 2000, 2000, 4000
   d) Any of the above

9) The Investor's Standard Settlement Instructions (SSI) contain all of the following information except:
   a) Investor's Security Account Number
   b) Global Custodian Bank's BIC Code
   c) Sub-Custodian Bank's BIC Code
   d) Security Trade Data

10) In contrasting confirmation / affirmation systems and trade matching systems, what function does a trade matching system perform?
   a) Affirms the Broker's confirmation
   b) Allocates the Investor's trade
   c) Compares the Investor's trade allocation and the Brokers confirmation
   d) Affirms the Broker's notice of execution

11) Of the following, which type of trade best describes the `market-side' of the trade?
   a) A purchase directly from another investor
   b) A purchase on a stock exchange
   c) A purchase vs. the Broker's trading account
   d) A purchase from a colleague

12) All of the following describe the benefits of a lock-in trade except:
   a) Eliminates the need for the comparison process
   b) Immediately notifies the submitting broker of the trade details
   c) Immediately reports matched and unmatched trades to the submitting broker
   d) Enables STP

13) A trade in which of the following execution systems results in a locked-in trade?
   a) Hong Kong's AMS
   b) Hong Kong's ITS
   c) London's SEAQ

d) London's Market-Makers

14) During the comparison process, Broker #1 knows a buy of 1,000 Raffles Center Ltd at HKD 6.00. Broker #2 knows the trade at HKD 6.25. On which report will this trade will be reported to Broker #1?
a) Only on the advisory report
b) Only on the unmatched report
c) On both the unmatched and advisory
d) On neither report since Broker #1 is correct

15) All of the following accurately describes the role of the Central Counter-Party except:
a) Assumes the broker's credit risk
b) Reports unmatched trades to the submitting broker
c) Monitors the risk management function
d) Reassigns executing counter-party to itself

16) All of the following participate in the clearance process except:
a) The clearing entity
b) The buying broker
c) The selling broker
d) The Institutional Investor

17) What is the reason for a Trade Guarantee Fund?
a) To protect against counter-party default
b) To protect against market risk
c) To protect against failed trades
d) To protect against credit risk

18) What is the primary reason a market has not implemented a trade guarantee mechanism?
a) The clearing house does not exist
b) The brokers high credit rating
c) The trading volume is stable
d) The regulators regularly review broker's net worth

19) A trade guarantee mechanism based on the broker's current volume includes all of the following except:
a) The broker's trading volume is tracked
b) The amount of the contribution is fixed during a periodic review
c) The amount of the contribution is based on the net value of daily trades
d) The daily computation is based on compared and locked-in trades

20) All of the following accurately describe a Continuous Net Settlement system except:
a) Only designated securities are eligible
b) Only compared trades are eligible
c) Trades must settle by the intended settlement date
d) The system reduces the number of failed trades

Part II

Settlement

Chapter 6
The Settlement Process

Part II: SETTLEMENT
Chapter 6
Settlement Environments

During the clearance process, the amount of securities and funds to be transferred is set. It is during the settlement process that the transfer of the securities and funds takes place. The intrinsic goals of an efficient settlement process are to effect the movement of both securities and the respective cash counter-values in a timely manner and to eliminate, or at least minimize, the risk of delivering the securities and not receiving the sale proceeds or paying for the shares and not receiving them. Markets attempt to accomplish these goals in different ways. As with executing an order, each market's settlement system has unique characteristics. Before dealing in a market, Brokers and Investors should understand the market's requirements for trade settlement.

This chapter explores the distinct and shared characteristics in global settlement systems. In this chapter we will examine the:
- Evolution of settlement practices
- Key Definitions
- Participants and their role in settlement
- Settlement of the securities
- Settlement of the funds
- Fail Control
- Things that can go wrong
- Effect of settlement systems in transition

The Evolution to today's Settlement Environment
The first 'settlement system' was directly between the buyer and the seller. The seller delivered securities to the buyer in the form of physical certificates, in registered form, and the buyer paid for them. The possibility existed that the certificates were not genuine; the buyer was at risk until the company (i.e., the company's registrar) verified the authenticity of the certificates. Share certificates were (and still are) usually pre-printed in small lots of 100, 200 or 500 shares; in some countries, shares are available in (only) 1 share certificates. Stacks of certificates were received, counted, checked for authenticity, and recorded - - a cumbersome and time-consuming task.

As market volumes increased, settlement was delayed for months as back-offices dealt with the avalanche of certificates that needed to be received, logged in, verified and delivered each day. Eventually, some Brokers agreed to 'net' deliveries - - that is, two Brokers who bought and sold the same security, would agree to deliver (and receive) only the difference between the purchase and sale amounts. They also agreed to net the amount due on the trade - - that is, the Broker who owed money on the trades would pay the difference. However, the settlement of the trade would only be final when the certificates were registered in the name of the new owner (called the beneficial owner) and the seller received the sale proceeds. The company registrar had the final word on the authenticity of the certificate and may have rejected certificates that did not pass inspection (i.e., signature was not valid or the certificate itself was mutilated or questionable). Payment for trades was typically made by check, which might have taken two or more days to clear. Only when the seller had a check that had cleared and the buyer had a certificate in their name was the trade considered settled.

Clearing Houses (as described in Chapter 5) simplified the process but early on, physical certificates were still used. Most markets agreed there had to be a better way. If physical certificates are used for settlement, risk and delays occur. In response to increasing volumes, even staunch advocates of ownership through physical possession grew more accepting of more efficient methods of settlement. To eliminate the physical movement of certificates, reduce risks and delays, markets sought an efficient way to settle a trade. This led to the development of the Central Securities Depository (CSD). Although some physical certificates exist in most markets, almost all countries have, or are in the process of switching to, book entry settlement (i.e., a computerized transfer of a position) through a CSD.

Today's settlement environment is a mixture of physical certificates and computerized book-entry in a CSD.
Depending on the country and the type of security, the securities settle in any of the following ways:
- Physical transfer of a certificate directly between counterparties or via a clearing house
- Book entry transfer with certificates held in the CSD
- Book entry transfer through a central or company registry
- Real Time Gross Settlement (RTGS)

The funds settle in different ways depending on the available payment mechanisms in the country and market practice. These practices include:
- Physical payment of a check
- Real time electronic funds transfer (EFT) payment
- Transfer of the net amount of funds or a final `net' transfer of funds via a payment netting system

Before we look at each of these types of settlement, let's first review a few key definitions and the participants in the settlement process.

Key Definitions
- Delivery Vs. Payment (DVP)
  There are two types of DVP practiced in the marketplace:

- o True DVP is the simultaneous transfer of funds and securities
  - To accomplish 'true' DVP, the entity must be a bank able to process both the settlement of the securities and the funds.
  - The terms of settlement usually include a provision allowing the bank to reverse the entries if settlement cannot be completed. In true DVP the reversibility of one side is strictly dependent on the return or refund of the other asset.
  - Examples of 'true' DVP are Euroclear versus Euroclear settlement or Clearstream versus a Clearstream settlement. (see Chapter 15 – Industry Organizations), who, since both are banks, are able to process the securities and the cash side of the trade. True DVP only applies if settlement is occurring within the Clearstream or Euroclear system. If only one side is a Clearstream or Euroclear participant and the counter-party is settling outside the system the settlement is dependent on the other settlement system (which may or may not be true DVP).
  - o DVP, as defined and accepted in the industry, is delivery vs. *verified* or assured payment. This is practiced by many CSDs that verify transfer of funds at a bank prior to moving the securities into the buyer's account.

- Free of payment (FOP)
  - o FOP is the transfer of the securities against no funds or the transfer of securities against a separate payment of funds. The transfer of securities with no related transfer of funds is most common when securities transfer in one country and the funds transfer in another country
- Book entry settlement
  - o Book entry settlement is the computerized transfer of a position from the seller's to the buyer's account (i.e., the participants).
- Real Time Gross Settlement (RTGS)
  - o RTGS is the simultaneous transfer of securities (i.e., each trade vs. the netted amount) and funds.

Who settles a trade?
To successfully settle a trade, two groups are needed – the group that authorizes the settlement of the trade and the group directly involved in the actual settlement of the trade.

Part II: SETTLEMENT
Chapter 6
Settlement Environments

In the group that authorizes the settlement of a trade are the:
- Investor
- Investor's Broker (IB)
- Global Custodian Bank (GCB)

Since, in an overseas trade, these parties are not typically members of the marketplace where the trade is taking place, they authorize their agent in the country of investment. As mentioned in Chapter 1, if this trade were taking place in their own marketplace, the IB and GCB (and, in some cases, the Investor) would be a member of the exchange or settlement system and would settle the trade directly. However, if they are not members of the overseas marketplace, the IB and Investor authorize their agent or GCB to settle the trade.

The group that directly settles the trade is:
- The Agent for the Investor's Broker (IB's Agent)
- The Sub Custodian Bank (SCB)
- The Local Broker (LB)
- The Settlement Agency
  (usually the Central Securities Depository – the CSD)
- The Market's Payment Bank and/or payment system
- The Bank used for the Foreign Exchange transaction
  (if different from the GCB or Agent)

The Sub Custodian Bank (SCB)
The SCB is the GCB's agent in the country where settlement will take place. The GCB receives instructions from the Investor or the IB and forwards them to the SCB. They are the ones that have physical possession of the certificates and/or are a participant of the CSD. They perform, on behalf of the Investor or IB, all settlement and custody functions.

The Agent
The agent is typically a SCB, a local affiliate of the IB or a local bank or Broker. An IB may decide to utilize a GCB for settlement or may opt to use their local branch or a non-affiliate. If they use a GCB, the SCB acts on instruction from the GCB (see above, the Sub-Custodian Bank). If the IB has chosen to use an affiliate or non-affiliate as their agent, the agent receives instructions from the IB. Like the SCB, they are the ones that have physical possession of the certificates and/or are a participant of the

CSD. They perform, on the IB's behalf, all settlement and custody functions.

The Local Broker (LB)

As the stock exchange and/or settlement member, the LB has direct access to the market's settlement system, They will be a member of the CSD (or settle trades through a Broker who is a member) and have an account at the banking system (or, again, settle through an intermediary).

The Settlement Agency

This is the entity responsible for maintaining and transferring the security positions. In most markets, the Settlement Agency is the Central Securities Depository (CSD). In a few markets, the Clearing House not only clears the trade (see Chapter 5) but also settles trades in the physical environment. Let's take a look at the role of each in the two methods of settlement - - book-entry and physical settlement.

Book Entry settlement through a CSD
Settlement within a CSD is called book-entry settlement. Traditionally, CSDs have been the repository of their participants' securities. The certificates are immobilized - - i.e., they don't move but are kept in the CSD's vault. Brazil and Hong Kong are among the many countries that maintain securities in a CSD.

Over the past decade, many CSDs have de-materialized the certificates, i.e., the certificates no longer exist in physical form. This is sometimes known as scriptless settlement and the system is sometimes called a Central Registry instead of a Central Depository. These CSDs maintain an automated record of ownership. The settlement process is the same whether the securities are immobilized or dematerialized – the only difference is the vault is empty.

Markets that have dematerialized certificates, break down into two further categories. Some have totally eliminated certificates while others have only eliminated the certificates during the settlement process. The distinction being the form of the security *after* settlement. For example, Denmark is an example of a market that has totally dematerialized certificates. In 1983 the VP (the Danish Securities Center) dematerialized all listed bonds followed by all listed shares in 1988. There are no physical certificates for listed securities. On the other hand, the U.K.'s CREST system and Australia's CHESS system are examples of markets that have eliminated certificates for settlement but a shareholder may still obtain a physical certificate for their wall, collection, etc. By requiring that the certificate be dematerialized for settlement, delays resulting from late deliveries of physical certificates are eliminated. In the U. K., after a trade has settled, an Investor may request a physical certificate be sent to them. Their Broker will instruct a withdrawal from CREST, who debits the Brokers position and instructs the company's registrar to issue a certificate. However, before selling these shares, the Investor must return the certificate to their Broker or the company registrar who cancels the certificate and sets up the position in CREST. With the position now back in the Broker's CREST account, the shares may be sold, with settlement via book-entry in CREST.

Physical Settlement

Some markets (fewer each day), also have an entity that acts as an intermediary (usually the clearing house) for the receipt and delivery of physical certificates. These may be certificates of companies that are not yet CSD eligible. In some cases, they are securities not widely held or traded and with low turnover; the CSD has delayed adding these to the list of eligible securities. In other cases, only equities are eligible in the CSD. Even if CSD eligible, many markets do not require (they encourage, but do not require) settlement in the CSD. As a result, occasionally Brokers will opt for physical settlement. Whatever the reason, Investors and Brokers should be aware that some trades may settle in the physical environment.

The Payment Bank or Payment system

This is the bank used by the Settlement Agency to receive or make payment for the securities. Payments are typically made via an electronic funds transfer (EFT) system, although checks are still used in some countries. Depending on the market, payment is made either directly between the SCBs, an exchange or CSD designated bank or a payment netting system.

Payment via a designated Bank

Many markets require payment at the CSD designated bank - - most often the Central Bank of the Country. For example, In Brazil, payment for settlement of equities and government bonds is made through the Central Bank. In Hong Kong, the exchange has approved more than 15 banks as 'designated banks.' The Investor's SCB and the Broker's Agent Bank is either a designated bank or clears payments through a designated bank. This allows a CSD, with procedures in place to verify payment before transferring the position for a DVP trade, to receive an automated verification of payment from the bank.

Part II: SETTLEMENT
Chapter 6
Settlement Environments

Payment via a Payment Netting System

A Payment Netting System receives instructions from their participants to debit their account and credit funds to the receiver's account. The system also monitors the participant's collateral and credit limits. Participants are typically the larger banks in the country. These banks are called the settlement banks or the payment banks. Other banks, in turn, maintain accounts with the settlement banks and authorize payments through them. The settlement banks pledge securities or deposit cash as collateral. They must have sufficient collateral to support their level of business (collateral requirements vary by system). In monitoring the credit limit, the system will not process a debit instruction if it causes the participant to exceed the account's credit limit, until there is a change in the situation that would permit the payment (e.g., additional collateral is deposited or an instruction for the receipt of funds is processed). Periodically during the day and/or at the end of the day (depending on the system), the debit and credit entries that were made to a participant's account are netted, producing one payable or receivable amount that the participant must settle at the account of the payment system.

For example, In the U. K., to settle a trade in CREST, the funds settle through the electronic credit transfer and netting system called the Clearing House Automated Payment system (CHAPs). Introduced in 1984, CHAPS debits or credits a participant's account as instructed - - including amounts resulting from settlements at CREST. CREST assures payment for securities (if a DVP trade) by utilizing the CHAPS' system of monitoring collateral and credit limits. Under the CHAPS system, the net amount due or receivable is calculated either 'real time' or 'end of day' depending on the plan selected by the participant. Real Time payments are netted periodically during the day, generating a report to the settlement bank; the settlement bank instructs payment (if a debit balance) or receives funds (if a credit balance) at the Bank of England. If the participant has opted to net all payments, a final amount is determined at the end of the day for settlement at the Bank of England. At this writing, CREST is implementing plans to also settle CREST trades vs. central bank funds at the Bank of England.

The Foreign Exchange Bank
This is the bank utilized by a Broker or Investor to buy or sell currency. As discussed in Chapters 2 and 8, an Investor might execute their currency transactions through their GCB; a Broker through their own trading desk or Agent; or they might prefer to use another bank. To settle the currency transaction, the bank must have the ability to settle both sides of the currency

transaction – a branch or agent bank in the Investors/Brokers home country and a branch or agent bank in the country of the foreign currency.

How does a trade settle?
Each market has developed a system for settling trades that is unique to that market and but also contains elements in common with other markets. What do they have in common? Almost all markets have a CSD. Most also have some certificates that are not in the CSD - - requiring a procedure for physical settlement. Most markets utilize the country's electronic payment system to transfer funds resulting from securities settlement. How are they unique? Each market has their own requirements for using the CSD and payment system.

The key elements, and the different ways of implementation, of trade settlement are:
- Preparing the Settlement Instructions
- Pre-matching and Matching of Instructions
- Delivering the Securities
    - Physical delivery of securities
    - Book-entry via the CSD
    - Real Time Gross Settlement (RTGS)
- Paying or Receiving the Funds
    - Real Time Electronic Funds Transfer (EFT) System
    - Payment Netting System
    - Check
- The Deadlines and Settlement Cycle
- Closing out open trades

Preparing the Trade Instructions
The first step to settle a trade is sending the instruction. The Investor and IB send the trade instruction to the GCB or Agent.

The Instruction contains the following information:
- Trade and Settlement Date
- Security Description / Code (ISIN)
    - The security to be settled must be clearly identified. Dual-listed securities, securities with similar names, different Series or Classes of the same security – all contribute to errors in settlement unless the security is identified by the security code (For additional information see the section on what can go wrong - later in this chapter). The International numbering system, one of the G30 recommendations (see

Chapter 15 - Industry Groups) is used in most countries for cross-border instructions.

- Quantity (see below – determining the amount for settlement)
- Settlement Amount
  - This is the cost or proceeds of the trade. The amount includes all fees, taxes, commission and accrued interest that are applicable to the trade.
  - The instruction will either be a DVP or FOP instruction. If the counterparty is expected to pay upon receipt of the securities, a DVP instruction is sent. If the securities are to be delivered free of payment, a FOP instruction is sent.
    - Some CSDs require all instructions be DVP. In this case, to instruct a CSD to delivery the securities free of payment, the instruction is sent with a consideration amount of 0.00.
    - During times of financial crisis, some markets required all settlement to be DVP; a requirement that was relaxed after the emergency passed.
- Currency Code (ISO code)
  - This is the currency of settlement.
  - Trades do not necessarily settle in the local currency of the country of investment. For example, trades executed in the U. K. may settle in a currency other than British Pounds (GBP) including Euro (EUR) and U. S. Dollars (USD).
- Instruction Type
  - This is the instruction to either 'receive' purchased shares or 'deliver' sold shares.
- Counterparty Account Number or BIC Code
  - Depending on the requirements of the CSD, the information that must be provided is either the Account number or code at the CSD, the full and exact name of the account, or the Bank Identification Code (BIC). The source of Counterparty information for the IB and the Investor are the Settlement Instruction Databases (discussed in Chapter 3 – Client confirmation).

Determining the Quantity for Settlement
Netting purchases and sales, which reduces cost and settlement risk, is common practice in the securities industry. As previously mentioned, before CSDs, Brokers agreed to net physical deliveries whenever possible. The two methods of determining the quantity of a trade for settlement is either Trade for Trade or Net Settlement.

- Trade for Trade is the transfer of each individual trade

- Net Settlement is the balancing of purchases and sales to generate one quantity for settlement (either a net receive or a net deliver).

In today's settlement environment, LBs net many of their transactions. During the clearance process (see Chapter 5) one net amount (per security) is determined for each LB. This information is reported to each LB and/or forwarded to the CSD for processing. Investors and most IBs, on the other hand, settle Trade for Trade and send instructions to their SCB/Agent on each individual trade.

In some markets, the IB's agent and the SCB are being invited to participate in the netting process. This reduces the number of settlement transactions for all concerned – the LB, the IB and the SCB. This does not change the way the quantity for settlement is calculated. The IB and Investor will continue to send their instructions as they have in the past. However it enables IBs, who may have purchased for one Investor and sold for another, to settle the trades simultaneously (their Agent will net these trades). The same for the SCB – it allows an SCB with instructions from one Investor to deliver and instructions from another to receive, to net these transactions. For example, Thailand's Net Clearing System links the Thailand Securities Depository (TSD), the LBs and the SCBs. The securities' net position is transferred at the TSD. Although netting has greater impact on the settlement of the LB's trades, netting also reduces cost and exposure for both the SCB and IB.

Pre-matching and Matching

Pre-matching of Instructions is the process used to compare the trade details sent by the Investor or the IB. In most markets, this step is not necessary for the trades executed by the LB as their trades were matched (compared) during the comparison process or were executed on a locked in basis (see Chapter 4 – Market Side). However, the pre-matching of instructions received by the IB and Investor's GCB or agent is crucial for trade settlement.

As described in Chapter 3 – Client Confirmation, the IB sent the confirmation of the trade to the Investor. The IB and the Investor matched their trade details. The Investor sent their trade instructions to their GCB who forwarded them to their SCB. At the same time, the IB forwarded their instructions to their Agent. Unfortunately, the instructions received by the SCB and the IB's Agent may not contain the same information that was matched by the Investor and IB. As noted in Chapter 3, if the instructions were sent by fax, the trade details had to be re-entered into the GCB's system. It is possible some detail of the trade was input incorrectly.

Part II: SETTLEMENT
Chapter 6
Settlement Environments

Faxed trade instructions, still sent by some Investors (especially Investors with few international trades) make pre-matching necessary, On the other hand, the use of ETC systems and a Central Matching System (described in Chapter 3) will improve (if not ensure) the probability of a matched trade instruction in the country of settlement. By using systems that support Straight Through Processing (STP), the same information that was matched between the IB and Investor is accessible to the GCB, the SCB, and the IB's Agent. The use of systems that support STP would make the need for pre-matching obsolete.

But, in the current environment, before entering their instructions to the CSD, each SCB contacts (usually by SWIFT or phone) the other SCB or Agent to verify that their instructions match. With current and anticipated volumes, this is almost an impossible task. Reduced use of faxes would certainly help alleviate this problem.

At most CSDs, the instructions from the LB, SCB or Agents are matched or affirmed at the CSD. And in some markets, this has eliminated the need for a manual pre-matching of instructions. However, in other markets, either a report of matched trades is not readily available from the CSD or other problems exist. As a result, trade instructions are manually pre-matched by the parties.

To be effective, pre-matching of trade instructions should occur on trade date or at least one day before settlement. This gives the agents an opportunity to resolve differences before the settlement date. But, considering time-zone differences and short settlement cycles, will the instructions reach the agents in time?
 Let's look at the example of the purchase of H.K. & China Gas in Hong Kong by a U. K. Investor.

- By the end of trade date, the Investor and the IB sends their instructions to their GCB and Agent. Hong Kong is closed by the time the instructions are sent from the U.K.
- On T+1, the instructions arrive on the desks of the agents in Hong Kong. Remember, in Hong Kong, the trade is due to settle two days after Trade Date (T+2).
- On T+1, the SCB and the IB's Agent attempt to match the instructions. If the instructions do not match, they will advise the IB and GCB (who will advise the Investor), of the problem. Since the U.K. business hours overlap with Hong Kong for a few hours, the instructions might be corrected and resent on T+1 and settlement can occur on T+2. If the Investor was in North or South America, where there is no time overlap with Hong Kong, a trade adjustment would be sent on T+2 - - the same day settlement is to take place.

Part II: SETTLEMENT
Chapter 6
Settlement Environments

- On T+2, the trade is due to settle. Fortunately, Hong Kong's CCASS can process an instruction on the same day it is received. This is not the case in many depositories. They require entry one day prior to Settlement Day (S-1) to settle the trade on the settlement date.

On exchanges that settle trades on T+3, most SCBs and Agents prefer to do the following:
- Pre-match on T+1
- Make any necessary corrections on T+2
- And submit the instructions to the CSD for T+3 settlement.
  In many markets, the first processing cycle is run overnight before the settlement date; in others the trade must be pre-matched by the day before settlement or the trade will not settle and the customer will incur penalties and charges for a 'failed trade.'

Part II: SETTLEMENT
Chapter 6
Settlement Environments

Receiving and Delivering the Securities

In this section, we will examine the characteristics of settling a trade in the physical environment and the book-entry environment including the advantages of Real Time Gross Settlement (RTGS).

Physical Delivery of Securities

Physical settlement requires the certificate to be delivered by the seller to the buyer. Before accepting and paying for the certificates, the buyer (or their agent) verifies that:

    a) The certificates are in good form with a valid signature
    b) The quantity is correct
    c) The description is correct. Special care should be taken when accepting delivery of securities with similar names or series and foreign or local registered shares. In markets were foreign and local shares (see Chapter 1) trade at different prices, it is important that the correct shares are received.

As noted previously, some physical settlement exists in most markets. Although decreasing, some securities (a particular type of bond or an equity issue) will still settle physically - - even if there is a CSD.

Book-Entry Settlement

Book-entry settlement is the electronic transfer of a position from the seller's account to the buyer's account at the CSD or registry. This is the most common form of settlement in the global markets. However, the methods used by CSDs vary by market.

Common Services of a CSD are:

- Receipt of Instructions
- Matching of Instructions (same criteria as in pre-matching)
- Verifying the position of securities to be delivered
- Debiting seller's account and crediting the securities to the buyer's account the securities
- Reporting completion of settlement to the participants
- Reporting change of ownership to the registrar (this step is discussed in Chapter 7 – Inventory Control and Registration)

Other Services offered by some CSDs

- Freezing seller's position upon trade execution
- On-line matching results
- Delivery vs. Payment
- Real Time Gross Settlement (RTGS)

Part II: SETTLEMENT
Chapter 6
Settlement Environments

The Basic Elements
The common elements in a CSD are the basic elements for settlement. The CSD receives the instructions, and if the instructions match, verifies that the seller has the securities in the account. If the securities are there, it debits one account and credits the position to the buyer's account. The CSD then reports the settlement results to the participants. You will notice, there is no mention of the buyer paying for the securities. Many CSDs are upgrading to include the verification of funds before transferring the securities. However, most CSDs only settle the securities side of the trade. It is the obligation of the SCB and Broker or their Agent to ensure payment for the securities delivered at the CSD.

The Basic Plus Elements
Other elements offered by CSDs include an on-line system that allows the participants to track the progress of the settlement process. They can view the match results and the debit and credit of securities and funds.

Other CSDs are contacted prior to the securities being sold (e.g., Poland and Korea). Upon receipt of the notification, they freeze the shares in the sellers account or move the shares to a settlement account. After execution, they process the settlement instructions received from the buyer and seller in the normal manner. These markets are called 'no-fail' markets because they have eliminated the possibility of a participant selling shares they cannot deliver.

The Elements that reduce Settlement Risk
Advanced CSDs offer Delivery vs. Payment (DVP) settlement. Typically, the CSD allocates (or locks or freezes) the shares in the seller's account. In some CSDs the position is transferred to a clearing or settlement account – but not to the buyer's account until payment is verified. As discussed in the section of Participants / Payment Bank, CCASS in Hong Kong only completes the transfer of the securities after receiving confirmation of the payment. CREST in the U. K. also completes the transfer after verification of sufficient collateral in CHAPS. In other cases, the CSD, upon receipt of the DVP instruction from the participant issues a debit or credit advice to the bank, In this case, after matching the instructions, the CSD transfers the securities from the sellers account to the buyer and instructs the bank to transfer the funds. After verifying that the participant has authorized payment, the bank debits the buyer's account and credits the seller's account and confirms payment to the CSD.

Part II: SETTLEMENT
Chapter 6
Settlement Environments

Real Time Gross Settlement

A major difference in CSDs is *when* the instructions will be processed. When they first started, CSDs typically began with one daily batch process. Instructions had to be sent the prior day and all instructions were processed by the CSD at a set time. Eventually, they increased the number of processes to 2, 3 or more a day. For example, if the instructions failed to reach the depository by the 10:00 a.m. cycle, the instructions might arrive and match by the 12:00 p.m. processing cycle. By providing multiple cycles, the CSD allowed participants to receive securities from one party (during one cycle) and deliver the same securities to another party (during the next cycle).

Some CSDs offer Real time settlement (RTGS). A critical advance, RTGS is continuous processing cycles (or, in some cases, so many cycles that they are in effect, continuous cycles). The CSD matches the instruction as they are received. On the settlement date, the transfer of the security position and the payment of funds is simultaneous. In addition to reducing the risk of a delayed settlement, a participant can enter settlement instructions any time during the day of settlement (CSD's deadlines vary). RTGS is sometimes offered at an additional cost – Brokers and Investors should weigh the reduction of settlement risk against the extra charge. Markets that offer RTGS include Australia, France, Germany and the U. K. In Europe, TARGET (Trans-european Automated Real time Gross settlement Express Transfer), is the RTGS payment system for transfers of the Euro currency.

Paying or Receiving the Funds
As noted above, funds are either transferred independently of the securities settlement or linked to the transfer of securities - - in either case the trade must be paid for.   Funding of securities transactions is handled in many ways. These are discussed in Chapter 8 – Financing. In this section we will look at the settlement or transfer of the funds.

The Process
The process differs if the funding is through the GCB or the Broker's Agent or if a third party (a F/X bank) is used.
If the funding is through the GCB or Broker's Agent,
- The Investor or Broker's trade instructions to their GCB/Agent initiates the funding of the trade. As per agreed procedure between the Investor and GCB or the Broker and their Agent, the currency will be purchased or sold or funding arrangements will be utilized – as discussed in Chapter 8 (Financing).

Part II: SETTLEMENT
Chapter 6
Settlement Environments

If the funding is through another Bank (the F/X Bank),
- The Investor or Broker must instruct, in addition to instructing the GCB or Agent, the F/X bank to transfer the funds to their SCB/Agent.

In both cases, the SCB and the Broker's Agent must be in a position to transfer (or receive) funds, based on the requirements of the CSD. (See the Payment Bank or Payment system earlier in this chapter.)

Contractual Settlement
To help their clients better manage their accounting and funding requirements, many Custodians offer contractual settlement, i.e., the posting of settlement on the expected settlement date instead of when it actually happens.
The SCB and Agent reserve the right to reverse the entries after a stipulated amount of time (typically 5 days) if the trade has not actually settled. This is a service that is provided exclusively by Custodians. It is addressed in Chapter 13 - Custody.

Deadlines and Settlement cycles
When should the trade settle?
The settlement cycle in most markets is a rolling 3 day settlement. However, the cycle varies by country and instruments within the country. Equities typically settle on Trade date plus 3 (T+3). International Bonds also settle T+3. Government securities typically settle same or next day. But there are exceptions. For example, the market in Israel settles on Trade Date, Taiwan on T+1. Of the countries we've been reviewing, Hong Kong settles trades on T+2, Brazil and the U. K. on T+3.

Fail Control
Trades that have not settled by settlement date are fails, and may cause additional trades to fail. If the seller does not deliver the securities to the buyer, the buyer may not be able to deliver the securities to the party they might have sold the securities to, and so on, and so on. If the buyer does not pay for the securities by settlement date, the seller is at risk until, one way or another, the open trade is closed.

As a result, many exchanges have regulations that authorize the exchange to step in and 'close out' the trade or charge the offending party a penalty. The regulations for Brazil, Hong Kong and the U. K. can be found in the box detailing the country's flow / procedures.
Exchanges have at their disposal three mechanisms to end the settlement risk associated with open trades.
1) Monetary penalties
2) Sell Out and Buy in
3) Suspension

Part II: SETTLEMENT
Chapter 6
Settlement Environments

Many exchanges charge the offending or failing party a penalty. The penalties typically start on the day after settlement date and are either a flat daily fee or are based on the value of the trade. (Penalties are discussed in Chapter 8 – Financing and Cash Management)

Sell Outs:
If the offending party has not delivered the securities or paid for the trade by a certain number of days after settlement, the exchange is authorized to close out the trade. If the buyer has failed to pay for the securities, the exchange or Broker will sell the securities and any money difference is charged back to the buyer.

Buy Ins:
 If the seller has failed to deliver, the seller is 'bought-in,' i.e., the securities are purchased by the exchange or the Broker and any money difference charged back to the seller (through the executing Broker)

Suspension:
In many countries, the exchange (or clearing house) is authorized to suspend the member Broker from executing any further trades. In some cases, the suspension lasts until the trade is closed out. In other cases, the suspension is for a determined period of time.

As settlement cycles shorten and potential for fails increase, and as market volatility increases, exchanges enforce these close out regulations with greater frequency. The reduction of settlement risk is critical to Brokers, Investors and settlement systems.

What can go wrong – and usually does?
Finally, let's look at some common settlement problems. Each market has unique characteristics that may cause difficulty if the Broker or Investor is not familiar with the procedures used. Some of the more frequent 'challenges' faced are:

1) Missed deadlines
   - CSD procedures stipulate the cut-off times for receipt of trade instructions and funds. However, the most important deadline is the one set by the agent or custodian bank. If the Investor and Broker miss the deadline set by their agent or SCB it is likely the trade will fail.

2) Settlement instructions
   - All markets require the counter-party settlement information be included with the trade instructions (i.e., advising the CSD the identity of the receiving or delivering party).

Part II: SETTLEMENT
Chapter 6
Settlement Environments

- Some markets require settlement information upon completion of the trade execution. These markets (e.g., Spain) book the trade execution complete with registration and custody details. If the information is not submitted in time, the trade is cancelled and rebooked (called a put-through) causing additional charges to be levied.

3) Securities with multiple listings
   - Many securities trade and/or are listed in more than one market. These securities may:
     o Trade and settle in the currency of the country where they are trading.
     o Trade in another marketplace but settle in the currency and country of issuance
     o Settle in the country where traded via a link with the CSD of the country of issuance.
   - Regardless of where traded or the currency of settlement, each security has only one ISIN code.
   - This impacts trade booking, settlement and inventory control issues.

4) Bank Accounts and Overdraft rules
   - One of the, if not the most important, aspects of settlement and fail control is funding (discussed in this Chapter and Chapter 8 – Financing). Regulations governing bank accounts should be researched and carefully monitored.
   - Markets may permit or prohibit local currency balances, foreign currency balances, overdrafts / credit lines. Some markets permit overdrafts but charge a sizable penalty if a payment creates a debit balance.

5) Currency controls
   - Currency Controls are restrictions on the inflow or outflow of currency. Some markets merely require the money transfer to be reported to the Central Bank or Regulatory Agency (e.g., Brazil). Other markets require reporting and approval of the transfer of currency.
   - Settlement may be delayed pending the approval. Markets that require the approval of the Central Bank also require documentation to prove the currency trade is related to a securities trade. When selling, the original purchase order must be produced with the new sale confirmation (e.g., Venezuela has instituted this and similar restrictions during times of financial instability).

6) Partial deliveries
- Partial delivery is the settlement of a portion of the trade. It occurs when the seller has an insufficient quantity of securities to deliver. Some markets require an entire trade to settle or the trade will fail. Other markets permit partial settlement. Partial delivery (against a pro-rated amount of payment) creates numerous entries each time a part is settled, additional tracking of the outstanding balance and management of residual cash balances.

7) Delivery vs. payment in a currency other than the local currency
- In some cases, usually at the request of the Investor, the trade will settle free of payment (FOP) at the CSD and payment is made separately in another currency (typically the Investor's currency). In most cases, the risk is assumed by the seller as they deliver securities in the country of issuance. After delivery has been verified, the buyer makes payment to the seller in the country and currency agreed upon.

8) Turnaround Trades – also called flip or back-to-back trades
- Turnaround Trades are trades executed by a Broker on behalf of another Broker or Investor. The Broker takes delivery of the securities and 'turns them around' or delivers the securities to the buyer. To minimize the risk, every effort is made to re-deliver the shares on the same day that the shares are received. If the Broker is unable to re-deliver the securities on the same day, the Broker incurs the failed trade and cost of funding.
- This problem has been reduced as CSDs offer multiple processing cycles. This problem is also solved by a netting system that permits the inclusion of the IB and the Investor's SCB (see the earlier section on trade netting). The individual market's settlement procedures can make this easy or impossible - so this risk is evaluated country by country.

Impact of Settlement Systems in transition
As you can see, market settlement practices are a combination of highly automated processes and laborious manual functions. Market settlement practices are constantly evolving as markets look for ways to improve the process. Some of these changes may not be noticeable to the participants while others necessitate alterations in the bank, Broker and Investors' settlement procedures.
The types of changes that have been taking place in many markets include custodian bank and agent access to on-line processing and verification of instructions and settlement; reducing the settlement cycle, improvements from one bulk process of instructions to real time processing and changing from a physical environment to CSD settlement.

Part II: SETTLEMENT
Chapter 6
Settlement Environments

When a market changes the settlement system, Banks, Brokers and Investors should determine what impact, if any, the change will have on their daily routine. Some of the changes will be permanent changes to the CSD's procedures. Other changes are temporary and must be followed only during the transition period.

Examples of Permanent Changes in Regulations and Structure
- The deadline for entering trade instructions
  - The deadline may be reduced as markets shorten the settlement cycle.
  - The deadline may be extended as settlement systems upgrade from once a day processing (which required instructions to be entered the previous day) to real time matching and settlement (which usually permit instructions to be entered on the same day as settlement)
  - Remember, the important deadline is not the deadline of the CSD or settlement agency, but the deadline set by the agent who must meet the settlement system's deadline.
- Changes in the trade instruction information or format
  - To improve the efficiency of the settlement process, the CSD may require new information in the trade instruction
  - Some examples:
    - A CSD may require ISIN codes to be used. Currently many markets accept either ISIN codes or their national code (e.g., Sedol or Euroclear and Clearstream's common code)
    - Markets that had previously accepted FOP instructions may now require DVP instructions
- Changes in sell-out and buy-in rules
  - In an effort to eliminate failed trades, markets implement stricter buy-in or close out procedures and tighter funding requirements. Exchanges / CSDs have increased penalties and/or initiated buy-ins immediately after the scheduled settlement date. The practice of allowing a grace period (the number of days between the settlement date and the day a penalty begins or a buy-in processed) is disappearing.
- Changes of when funds are required
  - Funding requirements may change as the system processes real time transfer of securities and money (the old system may have required the funds to be in place by the end of the day). In examining ways to reduce risk, some markets have concluded that an immediate credit of funds eliminates the exposure that exists as the seller waits to receive the cash proceeds. However, as a result, instead of netting the daily obligations and paying (or receiving) one

           net amount, the buyer's must make funds available as each
           settlement occurs.

- Changes in the membership criteria
  Some CSDs now permit direct or associate membership of foreign
  Brokers and Investors - - participants who are not members of the local
  exchange or clearing banks. Some Brokers and Investors might not
  consider direct membership cost effective; while others, because of the
  type and volume of their business, could benefit from direct
  involvement.

Examples of Temporary Changes during the Transition Period
In markets that are creating a CSD for the first time, or transferring securities that
were previously ineligible, there may be temporary changes to the settlement
process.

- What securities will be affected?
  - When transferring securities into a CSD, some markets switch all
    the securities at one time and others move securities gradually over
    time. Some markets move between 10 and 25 issues at one time.
    The entire move may take years to accomplish. Banks, Brokers and
    Investors must monitor when and what securities are impacted.
  - When the transition is to take place, the Exchange or CSD notifies
    the holders of record of the transfer. The notice includes the
    following information:
    - The description of the securities affected
    - The important dates - - the deadline for submitting
      certificates, if settlement is temporarily suspended, when
      settlement will resume.
    - The procedure to follow when submitting the certificates

- Is there a change in the settlement cycle during the transition period?
  Some markets have accomplished the move within the normal settlement
  cycle. Other, however, suspend settlement (typically for a few weeks) while
  the certificates are immobilized or dematerialized.
  - The book closure date
    During this period, settlement is suspended. The registrar
    receives the physical certificates, reconciles the record of
    shareholders and establishes a position at the CSD or central
    registry
  - The deadline date for deposit of the certificates and when
    settlement will resume
    Since settlement is delayed, payment will not be required by
    the normal settlement date, but instead is required on the
    new temporary settlement date. And - - probably more

important - - sale proceeds will not be available until the revised settlement date.

Summary
Over the past decade, major improvements have been made in settlement processing. Within a few years, with the advent of improved systems and the increasing maturation of emerging markets, even these will be replaced by new procedures that reduce cost and minimize risk. The use of systems that support STP will eliminate manual intervention and remove the need for pre-matching. The widespread use of a Central Matching Facility will give all parties access to the trade information. The CSD may be one of the parties accessing the trade data - - depending on the marketplace and the further development of matching facilities. The increasing inclusion of a central counterparty in the clearance process will, as well as reduce counter-party risk, facilitate one net transfer of securities and funds. Although the net settlement of the daily obligation is not true DVP, it will reduce the cost of funding and the quantity of payment instructions. A well-regulated market with securely capitalized Brokers will compensate for the risk associated with a non-true DVP environment.

BRAZIL SETTLEMENT PROCESS

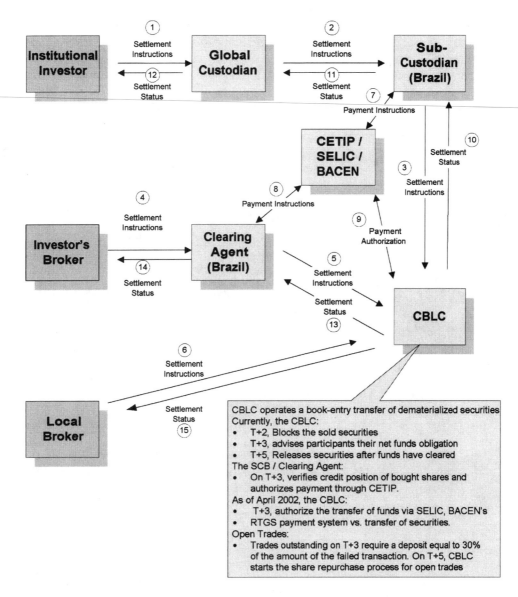

CBLC operates a book-entry transfer of dematerialized securities. Currently, the CBLC:
- T+2, Blocks the sold securities
- T+3, advises participants their net funds obligation
- T+5, Releases securities after funds have cleared

The SCB / Clearing Agent:
- On T+3, verifies credit position of bought shares and authorizes payment through CETIP.

As of April 2002, the CBLC:
- T+3, authorize the transfer of funds via SELIC, BACEN's
- RTGS payment system vs. transfer of securities.

Open Trades:
- Trades outstanding on T+3 require a deposit equal to 30% of the amount of the failed transaction. On T+5, CBLC starts the share repurchase process for open trades

Footnotes	
BACEN:	Banco Central do Brasil (Central Bank of Brazil)
CBLC:	Companhia Brasileria de Liquidacao e Custodia (Brazilian Clearing and Depository Corporation)
CETIP:	Central de Custodia e Liquidacao Financiera de Titulos (Payment netting system)
SELIC:	Sistema Especial de Liquidacao e Cuatrodia (RTGS)

HONG KONG SETTLEMENT PROCESS

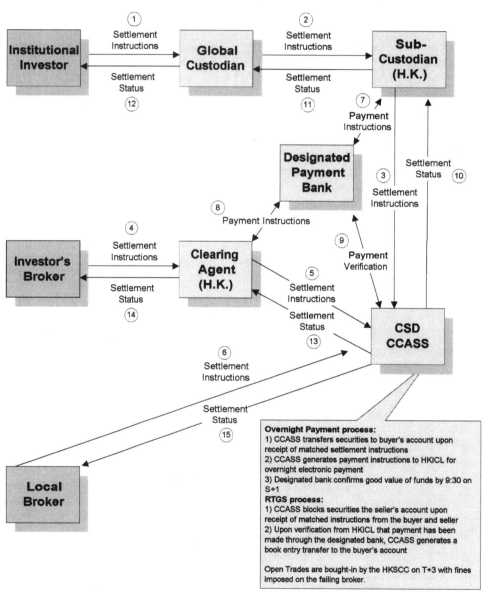

Overnight Payment process:
1) CCASS transfers securities to buyer's account upon receipt of matched settlement instructions
2) CCASS generates payment instructions to HKICL for overnight electronic payment
3) Designated bank confirms good value of funds by 9:30 on S+1

RTGS process:
1) CCASS blocks securities the seller's account upon receipt of matched instructions from the buyer and seller
2) Upon verification from HKICL that payment has been made through the designated bank, CCASS generates a book entry transfer to the buyer's account

Open Trades are bought-in by the HKSCC on T+3 with fines imposed on the failing broker.

Footnotes	
CCASS:	Central Clearing and Settlement System
Designated Bank:	CCASS designated bank for money transfers. Approximately 30 banks have been approved by CCASS
HKICL:	Hong Kong Interbank Clearing Ltd
HKSCC:	Hong Kong Securities Clearing Corp

UNITED KINGDOM SETTLEMENT PROCESS

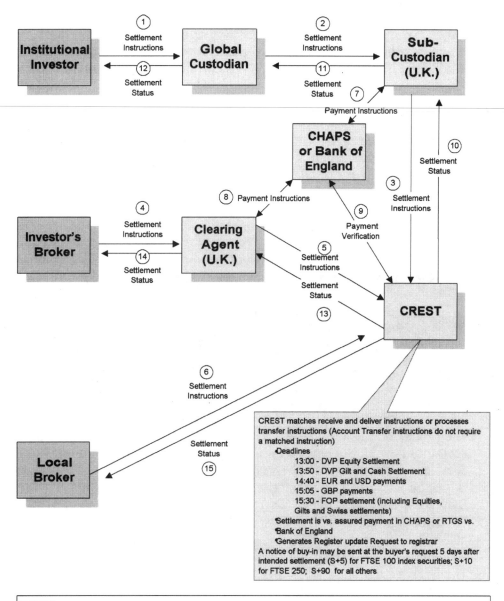

CREST matches receive and deliver instructions or processes transfer instructions (Account Transfer instructions do not require a matched instruction)
- Deadlines
  - 13:00 - DVP Equity Settlement
  - 13:50 - DVP Gilt and Cash Settlement
  - 14:40 - EUR and USD payments
  - 15:05 - GBP payments
  - 15:30 - FOP settlement (including Equities, Gilts and Swiss settlements)
- Settlement is vs. assured payment in CHAPS or RTGS vs. Bank of England
- Generates Register update Request to registrar

A notice of buy-in may be sent at the buyer's request 5 days after intended settlement (S+5) for FTSE 100 index securities; S+10 for FTSE 250; S+90 for all others

Footnotes
CREST: The Electronic Transfer and Settlement System for U.K., Irish and International Equities and U.K. Government Bonds
CHAPS: Clearing House Automated Payment System

Part II: SETTLEMENT
Chapter 6
Settlement Environments

CHAPTER PROCESS FLOW

The following reflects the flow of internal and external activities required to process the settlement of a trade. We refer to Investor, Broker and Custodian without specifying which broker or custodian is responsible. This way we hope to reflect the process rather than confuse our readers with 'who' is doing 'what,' 'when.'

Trade Details
Institutional Investor receipt of 50,000 H. K. China Gas (HKCG)
vs. payment of HKD 452,788.25
Broker delivery of 50,000 H. K. China Gas (HKCG)
vs. receipt of HKD 452,788.25
Trade Date: March 19, 2002
Settlement Date: March 21, 2002

Settlement Facility
H. K. Central Clearing and Settlement System (CCASS)

Settlement Agents
Broker: ABC Securities Ltd., H.K. (Securities)
Broker: HSBC, H. K. (Funds)
Investor: Deutsche Bank (Securities and Funds)

As part of the business profile, the following would be in place:
- The Investor's Custodian Bank, Deutsche Bank, H.K., has opened an account at the H. K. Depository, CCASS, for the purpose of effecting securities' settlement on behalf of the Investor.
- Deutsche Bank, H. K. has been approved by CCASS as a Designated Bank for the purpose of effecting payments for securities transactions.
- The Broker's Agent, ABC Securities Ltd., H. K., has opened an account at the H. K. Depository, CCASS, for the purpose of effecting securities' settlement on behalf on their clients, including our Broker.
- The Broker's agent Bank, HSBC, has been approved by CCASS as a Designated Bank for the purpose of effecting payments for securities transactions.

As a result of this trade, the following activities occur:
- Both the Investor and the Broker transmit their Trade Instructions for settlement of this trade to their Custodian Bank/Agent

- ABC Securities authorizes release of the shares from their account
- Deutsche Bank authorizes payment for the securities

On March 21, CCASS receives the Trade Instructions from the Buyer's and Seller's Agent / Custodian.

- Upon receipt of the trade Instructions from the Broker's Agent and the Investor's Custodian Bank, CCASS attempts to electronically match the instructions.
  - The following criteria, received from Deutsche Bank, must match the data received from the Broker's Agent:
    - Settlement Date   March 21, 2002
    - Counter-party ID   ABC Sec
    - Securities Code   HK0003000038
    - Instruction Type   Receive
    - Quantity   50,000
    - Payment Instruction   DVP
    - Money Value   452788.25
    - Participant's Account   21DUE
  - If the criteria matches:
    - CCASS blocks 50,000 shares of HKCG in the Account of the seller, ABC Securities Ltd., H.K.
    - Upon verification from the electronic funds transfer system, Hong Kong Interbank Clearing Ltd (HKICL), that Deutsche Bank, H. K. has paid HKD 452,788.25, the shares are automatically released to Deutsch Bank's Account.
  - CCASS settlement runs are at 11:00, 11:30, 12:30 and 3:30. This trade will settle only if verification from HKICL reaches CCASS before the last settlement run.

On March 21,
Deutsche Bank and ABC Securities' verify their settlement activity at CCASS via the on-line system.
If settlement has occurred the following entries are made:

139

Deutsche Bank Settlement account
Receives 50,000 HKCG

ABC Securities Settlement account
Receives HKD 452,788.25

ABC Securities Settlement account
Delivers 50,000 HKCG

Deutsche Bank Settlement account
Pays HKD 452,788.25

Part II

Settlement

Chapter 7
Inventory Control and Registration

Part II: SETTLEMENT
Chapter 7
Inventory Control and Registration

Inventory Control impacts many securities trading and processing activities. The primary function performed is the possession, accounting and control of securities that a Custodian Bank and Broker maintains on behalf of their clients and/or their proprietary accounts. This information is vital for customer protection as well as other considerations. The Custodian Bank and Broker must be aware of the "physical" location of securities they are holding to ensure that appropriate income and corporate action entitlements are received. Also when securities are sold or to be delivered it is critical for the Broker to know the location of securities.

In this Chapter we will examine:
- Where Securities are held
- The Role of Depositories
- Difficulties with physical securities
- The role of the registrar and types of registration

At times, uncommon now, the certificate representing ownership could be in bearer form with no reference to the current owner. The bearer certificate was passed from seller to buyer with possession of the physical certificate representing ownership. With many certificates registered in the shareholder's name, ownership of a security was based upon two actions. The first was the cancellation of the certificate delivered by the current owner (the seller). The second action involved the entry of the buyer's name on the books of the company and the issuance of a new certificate in the Investor's name. The certificate issued reflected the number of shares owned. A "Registrar" or "Transfer Agent" usually performed this function. These actions were critical, as beneficial ownership rights were not bestowed on the new Investor until completion.

Many Brokers or Custodians registered physical certificates in their own or nominee name (the name of the entity holding the securities) to facilitate the registration process. These names would appear on the 'books' of the issuing company as the "owners" of these securities. The Broker or Custodian would pass along income or corporate action information to the proper owner. Some market regulations require Brokers or Custodians to disclose the underlying beneficial owners. While other markets do not require this disclosure.

Physical certificates placed many constraints on the industry. Some were processing while others caused inefficiencies in establishing ownership and entitlement to ownership rights. As a result, market efficiency was impacted; spikes in trading volumes caused delays in processing new ownership records. Clearance and settlement was a cumbersome, though a manageable process, that involved high volumes of staff to count, verify and move paper certificates between buyers and sellers. The increased volumes, however, made the process impossible and stock exchanges were forced to close temporarily to catch up with paper work. This was unacceptable to the industry.

Part II: SETTLEMENT
Chapter 7
Inventory Control and Registration

In today's environment there are many methods of performing this function. We will review each and illustrate the characteristics of each. Some markets developed an infrastructure support, while others introduced regulations that eliminated or greatly reduced the use of physical securities. The flow charts at the end of the chapter reflect the current infrastructure in the three countries we are tracking.

WHERE SECURITIES ARE HELD
Securities are maintained
- In National Central Securities Depositories (CSD)
- In International Central Securities Depositories (ICSD)
- In vaults of Brokers or Agents and Custodian Banks
- By the Investors themselves.

Central Securities Depository (CSD)
All but a few markets have established a CSD to immobilize paper certificates. As mentioned in Chapter 6 – Settlement, CSDs either hold physical certificates or maintain ownership of securities in `book entry' form.

Physical Certificate Environment in the CSD
The German market addressed the maintenance of physical certificates in 1882 by introducing the Bank des Berliner Kassen-Verein - a cash and securities depository – The Kassenverein a concept meaning 'one box' provided a facility to German Brokers of common storage of the physical certificates. In essence this 'one box' concept immobilized physical certificates and established the concept of a Central Securities Depository.

The basic concept of immobilization is the storage and maintenance of all paper certificates in a central, secure location. When ownership of the securities is transferred, in the case of a buy and a sell, a movement of securities out (a debit) is processed versus the sellers account at the CSD. At the same time a movement into the buyers account (a credit) is processed at the CSD. This transfer is reflected on the books and records of the CSD.

Introduction of a CSD into local market infrastructures has been an important part of the evolution of safety and increased volume capacity in the global market. But physical certificates continue to strain securities industry processing. Through the introduction of securities regulations other changes have been introduced to make the market more efficient and safer. CSD have again been an integral part of these changes. Some of these changes have impacted the use and availability of physical certificates. The following sections reflect some of these changes and their impact on securities processing.

Part II: SETTLEMENT
Chapter 7
Inventory Control and Registration

Dematerialized Certificate Environment
In some markets regulations have eliminated or greatly reduced the use of physical certificates. In these markets physical certificates have been dematerialized. This means that the certificates are not readily available or do not exist at all (See Chapter 6-Settlement). The regulations have been amended to permit ownership without the issuance of a certificate.

These markets offer a 'book entry' environment. The CSD, in this environment, does not maintain physical certificates. But instead tracks ownership of securities through an automated 'book entry' system. This system maintains position and activity information for members and security issuers.

Book entry systems require a close relationship among the major participants in the securities industry. This includes the entities that issue securities including federal and local Governments and Corporate Issuers as well as the Corporate Trustees, Registrars or Transfer Agents, income and corporate action event Agents, Brokers and Custodians. But the CSD is usually the central point of coordination and dissemination of information among the participants.

For example an Issuer or their corporate trust Agent will advise the CSD of the security issue, issuance amount and the initial distribution amounts. In some markets, the CSD collects the monies due to the Issuer and credits the appropriate amounts to each member's account. On an ongoing basis the Issuer or their agent will pass along income or corporate action event information to the beneficial owners through the CSD. (This process is discussed further in Chapters 9 and 10 – Income Processing and Corporate Actions)

The daily operation of the CSD in a dematerialized environment will parallel the physical certificate environment except that there are no certificates involved in the process. This is huge benefit to the market as the CSD does not need space to house a vault for certificates. The audit function is a systems audit rather than a physical count and review of certificates.

There are many advantages of a CSD. The most obvious is that everyone knows where the securities are located. And the CSD greatly decreases the cost of maintaining securities. Individual firms do not need to maintain a vault or the associated staff that processes physical certificates. The movement and audit trail of paper is greatly decreased; reducing the time it takes to transfer securities from one participant to another. CSD provides benefits to all market participants.

A CSD relieves the risk, expense and effort of safekeeping physical certificates. And greatly reduces the cost and inconvenience associated with replacing missing or lost certificates and the delays experienced by processing and re-registration of physical securities. When a local Broker does not directly have a membership with a CSD, it usually has a relationship with a member firm so it deposits securities through the member firm. The member firm acts as the non-member firm's correspondent Agent.

In order to participate in a CSD, a Broker first must qualify for membership. Each market has it's own requirements, but in general a potential member must be involved in the securities as a central dealer, Broker or Custodian. Another important requirement is that each member be subject to the purview of a state or federal securities Regulator. This is an important point because it allows the CSD to defer major regulatory supervision to an organization that has already been charged with the oversight role. As a public entity, the CSD is required to issue an annual report of its financial records to its members.

Once membership is granted by the CSD, the member deposits eligible securities into the CSD to the benefit (credit) of their account. At the same time, the member notifies the registrar of the deposit. In most CSDs, the securities are held in the nominee name of the CSD for the benefit of the member. Each CSD has its own rules and regulations about which securities are considered eligible. In general, a security must have a certain level of liquidity and be registered with the local governing body. The CSD publishes a list of securities accepted for eligibility.

As additional securities are made eligible the list is updated. The trend is for depositories to increase their range of products that they will process, or to link with other national CSDs, to expand their services.

The CSD charges members a fee for storing securities, as well as a transaction fee each time securities or cash are processed. In addition, many CSDs require each member to pay into a reserve fund, based on the member's participation level, to protect the CSD against losses. In our high-risk business, even the CSD must have a risk management plan in place. Members of the financial industry often own local market CSDs.

Its members strictly govern stock and cash movements within the CSD. The members notify the CSD when securities should be transferred via manual or electronic delivery instructions. Most market participants have a direct electronic link with the CSD. The CSD in turn keeps in close contact with its members by issuing daily and intra-day reports reflecting the movement of all securities and cash in and out of accounts. It is essential that members reconcile their books and records with the depositories. Each member must perform a daily reconciliation between the CSD books and their own internal records. Any discrepancies must be researched and corrected immediately. The Custodian Bank and Broker track the location and movement of all securities.

Part II: SETTLEMENT
Chapter 7
Inventory Control and Registration

International Depositories (ICSD)

In addition to the domestic depositories, such as The Brazilian Clearing and CSD Corporation, The Stock Exchange of Hong Kong exchange-run CSD, CCAS, and CREST in the UK, there are two international central securities depositories, Clearstream and Euroclear. Both ICSDs have been successful in eliminating or greatly reducing the risks associated with international securities trading.

Cedel International (discussed in Chapter 15 – Industry Organizations) was established with the charter to reduce the costs and risks of settling securities in the Eurobond market. It has since expanded its role to minimize settlement risk of cross-border securities trading. In 1999 Cedel merged with Deutsche Borse Clearing (DBC) creating Clearstream.
Euroclear (also discussed in Chapter 15 – Industry Organizations) was founded in 1968 by Morgan Guaranty and is based in Brussels, Belgium. It was the world's largest clearance and settlement system for internationally traded securities prior to Cedel's merger with Germany's Borse Clearing

Both ISCDs maintain inventory in physical and dematerialized form. Following the regulations of the particular market, they hold securities either in physical form at their correspondent Bank in the country where the securities are issued; or, through their account with the domestic CSD, the securities are maintained in the CSD; or, if the securities were issued in `book entry' or dematerialized form, ownership is tracked electronically within their system.

CERTIFICATES HELD IN PHYSICAL FORM
Not all securities are eligible for a CSD. And in some rare cases there may not be an effective CSD in-place. When securities are not CSD eligible they must remain in physical form. Or in rare cases a member may choose not to join the CSD, either as a direct member or through an affiliated member firm. There are also Investors, both retail and institutional who prefer to take physical possession of their securities.

Physical Environment
Securities in physical form that are stored outside of the CSD, whether in a vault at the Broker or Custodian or in the Investor's possession, are said to be in physical form. Investors may store their certificates in many places such as a safe deposit box at a Bank, or in their personal files or framed or possibly under their mattress for safety. Their motivation for wanting to hold the physical certificate ranges from distrust of the Broker to the vanity of sharing their investment information with friends and neighbors.

Difficulties with Physical Securities
The widespread use of depositories has eliminated many of the problems connected with physical certificates. However, since physical certificates are still issued (either by

the Investor's choice or their non-eligibility at the CSD), a holder of a physical certificate can expect to have the following problems:

1) Difficulty when executing an order in a quantity other than a round lot
2) Delays while the authenticity of the certificate is verified
3) Delays and paperwork when replacing lost certificates
4) Delays in selling shares

Certificates are usually issued in round lots. For equities this means 100, 200, 500 or 1000 shares. If a customer sells 50 shares, the certificate must be sent to the transfer agent to be broken up into two certificates – one for 50 shares and one for the balance of the shares.

In order to process a certificate, it must be in good delivery form. Certificates, registered in the owners name must be properly endorsed by the current owner. To make the security `negotiable,' the Broker or Custodian Bank must guarantee the owner's signature. There are also problems with lost certificates, getting replacement certificates and meeting delivery deadlines.

Meeting the deadline for delivery by settlement date is impossible with the settlement date typically T+1, 2 or 3. If the security is not CSD eligible, expect a delay in settlement while the certificates are verified or authenticated. If the securities are CSD eligible, and the Investor has chosen to hold the physical certificate, the holdings must be sent to the CSD or the registrar for repossessing at the CSD. Many depositories that have switched to dematerialized entries permit a certificate (or a receipt of the security ownership) to be issued to the Investor. But the certificate must be re-deposited when sold. In most markets, the holdings must be shown in the depository prior to an order being taken by the Broker.

Despite these drawbacks of physical securities, they are unlikely to ever be eliminated. For the Investor that must have a physical paper, one solution would be to issue a presentable certificate (or receipt) that is not an official proof of ownership so the certificate does not need to be returned.

ADDITIONAL CSD SERVICES
The main business of depositories is the administration of securities, yet many depositories supplement their core business with value-added services to supplement their bottom line. Additional services that CSDs provide include the following. They are discussed in the Chapters noted.

Income Payments – Chapter 9 (Income Processing)
Corporate Actions – Chapter 10 (Corporate Actions)

Part II: SETTLEMENT
Chapter 7
Inventory Control and Registration

Funding/Pledges – Chapter 8 (Financing and Cash Management)
Proxy Voting – Chapter 10 (Corporate Actions)
Same-day Funds Settlement – Chapter 8 (Financing)
Securities Lending – Chapter 12 (Securities Lending)
Securities Registration/Transfer – This Chapter (see next section)
Tax Withholding/Reclamation Services – chapter 11 (Tax Withholdings)

HOW SECURITIES ARE REGISTERED

After a trade has settled (or, in some markets, simultaneous with settlement), the transfer of ownership is recorded by the registrar or transfer agent. The securities may not, in fact, be registered in the name of the `actual' owner (called the beneficial owner), but may be registered in the name of the party (called the nominee) holding the securities for the beneficial owner.

The method of registration depends on 4 factors:

1) The country's regulations: Do the regulations permit nominee ownership or must the securities be registered in the name of the beneficial owner? In some markets, nominee registration is permitted except to claim dividends or corporate actions.

2) The central depository's regulations and procedures: Must the securities be held in the name of the depository, the name of the participant of the depository or the beneficial owner's name?

3) The Investors' preference or requirements: Within the parameters of the country and depository's regulations, the Investor may prefer their name or their nominee's name as the registered owner.

4) The form of the securities: If the certificates are in physical form held outside a depository, the Investor's instructions dictate how the securities will be registered (in their own name or their nominee, within the parameters of the country's regulations).

Regulations effecting Registration
Or, is it required that the shares be registered? What are the implications if the shares are not registered?

Registration is automatic upon settlement for shares held in a CSD. As soon as the buyer pays for the shares and the position is credited to their account, the buyer has beneficial ownership of the securities. However, in the event of a corporate action, a dividend or interest payment or an Annual Meeting, markets differ on the regulations to obtain the entitlement.

> For shares held in a CSD, some markets permit nominee registration and others permit nominee registration except to claim dividends or corporate actions. A few markets require the securities to be withdrawn from the CSD and re-registered in the beneficial owner's name in order to receive the entitlement – including dividends, bonus shares or voting at the Annual Meeting .

If the certificate is not held in the CSD, must the owner register the shares? In most countries, to claim legal ownership, the shares must be registered in the shareholders name or a nominee name. Most markets require physical shares to be registered in the beneficial owner's name to receive corporate action entitlements. Frequently, the only time securities are sent to be registered is for a corporate action - creating huge delays at the registrar. This problem is further examined in the next section – Problems in Registration.

The CSD regulations and procedures
The country's regulations determine how a CSD will maintain their record of ownership. Registration of ownership is addressed in various ways based upon local or regional regulations. Basically there are two models prevailing at this time. We have named them based upon their geographic region.

Euro-merican Model
The most common method of registration is for ownership of the securities to reflect the CSD, Broker's or Custodian's name only. The Broker or Custodian receives notices from the CSD, Issuer/Agent and passes this information to the beneficial owner. The beneficial owner then decides on the appropriate action. Which is then passed back to the Broker or Custodian and then back to point of action.

Though Investors can register their ownership directly, most opt not to take advantage of this alternative. There are many reasons for this. Institutional Investors may not want to disclose their ownership. Both retail and institutional Investors, that hold shares in multiple companies, may not want to receive multiple mailings and then have to respond individually. These are the primary reasons for Broker or Custodian registration of security ownership.

In some cases, the Broker or Custodian Bank may register securities in their corporate names. For example ABC Securities might register shares in the name of `ABC Nominees.' This is a name that the Custodian or Broker has registered in a market for the purpose of registering securities. The prime motivation for the use of a nominee name is to comply with securities registration regulations. A custodian may use multiple nominee names in a market or across multiple markets.

Asian Model
Due to securities and civil laws prevailing in this region actual security ownership must be disclosed to the issuer, agent and regulators. Based upon this requirement Brokers and Custodians either registers securities in clients names directly or more frequently they build interfaces, via the CSD, to advise various interested parties of ownership as required.

As a result of this disclosure requirement, CSD registration practices evolved differently than the European or American markets. In many Asian markets the CSD permits Investors to have a direct account at the CSD. Singapore and Hong Kong are examples of markets that provide this service.

In these markets when an Investor purchases a security, the Broker or Custodian, once settlement has occurred, will advise the CSD of Investor information such as name, address, taxpayer identification and other profile data. The CSD then opens an account for the Investor. The securities are transferred from the Broker or Custodian to the Investor's account. The issuer in these markets can access this information and communicate directly with the Investor or can communicate via the CSD.

Some CSDs open multiple accounts for the Investor when the Investor has accounts with multiple Brokers. Other CSDs open one Investor account regardless of how many Brokers' accounts they may have.

WHO ARE THE REGISTRARS AND WHAT IS THEIR ROLE?

The primary role of the registrar is to record and maintain the list of holders of their securities. With this list, they transfer ownership when securities are sold, authorize dividend and interest payments, notify holders of corporate events - - annual meetings, mergers, acquisitions and distributions.   The registrar may be the company itself, although many have out-sourced this function to approved companies (i.e., registrars or transfer agents). In some countries, the CSD is the central registrar or the exchange has developed or appointed a central registrar for all listed securities.

Since most securities are held in a nominee name, the registrar does not have the list of actual owners. How does the registrar know who to pay dividends to or who to notify of upcoming events?
The most typical process used is:
1) The company announces the income or corporate action
2) The notification is sent to all holders (actual and nominee)
    a) In most markets the CSD notifies the registrar of the change in ownership at the time of settlement.
    b) In other markets, the CSD and other nominee holders submit a list of beneficial owners to the registrar upon receipt of the announcement from the registrar
3) The registrar processes the action, either
    a) to the CSD (if the CSD offers this service) or nominee holder for further distribution to the beneficial owner, or
    b) directly to the beneficial owner

Part II: SETTLEMENT
Chapter 7
Inventory Control and Registration

Problems in Registration
Many of the problems associated with lengthy registration periods have diminished as more securities are held at a central depository and the registration process is automated. However, some problems remain. The most notable are claiming entitlements (Discussed in Chapter 10, Corporate Actions), shares that have dual-registration and shares that are subject to foreign ownership limits.

Shares with Dual Registration

Almost all companies that issue shares are registered with one registrar in the country where the shares are issued. But, there are exceptions. A few companies have registrars in more than one country. These are companies that trade on more than one market and have a registrar in each country that they trade. These are call dual-registered shares (Again, these are very few – most shares that trade on multiple exchanges have only one registrar, the registrar in their home market.) The problem that dual-registration creates is the necessity for the shares to be registered where traded. If the shares are purchased in one market, they are sent to the registrar in that country for registration. If they are sold in another market, they must first be re-registered by the registrar in the market where the shares were sold. In many markets, this process has been simplified as CSDs and registrars develop links with other CSDs and registrars. On occasion, however, the physical certificates are mailed to the registrar - - creating delays and failed trades.

Shares with Foreign Ownership Limits

In some markets, the percentage of shares that can be owned by foreign Investors is limited (See Chapter 1 – Equity Products). For example, shares in utility, broadcasting and finance companies are typically considered protected industries and the amount of voting shares that a foreign Investor can own is limited. When the limit is reached, the registrar cannot register any further shares in the name of an Investor domiciled outside that country. Until such time as the registrar can transfer the ownership (e.g., another foreign Investor sells, or the regulations change permitting expanded foreign ownership) the buyer is not considered the holder of record for purposes of corporate events. To avoid settlement problems when selling shares that are at the registrar pending registration, the Investor should first determine that the shares can be recalled from the registrar by the settlement date.

Next
In the next chapters we begin the journey through the world of entitlements, beginning with income processing.

BRAZIL REGISTRATION PROCESS

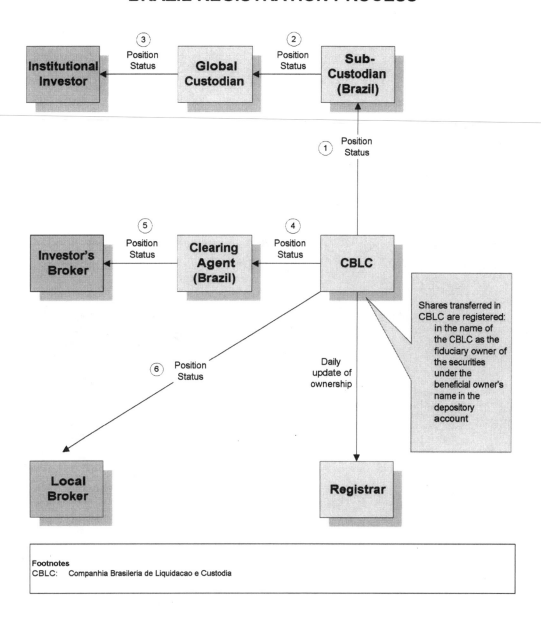

Footnotes
CBLC: Companhia Brasileria de Liquidacao e Custodia

HONG KONG REGISTRATION PROCESS

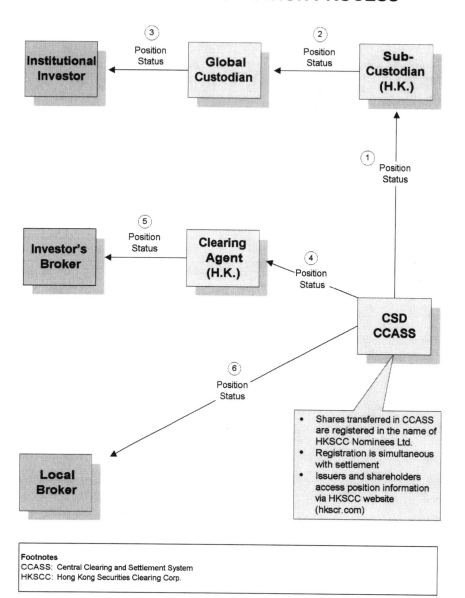

Footnotes
CCASS: Central Clearing and Settlement System
HKSCC: Hong Kong Securities Clearing Corp.

UNITED KINGDOM REGISTRATION PROCESS

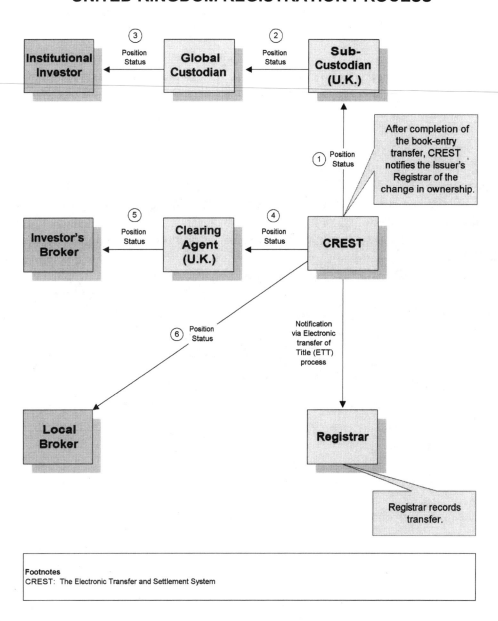

Footnotes
CREST: The Electronic Transfer and Settlement System

Part II: SETTLEMENT
Chapter 7
Inventory Control and Registration

CHAPTER PROCESS FLOW

The following reflects the flow of internal and external activities required to process the registration of a security. We refer to Broker and Custodian without specifying which broker or custodian is responsible. This way we hope to reflect the process rather than confuse our readers with 'who' is doing 'what,' 'when.'

On March 15, 2002 - Settlement Date
of a purchase of 100,000 BP (British Petroleum) by HSBC,
the shares are received to HSBC's account at CREST

As a result, the following activities occur:
- All securities held in CREST are held in the nominee name of CrestCo.
- CREST notifies BP's Registrar of the change of ownership immediately upon settlement.
- BP's Registrar records the transfer to HSBC and confirms the change to CREST.
- CREST reports to HSBC their position of 100,000 shares

On March 15,
upon notification from CREST,
HSBC records reflect the following position:

Firm Inventory or CSD account: **CREST account**
Receives 100, 000 BP   **Delivers 100,000 BP**

Questions
1) All of the following statements accurately describe an efficient settlement process except:
   a) Effects the movement of securities and cash
   b) Creates a DVP environment
   c) Verifies physical certificates are authentic
   d) Verifies receipt of funds before releasing sold securities

2) Which of the following statements accurately describe `true' DVP?
   a) The CSD transferring securities after verifying payment of funds
   b) The Central Bank simultaneously transferring government securities vs. funds
   c) The transfer of securities at the CSD vs. the net payment of funds
   d) The physical delivery of the certificates vs. a simultaneous receipt of a check

3) Which of the following settlements occurred in the book-entry environment?
   a) The name of the new shareholder is recorded on the book's of the registrar
   b) The seller delivers certificates to the buyer
   c) Sub-custodian Bank delivers the sold securities from their vault
   d) The CSD makes a computerized transfer of the position

4) All of the following statements accurately describe dematerialized settlement except:
   a) The CSD maintains immobilized certificates
   b) Settlement may occur via a Central Registry
   c) The CSD maintains an automated record of ownership
   d) Settlement occurs at the CSD via a computerized transfer of the position

5) The funds due on a purchase of Reuters Holdings shares are paid through a payment netting system. When are these funds due?
   a) The day before settlement date for value on the settlement date
   b) On the morning of the settlement date
   c) When the shares are delivered
   d) When the payment bank receives a report of funds due

6) Of the following systems, which offers the simultaneous transfer of securities and funds.
   a) Real Time Gross Settlement System
   b) Payment Netting System
   c) Electronic Funds Transfer System
   d) Check

7) A seller of 10,000 Raffles Center Ltd on the Hong Kong Stock Exchange is not able to deliver the securities by the settlement date. Of the following, what is the most likely result?
   a) The Broker's license is suspended until the trade is settled
   b) The Buyer may request the selling broker pay for the shares until delivery
   c) The shares are bought-in on T+3
   d) There is no procedure for failed trades in Hong Kong

8) All of the following statements accurately describe securities with multiple listings except:
   a) They are traded in more than one country
   b) They may settle in the currency of the country where traded
   c) They may settle in the CSD where traded
   d) They may have a different ISIN code in each country

9) The seller of 10,000 Reuters Holdings has only 5,000 shares to deliver on the settlement date. Assuming the country where Reuters Holdings (the U. K.) will settle permits partial delivery, which of the following statements accurately describes the settlement of this trade?
   a) 5,000 shares will settle vs. the pro-rated amount of payment
   b) New settlement instructions are required for the remaining shares
   c) A 5,000 share trade will failed
   d) All of the above

10) A Broker purchased 10,000 shares of Marks & Spencer in the U.K. What is the deadline for settlement instructions for this trade?
   a) The deadline set by their client's Custodian Bank
   b) The deadline set by their Clearing Agent
   c) The deadline set by CHAPs
   d) The deadline set by CREST

Part III

Post-Settlement

Chapter 8
Financing and
Cash Management

Part III: POST-SETTLEMENT
Chapter 8
Financing & Cash Management

FINANCING & CASH MANAGEMENT

This chapter explores the investment and loan of cash among Investors, Brokers and Custodians. The motivation for needing these services, as well as selecting one of the various alternatives, may be vastly different but all are usually related to securities trading and settlement activities. Topics addressed in this chapter include:

- Cash Management activities
- Foreign Exchange transaction lifecycle processes
- Activities creating need for financing
- Financing transaction lifecycle activities

FINANCING

Financing activities generally support the securities business of a Broker and Custodians, There are many business activities that require funding and there are many methods of meeting the requirements for funds available to Brokers, Custodians and their Investor clients. In this chapter we will explore the business drivers that create the demand for funds.

We do not address the financing methods that a Broker or Custodian utilizes to finance non-security activities. Our focus is on activities directly related to securities trading and settlement. At the conclusion of this chapter you will understand the drivers and principles associated with financing and cash management practices.

FINANCING REQUIREMENTS

Financing is the process that ensures that an Investor, Broker or Custodian has access to the cash they need to cover their securities trading and settlement obligations. The more markets an Investor, Broker or Custodian is involved with the greater the need for financing in multiple currencies. The primary activities that impact a Broker or Custodians financing needs are as follows:

- Securities Trading and Settlement activities
- Firm Fails to Deliver
- Client Debits
- Income Receivable
- Financial penalties/Haircuts

Part III: POST-SETTLEMENT
Chapter 8
Financing & Cash Management

Securities Trading and Settlement Activities

This requirement combines the individual requirements enabling trade and settlement throughout global markets. The three major participants, Investors, Brokers and Custodians have this same requirement. The need for funding may originate from a number of related activities. Investors that utilize contractual settlement, income and corporate action event processing, discussed in Chapters 6, 9 and 10, create the need for financing at the Custodian. Investors trading in markets with different settlement schedules often have the need to finance T+3 settlements requiring funds while awaiting T+5 settlements that will make funds available. There are many activities that create a Broker's funding needs but they use the same methods as Investors and Custodians.

Firm Fail to Deliver

A fail to deliver, as discussed in the Settlement Chapter 6, is a trade that has reached contractual settlement but for some reason the exchange of value has 'failed' to occur. This section will not pursue the causes of fails but rather examine the financial impact on Broker or Custodian. The 'cost' of a firm fail to deliver is the monies that must be paid to a client or proprietary trader for trades that were to settle but did not. Monies must be credited to the client or traders account even though the Custodian or Broker did not receive the funds from the counterparty. This situation is faced by Brokers primarily, but may impact Custodians as well. Investors that create this need, by failing to make the securities and or cash available for settlement, may incur financial penalties from their Broker or Custodian.

Client Debits

A Broker will incur this situation when they extend credit to a retail client that has not funded their account before settlement of a purchase. Many markets may call this transaction a loan, extension of credit or even a margin transaction. No matter what the transaction is called it requires the Custodian or Broker to acquire funds that they may not have anticipated.

Part III: POST-SETTLEMENT
Chapter 8
Financing & Cash Management

Income Receivables

An example of this is in Contractual Income accounts. The process is similar to contractual settlement; these accounts require the dividend or interest income on payment date regardless whether the Custodian has received the payment from the Paying agent. The investor pays a premium fee for this service. If the income has not been received from the transfer agent or CSD, the Custodian has a need to finance this transaction.

A Broker may credit their clients with a dividend or interest payment on Payment date even though they have not received payment. This usually occurs in large mature markets and is driven by investor demands. And as these investors expand into other markets will create this demand there as well.

Or in markets with physical certificates, a delay in registration may be encountered resulting in a missed payment requiring a claim procedure. Some Brokers and Custodians will credit the investor with the income event while they proceed with recovering the payment from the Paying agent or counterparty.

Financial Penalties

In some markets the regulators levy a penalty on Brokers for various nonperformance conditions. It can be based upon fail to deliver volumes, aged count difference which are discrepancies between physical certificates maintained and the internal accounting records or inventory difference Between the Broker and CSD or other noncompliance related situation. For example the Philippines Stock Exchange charges Brokers 200% of the trade value for trades that fails to settle. These charges are usually meant to 'motivate' the Broker to resolve the condition as soon as reasonably possible. These charges are known as Haircuts or Financial penalties. A market regulator defines each condition and a specific amount of money is assigned to each type of nonperformance condition. Once the condition is encountered the Broker must deposit the specified amount of money in a bank account. The Broker cannot use this money until the condition has been resolved.

Recap

These are the primary causes of the need for financing by Investors, Brokers or Custodians. There may be other causes, usually market specific, which are not germane to this type of text. In any case it is important for the Broker or Custodian to identify situation where funding is required and to resolve them as soon as practical. In some cases there may be an immediate solution where there is little or-f no costs incurred. While in other cases, the resolution may not be so readily realized so the condition exists for a long time before resolution.

Part III: POST-SETTLEMENT
Chapter 8
Financing & Cash Management

COMMON CHARACTERISTICS OF FINANCING

Duration

1. **Overnight:** Overnight financing needs are usually used to finance fails to deliver. An example is when a Custodian or Broker is unable to deliver a security on the same day they must pay for a security purchase, see Back to Back settlement description in Chapter 6.

2. **Term:** Term financing is commonly employed for longer term needs. For example a Broker may need HKD 10,000,000 for three months. Investors, Brokers and Custodians use this alternative for short tern securities investments when cash is unavailable.

3. **Open Ended:** Open-ended financing is used to finance requirements that have no predictable conclusion. An example may be expansion of a Broker's business in a new product or an entry into new markets. Investors may utilize this type of financing to bridge bonus, furniture or real estate payments. Investors or Broker may decide to 'borrow' the funds via a finance transaction, rather than use their own capital. Brokers borrow on term basis more often than Investors.

Interest Rates

A critical aspect of financing transaction is the interest rate charged to the borrower. As with most loans these transactions may be executed using fixed or variable rates. The borrower of the cash pays interest to the lender for the term of the loan. This charge is assessed and paid at the conclusion of the transaction

1. **Fixed Rate:** the rate of interest to be paid by the borrower is established at the onset of the transaction. This rate is not subject to change unless the rate itself is changed. Public rates that used across many markets include London Interbank Offering Rate (Libor) and the Brokers Call Rate.

2. **Variable Rate:** this rate is subject to change based upon the movement of the underlying index. These rates may change as frequently as daily, weekly, bi-weekly, monthly, quarterly, bi and semi-annually. A popular benchmark used in financing arrangements is Libor. These usually change monthly or quarterly.

Part III: POST-SETTLEMENT
Chapter 8
Financing & Cash Management

FINANCING METHODS

Investors, Custodians and Brokers have various means to raise funds. Banks are a primary resource but may not be able to make sufficient funds available to these participants. As a result three major methods used by the financial services industry to fund their securities investment activities. Sometimes the cause will point towards one method versus another. But the primary influence is the cost of funds, which simply put is the cost of borrowing. Each market has their own cost influences but the cost of funds is usually the prime motivation.

We address each of these and identify when one is used versus another and the associated characteristics. These are:

o Repurchase Agreements (Repos)
o Bank Loans
o Letter of Credit

REPURCHASE AGREEMENTS (REPOS)

Overview

A popular method of financing, for Custodians and Brokers, is a Repurchase Agreement. More commonly referred to as a Repo or in some markets as a Buy-Sell Back, these transactions use securities as collateral to obtain cash. Repo transactions require that the value of the collateral be greater than the cash lent. This 'over-collateralization is common on most loan transactions. It addresses two facts; one is that the securities are subject to fluctuation in value so therefore lenders want excess collateral value. The second need that the excess collateral addresses are the credit worthiness of the borrower. Though the securities collateralize the transaction, the lender wants to ensure that their cash is returned. As such, borrowers with lesser credit ratings will post more securities value than those with higher credit ratings. Typical over-collateralization will be in the range of 102-107% of the cash lent.

The securities will be used to borrow funds overnight and then the next day the repo is closed by returning the cash and receiving the securities back. These securities are then delivered and the sales proceeds received. Custodians may act as a principal in repo market, but more often act as an agent for their clients rather than themselves.

Investors, Brokers and Custodians may make excess cash available to borrowers. This is an alternate means of short term investing and can result in attractive returns across markets as compared to Money Market investments. Reverse Repos, also known as Buy-Sell Backs, which are lending rather than borrowing transactions are addressed in the Securities Lending chapter.

Part III: POST-SETTLEMENT
Chapter 8
Financing & Cash Management

Environments

The exchange of Repo cash and collateral exposes participants to many of the same risks associated with settlement. Exposure to these risks have spawned different environments. Each addresses risk in a different manner and impacts the transaction cost as well,

1.   Tri-Parte Repos

The most common environment is a "Tri-parte" repo. This environment includes a borrower, a lender and a tri-parte agent acting as an intermediary between the two counterparties. The tri-parte eliminates settlement risk by ensuring that both assets are received before the exchange of value.   The securities used as collateral and local customs will determine the organization that will provide tri-parte service.

The tri-parte role is most likely provided by the market's central bank, a local bank or a CSD or ICSD. The tri-parte agent charges a fee for the service provided. Many Custodians and Brokers will use various tri-parte agents based upon availability in local markets.

2.   Hold In Custody (HIC)

A second repo environment is "Hold in Custody". In this environment the borrower advises the lender that they will segregate the collateral on their 'books' and credit the positions to the benefit of the lender. This eliminates the physical exchange of security collateral simplifying the transaction flow. But it exposes the lender, by relying on the borrower to perform as specified, to losses. As a result well-financed participants within local markets commonly utilize this environment.

3.   Physical Repo

The third environment is a "Physical" repo, which requires the physical exchange of security collateral. The lender, or their agent which can be a CSD or Custodian, receives collateral from the borrower. Only after receipt of the collateral will the lender release the funds to the borrower. As a result the borrower risks the loss of their collateral in the event of failure of the lender to release the funds.

Part III: POST-SETTLEMENT
Chapter 8
Financing & Cash Management

Processing Steps

Brokers, Custodians and investors use Repos to obtain funds to support their trading and settlement activities. The Repo processing steps, within the different environments, are as follows:

- A need for cash is determined by a Broker, Custodian and or Investor (borrower)

- Broker or Custodian identifies appropriate collateral
  - Government bonds
  - Corporate bonds or equities

- Source of cash is determined (lender)

- Collateral (securities) are delivered
  - Repo 'Opening Leg'
  - Tri-Parte: to Central Bank, CSD or ISCD
  - HIC Repo: Borrower updates records reflecting securities pledged to lender
  - Physical Repos: to CSD, Custodian or Broker

- Lender remits cash to borrower
  - Tri-Parte: via Central Bank, CSD or ISCD
  - HIC Repo: directly to borrower
  - Physical Repos: to Borrower or via CSD, Custodian or Broker

- Beneficial owners (borrowers) entitled to income payments while Repo is open

- Borrower returns cash to the lender plus interest accrued
  - Tri-Parte: via Central Bank, CSD or ISCD
  - HIC Repo: directly to lender
  - Physical Repos: to Lender or CSD, Custodian or Broker

- Collateral is returned to the borrower by the lender
  - Repo 'Closing Leg'
  - Tri-Parte: via Central Bank, CSD or ISCD
  - HIC Repo: Borrower updates records reflecting completion of the Repo
  - Physical Repos: to Borrower or via CSD, Custodian or Broker

Part III: POST-SETTLEMENT
Chapter 8
Financing & Cash Management

BANK LOANS

Overview

Another alternative for financing is borrowing funds from a bank. This is the traditional method of raising funds. Most organizations have borrowed cash, for various reasons, from a bank. This type of borrowing is somewhat different. In these transactions the Broker or Custodian, and not the investor, will post securities to a bank as collateral for a cash loan.

In many markets this alternative is cumbersome and expensive. This is due to the large amount of securities that must be assembled to collateralize the required cash. There is the additional burden of posting this to the bank that is extending the credit. In addition during term and open-ended transactions many securities may be recalled to make deliveries requiring substitutions. Operating expenses are impacted due to the physical effort of assembling the securities and then the posting process to the bank. This is addition to the amount of over collateralization required. This ranges from 125-140% across global markets.

Environments

There are two methods of posting securities to the bank that is extending credit. They may not be available in each market due to local market practices. Bank loans can be returned at any time during the loan at the discretion of the borrower.

1.   **Physical**

Physical loans require that the securities move from the borrowers y the lenders possession. This is the traditional method of transacting loans and is similar to securities practices. Imbedded in this practice is the borrower's loss of asset exposure if the lender fails to make the cash available.

The process of physical bank loans in markets that have a CSD requires the borrower to move the securities from their account, via the CSD, to the lenders account at the CSD. In addition to the internal costs incurred by borrowers and lenders for processing the many securities that make up this transaction, the CSD will charges both the borrower and lender for the securities movement between accounts.

Each time the borrower has to recall a security needed for delivery while substituting another security, additional internal and external costs are incurred.

Part III: POST-SETTLEMENT
Chapter 8
Financing & Cash Management

2.   **Agreement to Pledge (AP)**

An AP loan addressees the processing efforts and expenses incurred in physical loans. It eliminates the physical movement of securities from the borrowers account to the lenders account. Instead, the borrower segregates the securities to be used as collateral for a bank loan on their books. This may be reflected by moving these securities positions, on the Brokers internal records, from a CSD or free account to a bank AP Loan account. This establishes that these securities are being used to collateralize an AP bank loan and are encumbered for use by the broker until the loan is repaid.

This type of loan is usually extended to Brokers with the highest credit rating. This is due to the fact that the bank trusts the Broker to maintain the correct and proper status of the securities pledged as collateral during the life of the loan. Yes the bank can audit the Broker to verify that the Broker's books correctly reflect the status, but it is difficult to do this on an ongoing basis.

LETTERS OF CREDIT (LC)

Overview

Brokers and Custodians do not usually use Letters of Credit to support their securities settlement activities. But Investors, and a few Brokers, may LCs to trade and settle securities transactions.

A bank issues an LC to an Investor or Broker based upon their expected need. The bank assesses a charge of ½ to 3½% of the value of the LC. The Investor or Broker executes a buy trade and presents the LC to settle the trade. The bank that issued the LC will extend amount. Once the bank has extended cash they increase the service charge to 7-12%. The Investor or Broker will pay this charge until they repay the loan.

SUMMARY

Beneficial ownership of the securities used to collateralize a Repo or Bank Loan does not change during the transaction. The Investor or Broker that own the securities pledged for these transactions does not give up their beneficial ownership rights. Any interest and cash and share dividends paid during the term of the loan accrue to the borrower that pledged the securities to the lender. As such they can be passed back as paid or settled at the conclusion of transaction.

In some markets, the UK and US for example, the central bank recognize a repo transaction and passes the interest payment on government bonds directly to the borrower, even though the securities are in the lender's account.

Part III: POST-SETTLEMENT
Chapter 8
Financing & Cash Management

CASH MANAGEMENT

There are many activities, provided by Brokers or Custodians, under the umbrella of Cash Management. Some are not addressed here because they are not directly related to securities trading and or settlement and as such do not add value to our handbook. These services include the following:

- Checking and other 'draw upon' accounts
- Overdraft privileges
- General purpose lines of credit
- Tax advice
- Real estate management

Settlement, though addressed in chapter 6, is a focus of Cash Management. Ensuring that Investors have the cash available for settlement is a critical issue for Brokers and Custodians. Not only are funds required, proper currency balances must be available to settle trades across markets. Most, but not all, markets credit funds on the day the cash is received (called same day funds). In a few other markets, the funds are available on the next business day (called next-day funds). As such forecasting future settlements, both buys and sells, is a crucial activity for Investors, Brokers and Custodians

The funds required for settlement can be made available through a number of methods. One is for the Investor to transfer the appropriate currency to the Broker or Custodian in time for settlement of a securities trade. The Investor may sell a security in the market at the same time they purchase a security and have the credit balance from the sale used to pay for the security purchased.

There are two other methods utilized by Investors to meet their currency need at Brokers and Custodians. The most common is the execution of a Foreign Exchange (FX) trade. The second method is for an Investor to arrange with their Broker or Custodian for settlement to be made across markets in various currencies by the Broker or Custodian. This is known as Single Currency Settlement

FOREIGN EXCHANGE (FX)

Overview

An FX is the sale of one currency and the simultaneous purchase of a second currency. Many investors, active across markets, often rely on a Custodian or Broker to Exchange currencies. Banks are the entity most involved in FX transactions. Large money center banks in each market process most of the FX transaction executed each day. The number of these banks depends on the size and the maturity of the market. The number could span from one or two banks in pre-emerging markets such as Viet

Part III: POST-SETTLEMENT
Chapter 8
Financing & Cash Management

Nam to three to six banks in Hong Kong to upwards of ten banks in Germany, the UK and the US.

A competitive concern about free trade is with a limited number of banks quoting exchange rates that the rates are not competitive. But today many of the large banks from mature markets actively quote exchange rates for 80% of the available currencies.

Exchange rates are quoted from one currency to another. For example UK Sterling to HKD quote would appear as GBP/HKD 13.25. This reflects that for the sale of each pound sterling receives 13.25 value in HKD. The USD is the natural offset for much of the FX market. The impact of this is that the above example actually reflects sterling to USD and USD to HKD. This is substantiated by the individual quotes for these currencies, which was 1.6987 Sterling to 1.00 USD and 1.00 USD to 7.80 HKD. This method will be subject to change over the next 2-5 years with the introduction and projected acceptance and success of the Euro on the continent.

FX activity is a major service of Custodians and Brokers. Each supports clients that are trading and settling trades in various currencies. FX rates are quoted in two markets. The difference in these markets is the FX settlement cycle. The Spot market, the majority of FX trades are executed here, settles on two days or less. FX trades executed in the forward market settle anywhere from three days to 5 years from the trade date.

The following transaction refers to sellers and buyers. The investor could be a direct participant in these activities. But more often it will be the Custodian, Broker or bank acting on behalf of the investor.

Transaction Processing

1. FX trades are executed in the OTC market. This market offers screen based quotes, which requires some communications, either verbal or electronic between the seller (the money center banks) and the buyer (Investor, Custodian or Broker), to negotiate and execute the FX.

    a. The communications between the seller and buyer includes finalizing the exchange rate for the transaction. This is an important aspect of the transaction to both the seller and buyer. The quote may have changed since the rates were posted. The buyer based upon the amount of the expected transaction may be able to negotiate a better rate based upon current market conditions.

2. Once agreement on the amount, settlement schedule has been completed the trade is entered onto the buyer and seller internal systems.

3.   The middle or back office for the buyer and seller receives notice of the trade and proceeds to preparation for settlement

   a.   Currently there is no Global Trade Matching facility for FX transactions in the global markets. This is subject to change as discussed in the summary section of this section. However, many Banks and large institutional Investors confirm trades via SWIFT or electronically match transactions using a Matching System (e.g., F/X Match). Less common, but still utilized, is the exchange of trade details via fax, telex or electronic data exchange.

   b.   This information is matched electronically or visually reviewed to determine that details from the buyer and seller match. Once agreement is determined, the counterpartys trade information is signed and returned via the method of receipt.

   c.   There is no central counterparty (CCP) and no trade guarantee as found in the security markets. Many banks and some institutions use a netting system (e.g., F/X Net) to Net trades. The netted amount is then processed for settlement.

   d.   Delivery instructions are exchanged during this process

   e.   Each participant advises the settlement banks to the buyer and seller

4.   Settlement occurs on the settlement date in the market of the currency. This is addressed in Chapter 5

FX Summary

Electronic trading alternatives are beginning to become more available in the FX market. Reuters 2000 is a popular trading systems used by investors, custodians and brokers. This will ease trading and in automate the recording of FX trades. As a result the sellers and buyers will be able to automate the preparation for and actual settlement activities. This will bring FX processing onto a par with many of the securities products.

Continuous Linked Settlement (CLS) is another advance in the automation and reduction of FX settlements. CLS expects to introduce their services during 2002. Essentially CLS will provide FX trade matching, trade netting and settlement services. See Chapter 15 for more about CLS.

As the industry nears T+1 settlement for global equities and bonds it will impact FX trading. Since some FX trades executed in the Spot market take two days to settle the FX will have to be executed one day before any securities trade settling T+1. More likely, it's assumed by industry sources in trading and settlement, to standardize FX

Part III: POST-SETTLEMENT
Chapter 8
Financing & Cash Management

trading to settle all FX Spot trades on a T+1 basis. This will ensure that appropriate funds are available for settlement.

Single Currency Settlement

Investors have adopted this type of cash settlement as an approach to reducing the cost of global trading. The concept is for the Broker or Custodian to utilize their individual currency balances to settle trades, on behalf of these Investors, and to settle a net amount of the buy and sell activity in the Investor's base currency. This approach permits Investors to 'settle' one amount daily in one currency. This currency is usually their base currency.

Utilizing this method permits Investors to minimize FX activity and related expenses, internal and external transactions and risks associated with holding multiple currencies. This method utilizes the currency balances that Brokers and Custodians have as a part of their role as intermediaries. And it positions these intermediaries to offer this valuable service to clients. These Investors pay an additional fee for this service.

INVESTMENT

Investors often need to invest cash balances held pending reinvestment or awaiting repatriation. The 'owner' of the cash may be the Investor or Broker. Custodians usually do not have proprietary funds available for investment. The source of Investors or Brokers cash may be from a sale, cash deposit, dividend interest payment, corporate action or a transfer from a related account.

The Brokers or Custodian offer, as part of their service, investment of free cash balances. These investments must generate a rate of return (interest) that is competitive and meets the investor's objectives. Often the rate of return offered is a primary consideration when the investor selects a custodian or Broker. Critical issues, and primary focus of the Broker or Custodian, associated with Cash Management are:

- o Safety of investments
- o Availability of diverse investments
- o Optimization of Returns (Interest rates)

Some markets restrict or do not permit foreign investors from earning interest on local currency balances. The motivation for this varies, but as a result may result in inhibiting investment activity.

Typical investment vehicles offered by Custodians or Broker includes national and or local government money market instruments or a money market mutual funds. Investments may be insured by an external source such as the Broker or Custodian in

Part III: POST-SETTLEMENT
Chapter 8
Financing & Cash Management

mature markets but often are not available in emerging or pre-emerging markets. Safety of the investment is a critical concern of the Investor.

The funds held for investors or Brokers, may be held in a number of currencies. Some investors may 'own' multiple currencies while awaiting reinvestment in local shares. While other investors convert all balances held to their national currency without delay. Investors that regularly own multiple currencies look to their Custodian or Broker to offer Investment opportunities for all the markets they trade. Investors that prefer to hold their national currency execute a foreign exchange (FX) transaction.

One major area of focus for the custodian and Broker is projecting the currency requirements of their investor clients. They need to 'look ahead' to identify any pending settlement of trades or taxes or other funds their client requires. As a specific currency is required, the Broker or Custodian executes a FX to ensure that the appropriate currency is available for settlement of client trades.

Part III

Post-Settlement

Chapter 9
Income
Processing

Part III: POST-SETTLEMENT
Chapter 9
Income Processing

Income, sometimes a primary reason for investing, consists of two types of cash flows. Dividends are declared on equity securities and interest is paid on bonds. Repayment of a bond at maturity can be considered income but in the truest sense it is the return of the capital

Income processing is the method of collecting income and disbursing payouts of dividends, interest payments that issuers pay stock and bond holders. The payouts of income processing may be predictable

In this chapter we will examine the various types of income and the following:
- Types of dividends
- Interest payment
- Principal repayments
- Critical dates associated with income processing

Some markets combine income and corporate action events. A primary motivation for this is that they both impact an account's holdings via a change in securities or cash held. This book treats these two events as separate and distinct actions. The basic difference, and the motivation for treating these events separately, is that income events are most likely to occur while corporate action events may or may not occur. After you complete this and the corporate action chapter you can make your own assessment of our approach and make your own distinction between the two events.

Types of Dividends

Dividends are usually declared and paid semiannually, but they can be declared and paid quarterly or annually. They can be paid in cash or in some case, as stock dividends or as stock splits, which are additional shares of stock.

Dividends can consist of cash and or security. Cash is the most common form of dividend. They are usually paid in the denomination of the country of the issuer. But they can be paid in other currencies as well.

Dividends paid in security form, can be referred to as property dividend, script or stock dividend, a stock split or a bonus share. We will review the characteristics of and the activities associated with cash dividends first and address stock dividend later.

Part III: POST-SETTLEMENT
Chapter 9
Income Processing

Cash Dividends

Cash dividends are not an obligation of a company that issues ordinary, common or registered shares. However, the issuer is usually obligated to pay a dividend on a regular basis on a Preferred issue. But since the most widespread security issued is ordinary and will use ordinary shares in our examples.

A company usually establishes a history of dividend payments. Many Blue Chip, or most recently Red Chip, securities enjoy a reputation for consistent dividend payments. This appeals to investors that need the safety of solid companies and a reliable cash flow to supplement their earnings or retirement benefits. In some markets, a company must pay a dividend in consecutive quarters or half years to maintain their exchange listing. Established companies usually pay dividends. This is due to the fact that many new or emerging companies reinvest their earnings and profits back into their core business. While an established company has a more consistent revenue stream and can more easily divert earning to shareholders without impacting their core business.

Dividends can be declared by companies that are earning a profit or companies that are experiencing operating losses. In these cases the dividends would be paid from retained earnings rather than current profits. A company usually establishes a quarterly or bi-annual history of declaring a dividend. The Board of Directors (BoD), at the Annual General Meeting, usually declares the first dividend payment. Though there may be a history of declaring dividends each must be voted and declared by the BoD. A schedule can be established for the remainder of the year to pay out the dividend. For example when the BoD of HK Gas declares a 2HK$ dividend it is usually paid in four quarters (actually 2 semi's – HK China Gas, as with most HK shares pay an interim and a final dividend) of HKD.50. The BoD in addition to declaring the dividend will also define when the dividend will be paid and the date when shareholders will be eligible.

Critical Dates

There are four critical dates associated with dividend payments as follows:

- Announcement/Declaration Date
- Ex-Date
- Record Date
- Payment Date

The Announcement Date is the date the dividend is declared. It can also be known as the Declaration date. The board of directors will announce the terms and amount of the dividend, payable date and record date.

The Ex-Date is the date established by the local trading entity. We will return to discuss this further on in this section.

The Record Date is the date on which entitlement to the dividend is established. Simply put, the trade date and settlement date of that trade must occur on or before the Record Date for the investor to be entitled to the dividend.
In certain markets, particularly throughout Asia, the Record Date is scheduled to occur on the date of the Annual General Meeting (AGM). Though the dividend amount may be pre-established it is subject to the vote and approval of the BoD during the AGM. As such it may be subject to amendment.

These amendments impact the processing activities because the expected dividend payment will not be made. This requires an adjustment to the expected dividend payment to ensure that the proper income is identified and collected.

The Payment Date is the date that the issuer, or their corporate agent such as a Paying Agent, issues the dividend payment. The payment can be issued via a bank transfer, wire draft or physical check.

The Ex-Date, the only date that the issuer doesn't determine, is established by the local exchange or marketplace once the dividend and associated dates are announced. The Ex-Date is influenced by the number of business days that occur between Trade and Settlement dates. The local marketplace will count back the number of days between Trade and Settlement date minus one resulting in the Ex-Date. In most markets ownership is established on settlement date so the Ex-Date is the first trade date that once settled will not be eligible for the dividend. This is illustrated by the following:

> Local market settles TD+3 – all business days
> Announcement Date – April 1st
> Ex-Date – May 29th
> Record Date - June 1st (less than or equal to settlement date)
> Payment Date – July 1st

Another event occurring on Ex-Date is an adjustment to the market price of the security in the trading environment. Logic dictates that once a dividend is declared, and assumed to be paid based upon the creditworthiness of the issuer, the trading price of the security is adjusted to reflect the pending dividend. And since the Ex-Date is the first trade date that will not carry the dividend payment the price is adjusted down to reflect that the dividend is not part of the transaction.

Part III: POST-SETTLEMENT
Chapter 9
Income Processing

In some markets, particularly throughout Europe, a common practice is for the Ex-date to occur the day after Record date. In France and Germany the Ex-date and Pay dates are scheduled for the same day. This environment often presents special challenges to brokers and custodians accustomed to trade based - processing schedules

This highlights the differences between Trade and Settlement dates and the associated entitlements of each. In France and Germany entitlement to the dividend payment is established on Trade date rather than Settlement date. And this practice is further extended into markets where the Ex-date falls on the next business day after the Record date.

To recap there are two methods of determining purchaser's entitlement to dividend payments. These are:

  o   Trade date eligibility: TD must occur before Ex-date
  o   Settlement date eligibility: SD must occur on or before Record date

Stock Dividends

Stock dividends, also called bonus shares, script or property dividends are less common than cash dividends but are found in many markets. There are a number of motivations for a company to issue additional shares. Stock dividends are issued to 'gift' shareholders with additional shares without creating a capital event. As a result each shareholder's percentage of holdings remains the same, because each stockholder receives a dividend in proportion to their original holdings.

Stock dividend increases usually range from 5 to 25%. For example, you owned 1000 shares of HK Gas with a current market value of HKD10,000, the BoD declares a 15% Stock Dividend. As a result your holding would increase by the 150 Stock dividend shares for a total holding of 1150 shares without any manual impact on the current market value. Of course, the market price will change, through buying and selling activity, to reflect the additional shares

Some dividend dates may be pre-established by the issuer. This results in a record date that may fall on a Saturday, Sunday or business holiday. The typical default, in most cases is to make this effective the immediate business day following the 'official' date.

Part III: POST-SETTLEMENT
Chapter 9
Income Processing

Participants, in addition to the investor, CSD, broker and custodians, performing income-processing activities include the Transfer Agent/Registrar who is responsible for maintaining a list of security owners and Paying or Disbursement agent. The investors will be the ultimate recipients of the income event. The Paying Agent is the entity that will issue the physical or electronic dividend payment to the owners of record.

CSD are critical participants in this process. Since they hold a majority of the issued securities they appear as the owner of record for income events. The CSD receives the payment, either shares or cash, from the Paying Agent and then passes the appropriate amounts to the membership in accordance with their holdings. To minimize loss of revenues and financing costs this process must occur and be completed on Payment Date.

Some CSDs may not receive the cash payment, for example in markets where the issuer knows the beneficial owner. In these markets the Paying Agent will issue payment to the beneficial owner either through an electronic payment to their bank account or issuance of a check.

Special Situations – Dividend Percentages

In a few markets dividends can be announced and paid as a percentages. For example an issuer may announce 10% cash divided. The question is then raised as to 10% of what; market value would be too subjective. The benchmark guiding this type of dividend is usually par or book value. In many markets 'book value' information is modified to reflect changes to the company's value. As a result in some markets 'book value; becomes the benchmark for dividends.

A situation that occurs, both in European and Asian markets, is the issuance of stock dividends that are not entitled to the first dividend payment after issuance. These are known as non-pari passu shares. Pari passu, a French phrase meaning 'equal in every way' so non-pari passu shares are not entitled to cash dividends until one year after issuance might be only a few to 6 months depending on when the dividend is paid.

In fewer markets, and hopefully fewer in the future, partial dividends are paid to shareholders. For example Indian companies that issue a secondary offering in July will pay a dividend of 10 rupee for shares issued before July but only 5 rupee for the shares issued in July. This causes operational and processing difficulties and can only be managed by maintaining two securities classes until the dividend is paid. After the payments are issued the company combines the two securities and considers them as one for future payments

Part III: POST-SETTLEMENT
Chapter 9
Income Processing

Many markets offer Dividend reinvestment Plans (DRPS). These plans permit an investor to reinvest their dividend payments so that they accumulate additional shares. This has been popular alternative to investors. But due to the small amounts reinvested often times fractional shares holdings result. This requires brokers and custodians to modify their processing systems to accommodate these fractional holdings. Of course an investor can't sell ½ a share but the broker or custodian will usually accommodate this situation with cash in lieu payment for the fractional shares.

Special Situations – Optional Dividend

A company that anticipates a need for cash, but seeks to reward their shareholders with additional shares utilizes this type of dividend event. The need for cash is usually for business expansion or a merger or acquisition. The request for issuance of additional shares is voted upon and approved by shareholders. Issuance of the new shares is completed via Script or a DRIP. Most Script and DRIP issues shares incorporate a discount from the publicly trades prices and allow for shareholders to acquire additional shares with no commission.

Interest

Interest is the cash flow, from bonds, paid to investors. It is an expense to the issuer for the loan of the cash from the investor and as such is income to the investor. Interest is an obligation of the issuer and if they fail to make a payment on time, they can be declared in default, which may impact their ability to borrow additional funds in the capital market.

As a rule interest payments are paid for the previous period. For example, a bond interest payment made on January 1st is for period of July 1st to December 31st. The bond begins an accrual of interest for the next period on January 1st.

Taxation of interest payments varies from market to market. It may be based upon the country/city of residence of the investor as well as the use of funds raised. We don't address this topic since tax and investment rules are subject to frequent change and interruptions.

Fixed Rates

Most interest payments are established at the time of issuance of the bond. This is reflected in the stated interest rate in the bond description. For example a HKD100,000 investment in Hong Kong Gas & Electric 6½ % due August 8, 2010 would pay 6½ % interest on the face value issued, resulting in yearly interest payment of HKD6,500 each year through August 2010. This payment is usually made twice yearly, as two payments of HKD3,250. Interest payments can also be made monthly, quarterly, and annually.

Variable Rates

Interest rates on variable rate bonds are subject to change based upon the associated benchmark of the bond issue. Examples of benchmarks are the 15 year German Bunds rate or the FTSE 100 index. The rate will change each time the benchmark changes. If there is no change in the benchmark, the previous rate continues in effect and interest payments are made at the last rate. Benchmarks can change monthly, quarterly, semi-annually or annually.

Zero Coupon

Zero coupon and money market bonds don't pay investors interest during their lifecycle. These bonds are sold at a discount from the face value. And upon maturity they pay their full-face amount to investors. Zero coupon bonds accrete interest daily from their date of issuance. This means their market value increases each day. This increase reflects the interest earned toward the full face value they pay at maturity. When an investor sells a zero coupon before maturity they will realize the accreted value through the day before settlement.

Securitized Products

Interest paid on securitized products such as asset backed or mortgage backed securities changes between interest payments based upon the principal outstanding. The principal investment of securitized products, also know as 'self-amortizing instruments' changes based upon scheduled and unscheduled repayment of principal. The scheduled payments are defined based upon the loan agreement in force and agreed to by the lender and borrower at the loan inception. For example when someone purchases a home they seek a mortgage from a lender that is usually a banker. The banks extend the cash on behalf of the borrower, while the borrower agrees to repay the loan. A schedule is prepared which outlines the date and amount of the repayment amount. This repayment amounts has two components, an interest and principal payment. The principal repayment reduces the interest amount and the outstanding principal. Any payment of principal in excess of the scheduled amount, also known as a 'prepayment' also reduces the outstanding principal, which, through a 'knock-on' impact reduces the interest payment.

Part III: POST-SETTLEMENT
Chapter 9
Income Processing

Critical Dates

Critical dates for interest payments are:

> Record Date
> Payment Date

Similar to dividends, investors must own the bond on or before the Record Date to be entitled to the interest payment. The interest payment is made on the Payment Date to the holder of record.

As you see, there is no Announcement or Ex-Date influencing the entitlement procedures for interest payments. There are two reasons for this. Since the interest amount and payment date is included in the bond indenture at the time of issuance and is not usually subject to change there is no need for and Announcement Date. There is no Ex-Date since bond interest is an obligation of the issuer and payment is expected. So interest payments are part of the cash consideration in trade details. This payment, called Accrued interest, is the prepayment of interest by the buyer to the seller on trades that occur between interest payment intervals.

For example, an issue with a January and July bond interest payment schedule, a trade with an August 1st settlement date will include an amount for the interest earned by the seller from July $1^{st.}$ The amount of this interest repayment would be determined by the amount of time since the last interest payment. In our example 32 days (July 31 days and 1 day for August) would have transpired since the last interest payment date. But charging for 32 days interest would be overcharging the buyer by one day. The calculation to determine the number of days interest the seller is entitled to is the first interest accrual date up to the day before settlement date. The day before settlement is used as the last interest accrual date since the seller delivers the bonds to the buyer who pays the seller, and therefore is the owner of the bonds on settlement date and is entitled to the interest.

The number of days is multiplied by the daily interest amount earned, resulting in the accrued interest. This is added to the market price the buyer pays for the bond and any additional costs including taxes, fees and commissions. Daily interest amount is determined by the dividing the interest paid for the period by 180 or the actual days in the period.

Bond's Accrued Interest Calendar may be either 30 days in each month and 360 days in a year (30/360) or actual days each month and 365 days in the year (actual/365) or actual days in both the months and year (actual/actual). In the example, if the Bond used a calendar of 30/360, the interest would be computed on 31 days – 30 days in July and 1 day for August.

Principal

Principal payments, which are repayment of capital invested, are not income. But in many firms this function is part of the Income processing operation. These payments of principal can be total in the case of a bond that matures or represent a partial payment for Securitized bonds or called bonds. We address these activities in Chapter 10 Corporate Actions.

Processing Income Payments

Processing income events may differ subtly among markets but the following are the general activities that are usually performed to collect and disburse the cash and or securities associated with income processing. Unique aspects of the three markets we are tracking throughout this handbook are reflected at the conclusion of this section.

The Participants involved in processing income payments are as follows:

- o Investors
- o Brokers
- o Custodians
- o Paying Agents who are responsible for the issuance of cash and or securities associated with income events
- o Register/Transfer Agent, a role previously discussed in Chapter 7
- o Market Data Vendors which are companies that collect and distribute income, corporate action event data as well as descriptive, pricing and statistical data

Process Steps

1. The starting point of income processing is the identification of the event. A market data vendor usually provides dividend and interest event data. Brokers, Custodians and Investors contract with two or more market data vendors to provides an array of data that they use to drive their internal analytics and processes. Multiple sources are used to ensure completeness and accuracy of these events.

2. This event information is stored in an electronic file often called a Security Master or Security Reference file. This data is maintained and may be retrieved by the security name or most likely a security number. An

example of market data is the specific security numbering system utilized for their local market.

3. At the end of the Record Date day, or Trade Date for markets that utilize Trade Date to establish entitlement, the broker or custodian will determine two conditions from their internal records. The first is to identify those accounts that are entitled to the income event. The logic used to reach this decision is the same as discussed in this chapter in the Critical Dates section.
The account must establish ownership of the security prior to Ex-Date or by Record Date. Another way of looking at this is to identify the accounts and the settlement date of the transaction creating this position and ensure when settlement date or trade date was on or before the Record Date that account was entitled to the income event. As a result the broker/custodian has identified the accounts that are entitled to the income event.

The second condition is to identify and balance the sources that will provide the cash for the income event. Typically the locations providing these include CSD, Custodian, fail to receive trades, securities out for registration, loan or bank collateral and client short accounts. These two conditions should equal so that the sources equal the entitled balances.

Once this is completed the broker/custodian/Investor tracks any activity that is processed that would effect the Record Date positions. This may include posting of late trade activity often referred to 'as of trades'. This type of activity may be caused by lost trade tickets or entries processed for a different account.

Any out of balance positions causing erroneous positions will also require adjustments that impact entitled accounts or the sources of income. Tracking the record date positions require a daily review to ensure that they security positions remain balanced and that the expected cash is received. During the time between Record and Payment Date the broker/custodian will process claims to the counterparty responsible for the Fail, Registration and or Short account. This process, also known as 'Due Bill' processing establishes a claim for the cash due from the particular condition. This 'Due Bill' is not effective until the Payment Date but delivery of the claim creates a 'Bill Due'.

There are exceptions to this for example in Japan the holder of record is not legally obligated to honor claims. Peru and Portugal have no formal claims process. Newer markets, for example Slovak Republic, with little dividend or corporate action activity have not yet developed claims procedures.

Unique to Taiwan is that the tax on the dividend must be paid prior to the dividend payment date. Though there are no fails in Taiwan it's another example of differences in processing income distributions.

4.   On Payment Date the appropriate cash balances will be received from the CSD and positions that were in loan on the Record Date. The broker/custodian will credit the appropriate cash amounts to the entitled accounts. In many cases the broker/custodian does not receive the full amount needed to balance the entitled accounts on payment Date. This is due the Fails, Registrations and Short accounts that existed on Record Date. The cash balances from these conditions will flow to the broker or custodian from Payment Date until some time in the future Brokers and Custodians must be vigilant in the collection of these balances as they may have used their own funds to pay their entitled accounts, in essence financing these balances, until the cash claimed is received.

In markets where the issuer or Paying Agent knows the beneficial owner payment will be made be made directly to those investors. And as a result will not create the need for financing by the broker, GCB or SCB.

At times broker/custodians will receive more cash than they require to pay entitled accounts. There are a number of causes for this; a security may be registered in a broker or custodian's name over the Ex – Date or Record Date or an unreconciled out of balance security position at the broker or custodian. In either situation the broker or custodian must hold these unallocated funds in an account until a claim is received or the out of balance security position has been identified and reconciled. In markets without a CSD this may be a common situation.

Contractual Income Processing

Custodians may offer contractual income payment processing. Simply put this process ensures that the investor or broker client of the Custodian receives the dividend or interest payment regardless whether the Custodian received the payment was made. The motivation for a client to request and a Custodian to provide this service is addressed in the Custody chapter 13.

Part III: POST-SETTLEMENT
Chapter 9
Income Processing

Withholding Income Payments

A portion of the income payment may be withheld, based upon tax treaty between investor's country of residence and the issuer country. This topic is addressed in Chapter 11

BRAZIL CASH INCOME PROCESS

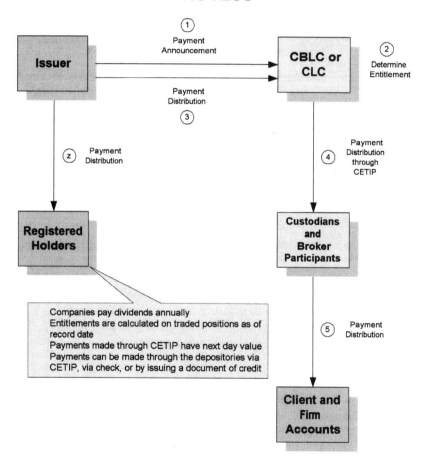

Footnotes	
BOVESPA	Bolsa de Valores (Stock Exchange) de Sao Paulo
BVRJ	Bolsa de Valores (Stock Exchange) de RIo de Janeiro
CBLC	Companhia Brasileira de Liquidacao e Custodia (Clearing House for BOVESPA)
CLC	Camara de Liquidacao e Custodia (Clearing House for BVRJ)
CETIP	Central de Custodia e Liquidacao Financeira de Titulos Privados (Cash clearance for corporate securities)

HONG KONG CASH INCOME PROCESS

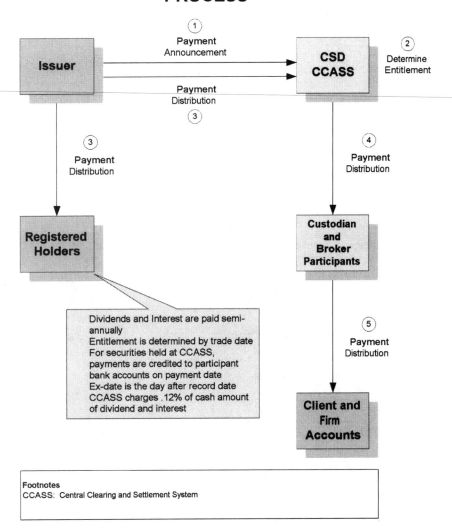

Dividends and Interest are paid semi-annually
Entitlement is determined by trade date
For securities held at CCASS, payments are credited to participant bank accounts on payment date
Ex-date is the day after record date
CCASS charges .12% of cash amount of dividend and interest

Footnotes
CCASS: Central Clearing and Settlement System

UNITED KINGDOM CASH INCOME PROCESS

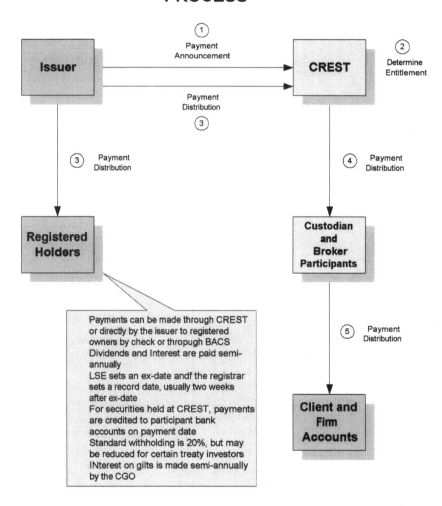

Part III: POST-SETTLEMENT
Chapter 9
Income Processing

CHAPTER PROCESS FLOW

The following reflects the flow of internal and external activities required to process a dividend payment. We refer to Investor, Broker and Custodian without specifying which custodian is responsible. This way we hope to reflect the process rather than confuse our readers with 'who' is doing 'what,' 'when.'

On July 1, 2002
H.K. & China Gas announced a dividend payment of HKD2 to holders of Record (date) September 2, 2002
Payable October 1, 2002

A dividend event, is announced and as a result the following activities occur:
- Local market establishes the Ex-Dividend date – September 1, 2002
- Market Data vendors collect information
- Brokers/Custodians update their Security Reference files with event information
  - This information is pended until
    - A change to the event details is received
    - September 2, 2002

On September 2, 2002
Brokers/Custodians review accounts that owned H.K. & China Gas shares as of the close of business September 2, 2002

Client AA holds 10,000 shares H.K. & China Gas Ltd.

- Broker/Custodian updates records to indicate dividend receivable for HKD20,000 from H.K. & China Gas dividend event
  - This receivable will reflect the location where the securities were maintained on September 2, 2002 (CCASS)

On October 1, 2002 the Broker/Custodian receives HKD20,000

Dividend Receivable account
Debited HKD20,000 for
payment received for
H.K. & China Gas Ltd.

Client AA account
Credited HKD20,000 reflecting
receipt of dividend on
H.K. & China Gas Ltd.

Part III

Post-Settlement

Chapter 10
Corporate Actions

Part III: POST-SETTLEMENT
Chapter 10
Corporate Actions

Corporate Action events are triggered, by a company's own action or by the action of another corporation, and result in a change in the corporate structure. Any change in a corporation's financial structure, from called bonds or a name change is a corporate action.

In this chapter we will define

- Types of corporate action events
- Motivations for triggering corporate event
- Impact on stockholders
- Processing flows

Types of Corporate Actions

Corporate action events fall into two categories, mandatory and voluntary. A mandatory event, which may be declared by the Board of Directors (BoD), without a formal shareholder vote, affects all stockholders of a security. Once enacted the shareholder receives the resulting outcome determined by the BoD.

A voluntary event is an offer, by the issuing or offering corporation, to shareholders that requires a response. It is the stockholder's responsibility to analyze the terms of the event and decide if it is in their best interest to participate. These events require the shareholder to respond to the event announcement. This response can be positive whereby the shareholder elects to participate in the event, or the shareholder can vote against the event or the shareholder may opt to respond and defer the decision to other shareholders.

In this chapter we address events commonly found in across markets. Often these events may be known by different names. Whenever possible we include this information in the appropriate section. There are unique events that may exist in particular markets that are not reflected in this chapter.

MANDATORY EVENTS TYPES

Call Provision

A call provision is a special feature of a bond or equity issue. It gives the issuer the right to redeem an issue. For a bond issue this may be before the scheduled maturity date. For an equity security, usually a preferred issue, it would be at the discretion of the BoD. Call dates for these securities may be specified in the prospectus of the issue or addressed with a call provision in a bond indenture. There maybe specific dates and amounts or percentages identified or there may be a general reference permitting calls to be made. Equity issues may be called to eliminate the need for a corporation to pay a specific dividend to shareholders.

Part III: POST-SETTLEMENT
Chapter 10
Corporate Actions

Bonds are often called when interest rates drop significantly enough that it would benefit the corporation to 'float a new' bond issue at the current prevailing (lower) rates. Or a corporation may also decide to call an issue if it is cash rich and would like to save the dividend or interest payments it is required to make to these security holders. By calling a security, a corporation reduces it's obligation for future payments.

The prospectus will reflect when a corporation can call a security. Besides listing callable dates, which usually do not begin until the issue is five years old, the prospectus will indicate the percentage of the security that a corporation may call at any one time and the call price. If the entire issue is called, a Full Call, the procedure is simple. Every investor submits their security and receives the cash payment. In the event of a partial call a lottery system is utilized to select investors that will have their securities called. To maintain fairness, since often it is not to the investors' advantage to have securities called, the lottery systems should not favor certain investors or the broker's own accounts.

Investors purchase these securities as a tool to lock in an interest rate that delivers a specific cash flow. Callable securities retain the risk that they will be called when interest rates drop. In order to compensate investors for this risk, the issuer often pays a call premium, a price that is higher than the security's face value, when it issues a call. The closer the security is to a maturity date, or the older the issue is, the less premium the issuer pays. Call events may be referred to as Redemptions in some markets as well.

Liquidations

When a corporation fails and closes their business, voluntarily or as a result of a bankruptcy proceeding, shareholders have a right to receive a disbursement of assets. Priority for payments in cases of bankruptcy may differ within markets but are usually are as follows:

1. Creditors (bondholders and other general creditors)
2. Preferred shareholders
3. Common or Ordinary shareholders

As you see, one benefit of owning preferred stock shares is that preferred shareholders have preference over common or ordinary shareholder in the liquidation of assets. When a corporation enters bankruptcy, it follows a prescribed legal procedure to liquidate its assets, if any exist, and pay off its creditors. The company's assets are converted to cash and are distributed to the holders in the prescribed sequence based upon local market laws. Because there is a rigid order in which creditors and shareholders are paid, and because a bankrupt corporation may lack sufficient assets, shareholders holding ordinary shares often receive little to no payment in return for their shares. Remember

Part III: POST-SETTLEMENT
Chapter 10
Corporate Actions

that stockholders are owners of the corporation, so in the eyes of the law, they are lower in repayment priority than the utility companies, suppliers, employee salaries and outstanding debts to other creditors. When a corporation announced that it is liquidating, shareholders have no choice but to take what they can get. This is a mandatory corporate action, since shares in the company do not exist after the liquidation is complete.

Maturity

When bonds reach their maturity date, the bondholder submits their holdings to the issuer or their agent for repayment of principal. This is a predictable, planned event and occurs without much difficulty.

The security is presented to the issuer or their agent and the principal amount is paid. It is important that the security be submitted for repayment of principal as close to the maturity date as possible so that the proceeds can be reinvested. There is no interest paid by the issuer from the maturity date and the date the security is presented. At times a maturity event may be referred to as a Redemption event.

Name Changes

Corporations may change their names for many reasons. A corporation may decide to reflect a major strategic change in their business or an additional product line with a name change, or it might decide to just modernize its image with a name change.

While a name change may not seem like a corporate action, it affects all existing stock certificates and book entry positions. All outstanding shares of the corporation must reflect the new corporate name in order to remain properly issued. The corporation will assign a transfer or corporate action event agent the responsibility for re-issuance of new certificates. The CSD, brokers and custodians will all be notified and all certificates must be sent to the agent for processing. In markets without a CSD this is quite a substantial effort. Book entry ownership will have the name changed on the books and records of the CSD as well as on the books and records of the company. The name change also impacts brokers and custodians, which must also reflect the name change.

Part III: POST-SETTLEMENT
Chapter 10
Corporate Actions

Reverse Splits

A reverse split is the opposite of a stock split, which is addressed later in this chapter. The board of directors of a corporation may decide that the price of the stock is too low to attract investors, so they announce a reverse split. Like a stock split, a reverse split is announced in terms of a ratio, such as 1:2 or 1:3. In a 1:3 reverse split, one share of stock will replace three shares of the stock. The per-share value will be adjusted accordingly so the investor's value of ownership remains exactly the same. The total number of shares outstanding will be one third of the original number, though each investor's share proportion will remain the same to the total number of shares outstanding.

Spin-offs

These events, also known as sub-divisions, are usually triggered by three influences, over diversification by a company, sale of a strong subsidiary to generate income or required by regulators as an anti-trust measure. This event involves a restructuring of the main corporation to reflect the separation of the corporation that is being 'spun off'. Shareholders of the corporation separating from the parent corporation will receive a pro-rata amount of shares in the new corporation based upon a formula developed by the BoD. The BoD may retain a percentage of the new corporations shares as an investment.

Stock Splits

Stock splits, also known as a sub-division, are capital events which change the financial infrastructure of a company, outstanding shares and requires an adjustment in the trading or market price of a security. When the BoD declares a 2 for 1 stock split, due to the size and impact on the holdings, it becomes a capital event. The definition of a capital event varies among markets but a common range is 25-30%. The motivation of the BoD to take this action can be a reduction in the current market to attract more investors. The impact of a capital event is as follows:

> Local market settles TD+3 – all business days
>
> Announcement Date – April 1st
> Record Date - June 1st (less than or equal to settlement date)
> Payment Date – July 1st
> Ex-Date – July 1st (July 2nd)

The Ex-Date moves to the same or in some cases the day after the Payment date. The rationale for this is you want to receive and process the additional shares before you adjust the price. For example in the following example 1000

Part III: POST-SETTLEMENT
Chapter 10
Corporate Actions

shares with a market value of HKD10,000 would result in the following for a 2 for 1 Stock Split

> 1000shares would become 2000 shares
> Market value would remain HKD10,000
> Unit price per share would be reduced from HKD100 to HKD50 per share

Because the Ex-Date occurs after the Record Date, industry participants must post an interim accounting of transactions that trade between the Record and Ex-Dates. This is due to the fact that the shares after Record Date are for post Stock Dividend or 'Split' shares and payment must be made accordingly. The interim accounting accommodates this situation and ensures that everyone receives/ delivers appropriate shares and renders/receives proper payments.

As a result of the split, there is no gain for the investors. The value of their holdings in the corporation remains exactly the same, with no increase in their investment. However, as time goes on, each increase in the stock price increases each of their new shares. For example, if the stock were selling at HKD 300.00 per share, and the stock increase 1 point; each share would increase in value HKD $3.00. After a 3:1 split, with each share worth HKD 100.00, a 1 point increase in the stock price would result in a $1.00 increase per share, making the 3 new shares worth HKD 303.00

A stock split increases an investor's potential for future earnings as well as potential for increased dividend payment. It is also an indication that the corporation is doing well.

Part III: POST-SETTLEMENT
Chapter 10
Corporate Actions

VOLUNTARY EVENTS

Acquisitions Offer

There are times in the life cycle of a corporation when change is required. As new products are introduced or a company's needs change, a company may choose to reorganize. This event may also be known as a Merger or Takeover.

This process may result when two or more corporations; combine resources, agree for one to acquire the assets of the others or decide to merge. In order to complete the Acquisition, the board of directors and the stockholders of the involved corporations must vote for the acquisition. These events are usually friendly. But they can be unfriendly as when one corporation acquires sufficient shares to become a majority shareholder of another corporation.

Conversions

This event, driven by shareholder preference, is the exchange of one security type for another of the same issuer. For example it may involve the conversion of bonds to equity shares or preferred shares for common shares. In all cases this event is influenced by the holders preference for a type of security.

This event is associated with bonds and or preference shares that are issued with a conversion feature. This is a 'credit enhancement' used by issuers permitting holders to convert their holdings to another holding type. The motivation of the issuer to offer a 'dual security' since the holder can, at their discretion, effect a conversion. The investor is attracted to this feature for the same reasons and these securities usually trade at higher prices than similar securities without this feature.

The rate of exchange between the primary and underlying security is established at issuance as well as the conversion price. The convertible security, either a bond or preferred share, will include the details of the conversion. This includes the value of the bonds (an absolute par amount) or the number of preferred shares required to convert to a specified amount of the ordinary or common shares. For example HKD 100,000.00 bond may be convertible for 10,000 shares of HK Gas. Convertible issues may also require a cash payment to the issuers as part of the conversion privilege. So further to our example is HKD100, 000 of HK Gas bonds AND HKD10,000 must be presented to the issuer or their agent in order to effect the conversion to 10,000 HK Gas ordinary shares.

Part III: POST-SETTLEMENT
Chapter 10
Corporate Actions

Exercises: Warrants

A warrant can be associated with common, ordinary and preferred shares or bonds. A warrant provides the holder with the right to purchase a specified amount of common or ordinary shares at a specified price for a fixed period of time. The fixed price is usually higher than the market value of the stock at the time the warrant is issued. The warrants may expire, usually, 5, 10 or 15 years in the future by which time the owner must exercise the warrant or it will be worthless, or it may be issued un perpetuity. A warrant is considered an issuance sweetener, making the offering more appealing to investors.

The appeal of a warrant is that over time, it is assumed that the price of the underlying security will increase during the life of the warrant. As the underlying security price increases, the warrant increases in proportion to the exercise privileges. This situation offers the holder the choice of exercising the warrant and receiving additional shares at a reduced cost or selling the warrant realizing the profit.

If the stock price doesn't increase above the warrant exercise price, it would not make sense to exercise the warrant. Warrants can be detached from the security and traded on the market as a product onto itself. The warrant has no intrinsic value until the price of the stock exceeds the price of stock purchase allowed by the warrant.

A warrant is similar in characteristics to an Equity Option. A major difference is that it is issued by the issuer of the underlying security and is usually categorized as an equity derivative.

Odd Lot Buy Out or Buy Back, Round Up

Most markets haven established lot of trading. This can be defined as 1, 10, 100, 1,000 or 10,000 shares. Any amount less than the established amount is considered an odd lot. Fractional share holdings are also considered odd lots. An odd lot is usually defined as 1 –1000 shares, but it can be as much as 20,000 shares in emerging markets. Odd lots exist because many investors do not have the resources to purchase round lots or as a result of stock dividends or corporate action events.

A corporation may offer an 'odd lot buy out' to investors. Or they may offer to sell shares of stock from its treasury allowing investors to 'round up'. When purchasing odd lots, the corporation may pay a slight premium over the market price to entice investors to sell back their shares. It will sell shares at a reduction from market price to entice investors to round up odd lots. The odd lot investor has the option of ignoring or participating in the offer.

Part III: POST-SETTLEMENT
Chapter 10
Corporate Actions

Put Features

A Put is similar but different from a Call. The similarity is that it is a privilege but it's at the discretion of the investor, rather than the issuer, to redeem the security. The Put feature is usually associated with bonds. It's a credit enhancement that permits the investor to 'put' the bond back to the issuer. In this case the issuer will redeem the bond for the face value. Unlike a Call, a bond issue with a Put feature will not pay a premium to the investor.

Issuers often utilize it without a history in the capital markets. It allows the issuer to offer a lower rate in combination with the Put feature that enhances the credit by permitting the investor to return the bond to the issuer for par value. . Issuers with a history of defaults and or late interest payments may also use it.

Subscription Rights

A subscription right offering gives existing shareholder the right to purchase additional shares of a new issue of common or ordinary shares before it is made available to the public. Usually one share entitles the stockholder to one right, which is equivalent to one share purchased. The corporation, however, is not bound to a one share one right rule, and may issue rights in any ratio it chooses. The ratio is determined in advance of the offering and is part of the information reflected in the prospectus. To encourage an investor to exercise his rights, the corporation may offer shares at a price below market value (discount).

Corporations may issue rights to comply with laws that guarantee investors the right to maintain a proportional share of interest when a new issue is introduced. This is called the investor's preemptive right. Corporations have found even when there is no legal requirement, it is 'good business' to offer current investors the right to purchase additional shares.

The lifecycle of a right is short-lived – somewhere between 15 10 and 60 days, with most expiring in 15 days. If a stockholder does not respond within the designated timeframe he loses his right. To exercise a right, the stockholder must return the rights forms with proof of ownership. While the rights offer is open, rights may be traded and transferred in the marketplace. But in some markets rights are not traded, such as Mexico, Taiwan, Thailand has both transferable and non-transferable rights (NTR). Also some foreign shareholders may be excluded from selling and / or subscribing the rights in some countries (example: In Great Britain often non-European holders are not permitted to participate. In these situations, the restricted foreign holders are credited with their share entitlement but their only option is to sell the rights at the market price. If there is no demand for the rights, some companies will distribute Liquidation Proceeds). Participation Restriction would be disclosed in the prospectus. These restrictions may cause processing errors due to a misunderstanding of the conditions related to the issuance of the rights. And while shareholders sell the rights, they still maintain the ownership of the original shares. as the right is separated from the original shares. Once a right expires, it is worthless.

Tender Offer: Purchase Offers

A tender offer is an offer to exchange shares in a corporation for cash. The organization making the tender may want to take control of the corporation, in which the shares are owned, through the acquisition of a majority of the shares. The tender offer may come about from friendly negotiations from a potential buyer who is also trying to accumulate additional shares of a company. A corporate suitor who acquires more than a certain percentage of a target company may be required to file its intentions with the securities regulator, the target company and the stock exchange where the corporation's shares are traded.

A tender offer is sent to all shareholders of the corporation. The offer includes the price, which may be above market price, or at a premium. The increased price is an incentive for shareholders to tender their shares. It also includes the date by which the stockholder must respond to the offer. If a shareholder chooses to participate in this voluntary event offer, they advise their consent and or sign the tender offer, forward stock certificates if a physical market and advise their broker and or custodian. The broker and or custodian will process the event directly with the tender event agent.

Voting Rights and Proxies

Many common or ordinary shareholders may vote on a corporation's activities. As you recall, a shareholder is an owner of the corporation. The right to vote is a characteristic of common or ordinary share ownership. A shareholder votes for a range of policies of the corporation, including change of corporate structure, new share issuance, mergers, acquisitions and election of the corporation's board of directors. The board of directors is responsible for the direction of the corporation and decides if and how much of a dividend the company will pay to its stockholders. The board of directors in effect reports to the stockholders.

Most of the opportunities to vote take place at the corporation's annual meeting, which most shareholders do not to attend. In order to enter a vote, a shareholder may vote by proxy. Prior to the annual meeting, the investor relations department of the corporation sends out proxy materials to shareholders. Because the corporation may not know all shareholders, if the shares are held in book entry or street name, the corporation sends proxy materials to the holders

Part III: POST-SETTLEMENT
Chapter 10
Corporate Actions

of record, the registered holders and depositories. The corporation often hires a proxy agent to help locate all holders of the security and disperse the materials.

The proxy materials explain the issues at hand and may contain a recommendation on how the board of directors would like the shareholder to vote. Most corporations follow the one share, one vote rule. If a shareholder owns 100 shares of the corporation, they are entitled to 100 votes. Naturally, this method gives large shareholders more weight in the election outcome. To respond to a proxy, the shareholder indicates their vote on the printed material; returns the material to the proxy agent, who tallies the votes, and enters the votes at the annual general meeting (AGM).

In mature markets this information is standard. In emerging and pre-emerging markets BoD issues and other information may not be available before the meeting. This creates a hardship to custodians and brokers because they are unable to provide local or offshore investors with this critical information in advance of the AGM.

Many countries require the physical presence of the shareholder or their legal representative (Power of Attorney) at annual meeting. They may also require a certification of ownership, which is provided by the CSD; The CSD freezes the shares once this certificate is requested and releases them after the AGM. As a result the shares cannot be delivered until after the AGM.

Part III: POST-SETTLEMENT
Chapter 10
Corporate Actions

PROCESSING CORPORATE ACTION EVENTS

Dates

Every corporate action event has associated dates for entitlement and processing. Some corporate actions are date sensitive, especially voluntary actions that an investor must respond, in order to participate. If an investor misses the response date, they miss the opportunity to participate in the corporate action. To qualify for a corporate action, an investor must be a holder of record (recorded on the books of the Registrar)

Announcement Date
The date that the corporation's Board of Directors announce the corporate action event to the general public.

Record Date
The optional date established by a corporation's board of directors, on which an investor must be recorded as the shareholder of the security to be eligible to qualify for the corporate action event.

Response Date
A date, defined by the issuer, by, which an investor must respond in order to participate in the corporate action event. For voluntary corporate actions, the agent must be advised as to the wishes of the investor. The GCB, SCB and brokers often establish an earlier response date for their clients so that they will receive the information with sufficient time to meet the Issuers response date. Distribution/Effective Date is the date the proceeds or new securities, resulting from the event, are distributed.

Part III: POST-SETTLEMENT
Chapter 10
Corporate Actions

Process

While many markets have instituted changes to streamline corporate action event processing via regulatory and securities laws, it is multi-stepped, error prone process involving multiple participants.

The first step is to identify and collect the relevant information associated with corporate action event. Typical sources of this information include, CSD, ICSD, Issuers, transfer and/or income agents and Market Data Information Vendors (MDIV). In most markets utilize a combination of these sources to gather corporate action events. This is due to a lack of central source of this information in a market and the difficulty in gathering the relevant information associated with each event.

Once the GCB, SCB or broker has gathered this information it will be stored in a securities information reference file within their system infrastructure. It will be maintained there until the effective date of the event for mandatory events. Voluntary events require immediate action for investors currently holders of the security involved in the corporate action. We will review the processing steps associated with the voluntary events first and then proceed to the Mandatory/Voluntary steps following that.

Typical information associated with the announcement of a corporate action includes the following:
- o Event Type
- o Issuer
- o Security description and identifiers
- o Event terms and descriptions
- o Corporate Action Event agent (often different than transfer or income agents)
- o Critical Dates
- o Payout/Rate
- o Payout currency

The Issuer, for a specific event, appoints the Event agent. Typical duties of a 'Corporate Action Agent' are the compilation of shareholder records, notification and tracking of shareholder responses and voting records. The agent, usually a bank ensures objectivity in the process.

Part III: POST-SETTLEMENT
Chapter 10
Corporate Actions

Voluntary Event Processing Steps

The voluntary flow has added steps because the GCB, SCB or brokers must notify their customers and await a response from the customer. Because the customer has a choice of participating in the corporate action, their input and instructions are required before proceeding can begin.

1. The GCB, SCB or broker analyzes the terms and conditions of the corporate action event
    - ✓ May recommend to their clients to accept or reject the opportunity
    - ✓ May decide to withhold a recommendation
    - ✓ The issuer contacts shareholders directly if their name/address is known

2. The GCB, SCB, broker identifies clients holding the impacted security
    - ✓ Also to determine where the security is located
    - ✓ This determines entitlement of client and firm accounts

3. The Investor is notified of the corporate action event details
    - ✓ SWIFT, postal system, fax, email
    - ✓ Euclid
    - ✓ Cedcom

4. The Investor reviews event details, considers any recommendation, forwards their instructions to the GCB, SCB or broker
    - ✓ SWIFT, postal system, fax, email
    - ✓ Euclid
    - ✓ Cedcom

Mandatory/Voluntary Event Processing Steps – from this point forward the processing cycle is the same for Voluntary and Mandatory Corporate Action events

5. The SCB or broker forwards instructions to the CSD or the Event agent.
    - ✓ SWIFT, postal system, fax, email

6. The CSD will forward the instructions to the Event agent

7. Event agent processes the event
    - ✓ Cancels old securities
    - ✓ Issues new securities
    - ✓ Issues cash payments

8. New securities delivered, and or cash payments made, to the CSD or SCB or broker
   - ✓ CSD reflects the receipt of cash and/or securities in members accounts
   - ✓ SCB or the broker reflects the receipt of cash and/or securities to their internal client and or firm accounts
   - ✓ SCB or the Broker claims versus other SCB and Brokers for appropriate entitlements

When the CSD or the registrar credits the investor with a corporate action event they credit the investor of record. There are two circumstances when the investor of record is not the current owner.
1) A trade has not settled by the expected settlement date
2) Securities in physical form and are pending registration to the new owner.

Claiming an entitlement from the previous owner is not always easy or possible. Some CSDs claim the entitlement from the previous owner when the trade does finally settle. Others do not – they leave that to the buyer to claim from the seller. In some markets the buyer is not entitled to an entitlement unless their securities are in their name (nominee or beneficial owner) by the record date

In many countries, physical certificates are not sent to the registrar each time the shares are purchased but only when an event is about to take place. To vote at an annual meeting, to collect a cash or stock dividend, the shares must be registered in the recipient's name. If the investor plans to sell the shares in a short period of time and does not intend to hold the securities long enough to collect a dividend (etc.) the securities are typically not submitted for registration. This is especially true if the re-registration will take a long period of time. If the investor were to sell shares that are in the process of being registered, the shares would be unavailable for delivery and would, more than likely, result in the cancellation of the sale through a buy-in. To avoid this situation, the shares are only registered for a corporate action. Unfortunately, if this is not done in time, the owner may not be entitled to the corporate action.

Contractual Corporate Action Processing

Many Custodians offer contractual Corporate Action processing as a service. Simply put this process ensures that the investor or broker client of the Custodian receives the corporate action result, either cash and or securities, regardless whether the Custodian received the resulting cash and or securities. The motivation for a client to request and a Custodian to provide this service is addressed in the Custody chapter 13.

Part III: POST-SETTLEMENT
Chapter 10
Corporate Actions

Processing

The process of identifying and processing Corporate Actions is problematic and costly across the global industry. This is due to a number of issues:

Lack of standards – Manual Steps – Lack of Automation Support

Within many markets there are few regulations and even fewer standards addressing the disclosure of events and required information. Data is collected manually from diverse sources and is 'touched' by many hands during the editing, validation and entry into the distribution system.

There are little or no central repositories of event information. Most investors, brokers and custodians subscribe to multiple data sources. As a result there are conflicts found in the event information received from the different sources. These conflicts must be reconciled and resolved before processing. Cross border activity increases the challenges that industry participants face in processing these events between investors, agents, brokers and custodians.

SWIFT 15022 will address many of the communications related issues. But more standardization is required to remedy this situation. As we have experienced, changes must evolve within each market and then across markets. Markets, seeking to attract 'off-shore' investors, must establish disclosure criteria to ensure that accurate and complete information is available to investors in a timely manner. And those investors have ample opportunity to understand the full impact of these events.

Brokers and custodians, as direct participants between Investors, companies and agents must apply the same level of automation that they have to trade and payment processing. And the Regulators in each market must begin to focus on the critical issues and encourage brokers, custodians and agents to communicate and process efficiently to the benefit of the investors.

Once the local market needs are being addressed each participant's constituency can begin to examine cross border issues and address those as well.

BRAZIL CORPORATE ACTIONS PROCESS

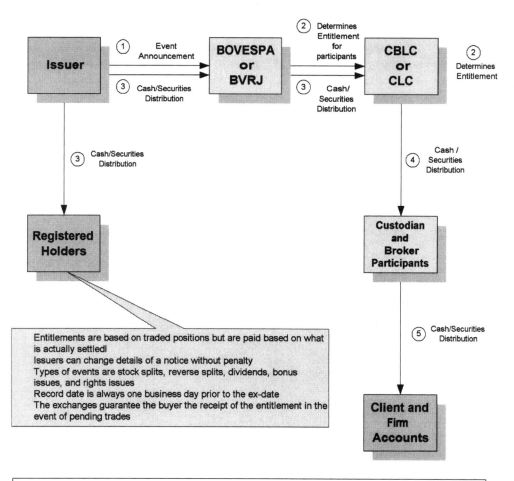

Entitlements are based on traded positions but are paid based on what is actually settledl
Issuers can change details of a notice without penalty
Types of events are stock splits, reverse splits, dividends, bonus issues, and rights issues
Record date is always one business day prior to the ex-date
The exchanges guarantee the buyer the receipt of the entitlement in the event of pending trades

Footnotes	
BOVESPA	Bolsa de Valores (Stock Exchange) de Sao Paulo
BVRJ	Bolsa de Valores (Stock Exchange) de RIo de Janeiro
CBLC	Companhia Brasileira de Liquidacao e Custodia (Clearing House for BOVESPA)
CLC	Camara de Liquidacao e Custodia (Clearing House for BVRJ):

HONG KONG CORPORATE ACTIONS PROCESS

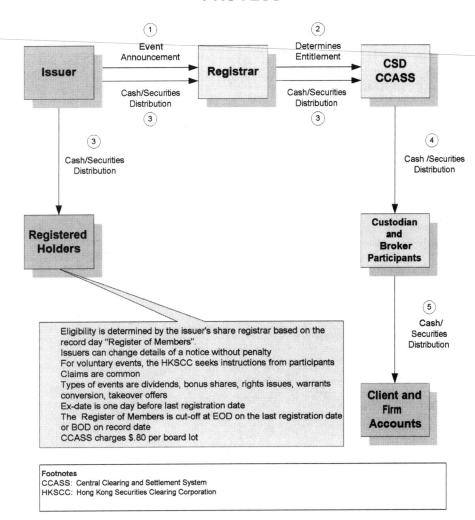

Eligibility is determined by the issuer's share registrar based on the record day "Register of Members".
Issuers can change details of a notice without penalty
For voluntary events, the HKSCC seeks instructions from participants
Claims are common
Types of events are dividends, bonus shares, rights issues, warrants conversion, takeover offers
Ex-date is one day before last registration date
The Register of Members is cut-off at EOD on the last registration date or BOD on record date
CCASS charges $.80 per board lot

Footnotes
CCASS: Central Clearing and Settlement System
HKSCC: Hong Kong Securities Clearing Corporation

Part III: POST-SETTLEMENT
Chapter 10
Corporate Actions

UNITED KINGDOM
CORPORATE ACTIONS PROCESS

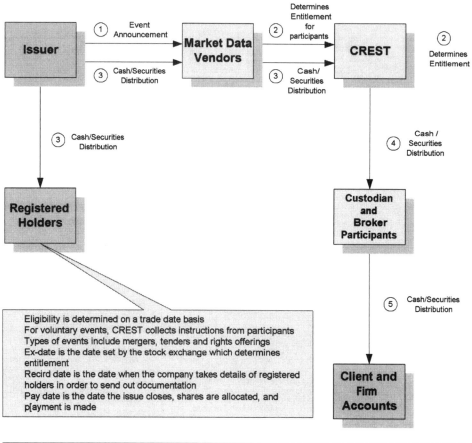

Eligibility is determined on a trade date basis
For voluntary events, CREST collects instructions from participants
Types of events include mergers, tenders and rights offerings
Ex-date is the date set by the stock exchange which determines entitlement
Recird date is the date when the company takes details of registered holders in order to send out documentation
Pay date is the date the issue closes, shares are allocated, and p[ayment is made

Footnotes	
LSE	London Stock Exchange
CREST	Depository for the LSE

Part III: POST-SETTLEMENT
Chapter 10
Corporate Actions

CHAPTER PROCESS FLOW

The following reflects the flow of internal and external activities required to process a corporate action and maintain accurate records regarding the status of a client's security position. We refer to Investor, Broker and Custodian without specifying which broker or custodian is responsible. This way we hope to reflect the process rather than confuse our readers with 'who' is doing 'what', 'when'

On April 1, 2002
H.K. & China Gas Announced the ACQUISTION of Asian Gas Ltd.
1 share of Asian Gas Ltd. = .5 share of H.K. & China Gas
Shareholder voting to be completed by July 1, 2002
Shares due at Event Agent by August 15, 2002
Effective September 1, 2002
Event Agent: HKSB

Acquisition, a Corporate Action event, is announced. As a result, the following activities occur:

- Market Data vendors collect and distribute this information to clients
- Brokers/Custodians update their Security Reference files with event information
- Brokers/Custodians review accounts that own H.K. Gas and/or China Gas shares
- Brokers/Custodians notify/advise accounts holding H.K. Gas and/or China Gas shares

---

Client AA holds 10,000 shares Asian Gas Ltd.

- Mandatory events require no response from investor
- Voluntary events require investor response

Client AA advises their consent and
approval of ACQUISTION of Asian Gas Ltd. on May 1, 2002

- Broker/Custodian updates records to indicate receipt of response from Client AA

213

Part III: POST-SETTLEMENT
Chapter 10
Corporate Actions

- Broker/Custodian, acting as a proxy, indicates Client AA approval of the acquisition

---

On August 15, 2002
the Broker/Custodian delivers the 10,000 shares
of Asian Gas Ltd. to Corporate Action Event Agent

Broker/Custodian Inventory account
Debited 10,000
shares of Asian Gas Ltd.
to be sent to HSBC

Corporate Action Pending Event account
Credited 10,000
shares of Asian Gas Ltd
sent to HSBC

On September 2, 2002
the Broker/Custodian update their records
to reflect that Asian Gas Ltd. has been ACQUIRED and
is no longer owned by Client AA

Corporate Action Pending account
Debited 10,000 shares of
Asian Gas Ltd

Client AA account
Credited 10,000 shares of
Asian Gas Ltd.

On September 2, 2002
the Broker/Custodian update their records
to reflect receipt of the H.K. & China Gas shares for Client AA

Client AA account
Debited 5,000 shares
H.K. & China Gas

Broker/Custodian Inventory account
Credited 5,000 shares
H.K. & China Gas

Part III

Post-Settlement

Chapter 11
Tax Withholding

Part III: POST-SETTLEMENT
Chapter 11
Tax Withholding

This chapter explores the basic concepts relating to the taxation on income derived from foreign investments. It is not intended to provide all tax regulations but a glimpse into the world of paying tax on dividend and interest income. Although tax regulations vary by country, taxes are typically deducted from income obtained from dividend payments, interest payments and in some cases, capital gains.

This chapter describes
- The Double Tax Agreement (DTA), also known as the Double Tax Treaty
- The Methods used to deduct the tax
- Requirements for obtaining tax relief
- The roles of the Investor, the Custodian Bank or Agent and the tax Authority
- Franking and other tax issues

Many of us are acquainted with the time honored tradition of paying taxes on our income. When we invest in the international markets, the tax Authority of the country where we are investing may require taxes be paid on dividend and interest income. The tax Authority of the country in which we are a resident also may require taxes be paid on the same income – as a result we are double taxed. (There are some exceptions, but more on that later.)
For example, the Investor who purchases Electrobras in Brazil will pay tax on a dividend received on the shares at a rate of 15% to the tax authority in Brazil. If the Investor is from a country other than Brazil they may also be required to pay tax on that dividend to their own tax Authority (e.g., a U. S. resident will declare the dividend income and pay taxes on that income to the Internal Revenue Service).

The Double Tax Agreement
To reduce the amount of tax paid on income derived from foreign investments, many countries have bilateral agreements that stipulate the maximum amount of tax that must be paid by the foreign Investor. The agreement between the country of investment and the shareholder's country of residence is called the Double Tax Agreement or Double Tax Treaty. The agreed amount of tax is called the Treaty rate or the preferred tax rate. The rates in these agreements range from no reduction in tax (i.e., the foreign Investor pays the full tax) to exemption of all tax (i.e., the foreign Investor pay no tax in the country of investment). But the Treaty rate in most countries is typically 15%. For example Switzerland has treaties with most countries that stipulates a treaty rate of 15%. The full rate on Swiss income is 35%. Under the treaty, a foreign Investor can reclaim 20% - leaving the Swiss government with 15%. The rates differ by instrument – the rate paid on a dividend from an equity investment may be different from the rate paid on interest from a debt investment. The rates differ by Investor. For example,

Part III: POST-SETTLEMENT
Chapter 11
Tax Withholding

some countries acknowledge the tax-exempt status of some institutional clients (e.g., Charitable Institutions) and reduce or eliminate the tax obligation and others do not recognize their home-based tax-exempt status.   See box for details on the exampled countries.

Tax Deduction Methods
There are two methods of obtaining tax relief. Either, the Investor claims a refund of excess taxes paid (called the Tax Reclaim Method) or the reduced tax (the amount stipulated in the treaty) is deducted from the income payment (called the At Source Method). Both methods have their own set of problems. In fact, because the methods are so cumbersome, for the last decade, Banks, Accountants and Brokers have been working diligently to try to simplify the process.

As far back as 1990, the ISSA (now called the International Securities Services Association – see Chapter 15 for more information on the ISSA) sponsored a workshop on tax relief practices. Here is what some participants had to say about the process. "Inefficient and bureaucratic methods of obtaining treaty relief at source," said one. "Complicated methods for processing the necessary documentation through different government departments" said another. A third one summed up the process with the following statement "different documentation requiring different information in different countries."

The recommendations that resulted from that symposium included the development of a model that would allow Investors to obtain treaty benefits in an efficient manner - - treaty relief at source, standardized documentation and processing through one central agency per country.
Source: Taxback, An International Survey of the Status of Tax Reclamation Procedures within the European Union by KPMG Peat Marwick

In 1994 the TAXBACK group was formed. Spearheaded by KPMG, the group included, among others, representatives from Barclays Bank, Chase Manhattan Bank (now J P Morgan Chase), Chemical Bank (also now J P Morgan Chase), Citibank, HSBC, Northern Trust and Royal Bank of Scotland. Their goal was to focus attention on the problem and establish ways in which the tax reclamation process could be made more efficient. The working group set a number of goals including an agreement to share market information, arrange meetings with various Revenue Authorities and prepare an international survey that would bring out the problems faced by the Revenue Authorities.

Chris Gilbert, of J.P. Morgan Chase, summed up the tax relief environment during this period. Broadly speaking, he said, the western European countries operated a tax reclaim system. Elsewhere, relief at source had been the norm, although there were a number of variations in terms of the mechanisms adopted

Part III: POST-SETTLEMENT
Chapter 11
Tax Withholding

to achieve that relief. An active member of the TAXBACK Group, Mr. Gilbert said the group's long-term objective was to move all countries to an operationally efficient relief at source system. Short term, the group worked to improve some procedural aspects of the tax reclaim systems operated by the tax reclaim countries.

Their efforts have resulted in the simplified (although still nightmarish) process of obtaining tax relief.

The Tax Reclaim Method
Using the Tax Reclaim method, the full amount of tax is deducted and the Investor must file for a reclaim of the excess tax paid. (Note: countries that deduct reduced rates of tax at source are listed in the next section. In all other countries, to receive tax relief, a reclaim must be filed.)
Procedures for reclaiming excess tax or receiving the preferred rate vary by country (and instrument). But in most countries, the process goes like this.
1) A reclaim form is obtained from the country of investment
2) The form is completed; listing the Investor's name and address with country of residence, the description of the securities held and the income.
3) For some countries, the form must be certified by the tax Authority of the Investor's country of domicile
4) The certified form is submitted to the tax Authority of the country of investment.

Tax Deducted on Dividend Interest:

- Brazil: The Standard rate of 15% is deducted at source; the rate may be reduced if a treaty exists between Brazil and the Investor's country
- Hong Kong: None
- United Kingdom: None; however, a tax credit of 10% is deducted at source from dividend income; this tax credit is available to U. K. investors

---

The At Source Method
Treaty relief at source means the amount of tax deducted from the dividend or interest payment is the treaty rate of tax and no reclaim is necessary.
The documents for claiming tax relief a source are broadly the same as for tax reclaims (see procedures above). The difference is that the documents must be

filed by the deadline that precedes the income payment; thereby allowing the reduced treaty rate to be deducted from the dividend or interest payment. Examples of countries that pay income less the treaty rate or `at source' are Australia, Brazil, Canada, Finland, France, Italy, Japan, Netherlands, New Zealand, Norway, Poland, So. Korea, Sweden, Taiwan, Thailand and the U. K.

How does a Shareholder obtain tax relief?

The Role of the Investor and Broker
To obtain tax relief on dividend or interest payment, the Investor and Broker starts the process when the decision was made to invest in the country. When deciding to invest in a country, the Investor / Broker researches the requirements for that country (see Chapter 1). Included in the requirements are the procedures to receive tax relief. The Investor and Broker determines:
1) If the country has a Double Tax Agreement and the terms of the Treaty
2) The required documents
3) The filing deadline
The Investor's Custodian Bank or Broker's Agent has this information and will provide it to the Investor and Broker.

The Double Tax Agreement (DTA)
If the country of investment does not have an agreement with the Investor / Broker's country of residency, the point is moot. - - The shareholder pays the full tax.
If an agreement is in place, the DTA stipulates the amount of the tax payable by a shareholder. The DTA is very specific. It includes the tax rate due on income from equity investments as well as debt investments; it also contains exceptions. These exceptions, usually found in the treaty's footnotes, detail the reasons why a rate would be different from the normal rate. The reasons include the length of time a shareholder has held the security or the percentage of shares held by the shareholder. It is one of the reasons why the amount expected is sometimes different from the amount actually deducted from the income payment (for more reasons see the next section, Franking and other issues).

The Documents required
A Tax Reclaim Form is required to be submitted to the tax / revenue Authority of the country of investment. The important issues here are who must complete the form, the language in which the form must be completed and if the form must be certified. Normally, the Investor's Custodian Bank or the Broker's Agent will complete the tax reclaim form if the Investor / Broker has signed a Power of Attorney authorizing the Bank to act on their behalf. However, in some countries, the Power of Attorney

only permits the Bank to collect the payment and the Investor / Broker must sign the tax reclaim form. In other countries, the Power of Attorney permits the Bank to sign and file the form and collect the payment. In most countries the form must be completed in the language of the country of investment. It must be translated if the form was completed in the Investor / Broker's language. Most countries require the tax reclaim form to be certified by the shareholder's tax / revenue Authority, verifying residency and the tax status of the shareholder.

The Deadline for filing
In countries that require a reclaim, the documents may be filed many years after the payment (requirements vary from 1 year to 7 or 10 years). However, as already mentioned, to obtain relief at source, the documents must be filed prior to the revenue agent processing the payment. If the form is not filed before the dividend or interest is paid, the full amount of tax is deducted. If that country has arranged an `at source' deduction, they may or may not permit a reclaim.

Posting the Income
When the income is received via the Custodian Bank or Agent, the Investor and Broker post the income to their account. The income should be the amount the Investor / Broker was expecting, but may not be (again, see the next section). If a reclaim has been filed, the Investor / Broker tracts the anticipated income. The time lapse between the filing of the reclaim and the time it is actually paid may be as short as 1 or 2 months or as long as 1 or 2 years, or - - as many Investors have realized - - they may never see it.

Part III: POST-SETTLEMENT
Chapter 11
Tax Withholding

The Role of the Custodian Bank or Agent
Who actually files for the reduced treaty rate? Investors and Brokers could file this documentation to the tax / revenue Authority – buy they typically avail themselves of the services of their Sub-Custodian Bank or Agent. There are also tax consultants who perform this service for clients. The Bank, Agent or consultant service researches the tax laws of the country and provides the information on requirements and documentation to their customers.
The functions performed by Custodian Bank, Agents and consultants are:
1) They research the market's requirements
2) They obtain the required tax reclaim form from the country of investment
3) They complete the forms and if necessary, obtain the shareholder's signature
4) Submit the forms to the tax / revenue Authority of the shareholder's country for certification and then forward the form to the tax / revenue Authority of the country of investment
5) They credit the income to the client when received or on the payable date (see Contractual Settlement in Chapter 13 – Custody).
6) They report tax reclamations. Typically these reports track the reclaims payable and when the reclaim has been filed. The report allows the shareholder to track future revenue.

The Role of the Tax Authority
The Tax or Revenue Authority of the country of investment is the entity that is responsible for collecting the tax. Each country's requirements are different but typically, the Authority:
1) Receives and reviews the tax reclaim form
2) Approves the preferred treaty rate if the tax is deducted at source
3) Processes the reclaim if that is the method used in the country
4) Pays the reclaimed amount

Franking and other issues
In many countries, especially those using the `at source` method, the process is quite straightforward and the correct amount of income is received by the expected date. However, in other countries, determining the amount of tax that should be paid on income is fraught with ambiguity and constant modifications. Although the process has improved, some of the issues that still remain are 1) what is the correct tax rate, 2) what are the factors that effect the tax rate and 3) why is some reclaimed income never received.

Determining the correct tax rate
You have received notification of the payment of a dividend with the amount and payable date. You know the tax rate for the country involved. So why, when the

dividend is paid, do you not receive the expected amount? There are many factors that affect the rate of tax on a particular item.

Factors affecting the tax rate

1) Tax rates change from year to year and internal records should be updated to reflect the country's *current* tax rate

2) The quantity of shares owned by the Investor will affect the amount of tax. Many regulations reduce the amount or exempt Investors who hold more than 10% or 25%.

3) Treaties are `reinterpreted' each year. One common revision is the removal or reinstatement of exempt status (just because the tax-exempt status was honored one year, don't count on that provision remaining constant)

4) Franked dividends. A Franked Dividend is a dividend paid from previously taxed earnings, i.e., the corporate tax. If it has been previously taxed, the tax rate on the dividend income is reduced. If not reduced, the result is the income would be taxed thrice – once before paying the dividend, once as dividend income and finally by the Investor in their own country. The problem arises from the regulations governing corporate tax. What corporate earnings are taxable? Is foreign income taxable? If not, only a portion of the dividend income is franked. But what portion? Is 50% of the dividend franked? Thereby reducing the tax on that dividend by 50%? Tax accountants should be consulted to determine the applicable rate of tax for an individual item.

Other Factors affecting the reclaim process

1) Who must sign the reclaim form? The beneficial owner of the shares (either directly or through their Power of Attorney) is required to sign the form. However, who is the beneficial owner? This is not always clear. On individual holdings it is easy to determine the owner of the shares. However, who are the owners of the shares held in trust or through Mutual Funds, Unit Trusts or Depositary Receipts? Many countries recognize the Mutual Fund or the Unit Trust as the beneficial owner. But occasionally countries have requested the names of the owners of the funds or trusts or depositary receipts – a truly nightmarish undertaking which so far has been averted.

2) Taxes due on stock dividends. In some countries, taxes must also be paid on stock dividends; in others they are exempt or payable only on optional stock dividends. The rate is typically the same as for cash dividends. The process for the payment of tax on stock dividends varies by country. The most common practice is to reduce the number of shares received (i.e., in effect, the value of the shares is used to pay the tax). In some countries, the tax is paid

in cash upon receipt of the shares. And, in a least one country (Taiwan), the tax must be pre-paid; the funds must be paid before the stock will be credited to the shareholder's account.

3) Combination of `at source' and `reclaim method.' One method may be used for dividend income but the other used for interest income. In France the dividend tax is deducted at source but the corporate tax credit must be reclaimed. For example, France deducts 15% of dividend income (the French DTA rate with most countries) at source. However, the tax credit (called the Avoir Fiscal) must be reclaimed.

Assuming a French company pays a dividend of   € 100.00
  - a) 15% (the treaty rate) is withheld at source   - 15.00
  - b) 25% (The Avoir Fiscal) is reclaimed*   + 25.00
  - c) less 15% of the Avoir Fiscal (15% of 25)   - 3.75
  - d) Dividend amount with reclaimed tax   € 106.25

* The criteria for eligibility is changing, reducing the amount of *Avoir Fiscal* that may be reclaimed each year.

Waiting for Income
Unfortunately, some reclaimed income may take years to be received or may never come. One reason is the sheer backlog of claims that have been filed. Another reason is the disagreements between countries over the tax relief they are expected to give. For example, if a country determines that the other country does not reciprocate the tax break, they may suspend payments pending the resolution of the disagreement.

In summary, because of the efforts of the TAXBACK Group, Brokers, Custodian Banks, Consultants and Tax Authorities - - shareholders receive a higher rate of return on their investment, i.e., they receive their entitled tax rate with a less costly and cumbersome process. In countries that have implemented `at source' tax treatment the process is relatively efficient. Many countries that still require a reclaim are prompt in refunding the tax amount; albeit some, because of operational procedures or budgetary constraints, are slower to process the reclaim.

Part III: POST-SETTLEMENT
Chapter 11
Tax Withholding

CHAPTER PROCESS FLOW

The following reflects the flow of internal and external activities required to process the tax paid on dividends. We refer to Investor and Custodian without specifying which custodian is responsible. This way we hope to reflect the process rather than confuse our readers with 'who' is doing 'what,' 'when.'

An Institutional Investor, domiciled in the U. K.
holds 10,000 of Electrobras.
Electrobras pays a gross dividend of Real 2.5
on the Payable Date, June 27, 2002.

As a result, the following activities occur:
- In Brazil, dividends remitted abroad on securities held by foreign Investors, are taxed at source at a rate of 15%.
- Electrobras pays the dividend to the holders of record
    - 15% (0.375) is deducted before distribution
    - The dividend net rate is 2.125
    - Investor's position of 10,000 is entitled to receive Real 21,250.00

The dividend, Real 21,250.00,
is received by the Investor's Custodian Bank and
credited to the Investor's cash account.

Investor's Cash account
Receives Real 21,250.00

Custodian Bank Dividend account
Pays Real 21,250.00

Part III

Post-Settlement

Chapter 12
Securities Lending

Part III: POST-SETTLEMENT
Chapter 12
Securities Lending

This dynamic business has become the focus of investors, direct market participants, custodians, utilities and application services providers (ASP). The driving motivations of this focus are ongoing client support, potential source of financing, source of new revenues, and business opportunities.

In this chapter we address these issues and present this complex business and how it is changing the landscape of global securities processing. Specific topics will include:

- Participants and their roles
- Drivers responsible for expansion of this activity
- Review of the lifecycle transaction process flow
- Perspective of how this business will impact future processing activities

This business activity has evolved from a simple operations focused function, for fail avoidance, to a vital investment alternative for investors. You can trace the roots of securities lending to short selling on European exchanges. Though believed to be less then prudent and ethical, short selling has existed in various forms and is a popular activity in many markets.

A securities lending transaction is one in which securities are borrowed and collateralized with cash or securities. During the life of the loan the Lender is able to use the cash to earn interest income. And the Borrower can use the securities to satisfy their obligations or re-lend, also known as on-lend, the securities to other counterparties.

HISTORICAL PERSPECTIVE

Through the 1960s this activity took place in the back office mainly supporting short sales and fails. Certificates were exchanged between the borrower and lender as the concept of a CSD had not been yet established. During the early 70s substantial changes were introduced including rebates and direct lending by institutional investors. But lending was still primarily a service provided by custodians and brokers limited to equities.

During the mid to late 70's there were many revolutionary changes in lending practices. First there was the introduction to the use of bonds. This was via reverse repurchase agreements (repos) and bonds borrowed transactions. This permitted dealers to use bonds as collateral for loan transactions instead of cash, which often resulted in capital charges.

Lending activity expanded to include matchbook lending. This permitted dealers and custodians to exploit their access to the demand side of the market and earn revenue on the difference between the cost of borrowing and lending income. Today this activity is sometimes referred to as Conduit business. This type of business is conducted using both equity and bond securities.

Part III: POST-SETTLEMENT
Chapter 12
Securities Lending

New intermediaries were introduced. 'Finders', came into existence during this time. These finders assisted borrowers to locate securities and lenders to identify borrowers. These 'Finders' offered an 'outsourcing' service to participants that did not have, or preferred not to have, sources of securities required by their clients. Or conversely located counterparties that needed securities available for loan from their clients.

Lenders also began to look beyond their borders for business opportunities. Brokers in London started to make markets in European securities. Since short selling was popular in the UK markets, this strategy was employed for non-UK securities. This investment alternative, often not available in local markets, and the liquidity that it provided, permitted investors to arbitrage between their local markets and London, This activity created the need for delivery in the local market and as a result lending activity expanded.

During the 1980'2 the expansion of lending continued throughout Europe and in Japan and Hong Kong as well. As lending activity increased, new risks associated with lending practices were identified. This was a result of existing settlement schedules and infrastructure support found across markets. Counter-measure practices to address these risks were introduced. Tri-Party transaction processing was a response to offset or minimize some of the risks associated with the exchange of securities and collateral. Tri-Party arrangements positioned a third party, often a bank, to serve as an intermediary in the transaction. The tri-party received the securities and, collateral and was responsible for oversight of the transaction. Initially this practice was followed for bond transactions but are soon was expanded to include equities as well. Today a CSD, transnational organization such as Euroclear or Clearstream or a major bank provides the role of the Tri-Party.

Beginning in the 90s through today has been a period of continued expansion of lending transaction volumes, type and number of participants, including institutional and high net investors. Lending and borrowing has expanded to Australia, Korea and Singapore. At the same time there has been a reduction in the fees, which is the cost of loan to the borrower. This is a result of advances in reducing the cost of processing these transactions in the global market as well as the competition for business. The continued focus of brokers and custodians continues to be on the type of business their clients transact and how they can offer securities lending and other collateral management services to support their activities.

A simple example of a securities lending transaction involves a borrower who has a need for a security, a lender who has the security the borrower is seeking. As in other execution environments, the borrower and lender may come together directly without a third party. Or they may enter the transaction through the assistance of a third party intermediary.

Part III: POST-SETTLEMENT
Chapter 12
Securities Lending

PARTICIPANTS

Let's identify the roles of the participants and related services as we proceed through this function,

> A **Borrower** can be a participant involved in investment activities, including an investor, broker, custodian, an industry utility or other participant that requiring a security.

> A **Lender** can be an investor, broker, custodian, an industry utility or any other participant that has the right to lend a security

> An **Intermediary** can facilitate a security lending transaction. A broker, custodian, an industry utility or other entity can act as an intermediary. In some markets 'Finders' act as the intermediary and their role is finding someone with a security to lend and/or someone that needs the security.

As you see the participants, except for the intermediaries, involved in securities lending activities are the same that have been involved in previous chapters. The crucial issue to understand about this activity is that the need and opportunity has to exist for the borrower and lender to enter into a transaction. In this chapter we will present these 'drivers' and frame the environment in which these transactions develop,

The basic need for a securities lending transaction is 'Motivation'. The borrower usually creates the demand for securities lending activity. Borrower's needs are based upon a situation that creates the need for a security. This can be from any number of business conditions. The most common reasons to borrow a security are:

> ➤ Arbitrage: trading scenario involving the simultaneous purchase and sale of a security, in or across markets, at different prices
> ➤ Fail Resolution: operational need resulting from the inability to make a delivery of a security sale
> ➤ Short Sale: trading strategy where an un-owned security is sold with the expectation that it can be bought, at a future date, at a lesser price
> ➤ Matchbook: simultaneous borrow and re-loan of a security
> ➤ Financing: loan of firm securities to raise cash

As you see from these motivations the need of the borrower usually creates the demand for securities lending. But it may be the lender, seeking to raise cash, that that drives the lending transaction. In general the need for securities lending is generated from a trading strategy such as an arbitrage or short sale or from operations for fail avoidance.

Part III: POST-SETTLEMENT
Chapter 12
Securities Lending

PROCESSING A TRANSACTION

The Need

Once the need has been identified the next step in the lifecycle is to locate a source. Once the investor has employed an investment strategy or made their security available for lending, their direct involvement ends. Most investors rely on their custodian or broker to represent their interests in the lending transaction. The custodian, broker or industry utility, most often the CSD, are the primary participants in the remaining processing security lending activities.

Sources of Security

Once the custodian or broker has identified the need, the next step in the transaction is to locate a source of the security. Internal resources are the first source reviewed. For brokers this may be their proprietary positions or securities purchased on margin. Custodians, which don't own securities, and brokers that don't currently own securities review the holdings of their investors to determine accounts with the desired securities. When the securities are located, the status of these accounts is reviewed to identify accounts that permit the loan of their securities.

Accounts that permit their securities to be loaned, share in revenue earned by the custodian or broker. The custodian or broker often acts as a principal in these transactions. This insulates and protects the investors from potential losses of the security or cash earned from the transaction.

If the securities are not available from an internal source, brokers or custodians will query other sources on the availability of the securities. This may be accomplished through prior knowledge of brokers or custodians holding these securities or may be through solicitations to other counterparties. This process is usually conducted via telephone but may be pursued via an automated facility commonly shared by market participants. The facility would reflect securities available for loan by participants. Once located the borrower would contact the potential lender directly or through the facility.

A CSD, and ICSD or a system provider may provide this service. This type of location service will expand in the future. Some firms, in Europe and Asia, have announced a cooperative effort to advertise securities available for loan. Membership and participation in these cooperatives are unclear but is expected to be open to lenders and borrowers in the expectation that more supply and demand will be needed to ensure success. Alternative methods will continue to be introduced as the participants, especially the Institutional Investors, to reduce the costs conducting this activity, utilize the power of the Internet.

Once a lender and the security are located, arrangements are negotiated regarding the collateral type and margin, delivery venue, rebate and sometimes other entitlements.

Part III: POST-SETTLEMENT
Chapter 12
Securities Lending

Exchange of Collateral for the Security

The next step in the transaction is the exchange of collateral. In a Tri-party environment, which often is the CSD, the securities are delivered to the tri-party agent by the lender. The borrower delivers the collateral to the tri-party agent as well. This collateral could be either cash or securities. Once the tri-party agent has received the securities and collateral they deliver the securities to the borrower. The cash collateral is passed along by the tri-party to the lender. If securities are used as collateral it may be held by the tri-party agent for the duration of the loan transaction or passed to the lender for reuse.

When the transaction occurs in a physical environment the borrower delivers the collateral to the lender. This is the procedure used for either cash or securities collateral. Once the lender, or their agent, has received the collateral the security is delivered to the borrower.

This procedure protects the lender from the loss of an asset since they don't release the security until they have received the collateral. But it exposes the borrower to the loss of their collateral. But since the borrower needs the security they usually accept the risk. And for this reason many markets are instituting tri-party processing via local CSD, an ICSD or via a local bank.

As with most loan transactions, the value of the collateral exceeds the value of the lent asset. The current prevailing rate is 105% of the value of the securities lent. For example for a loan of securities valued at HKD 1,000,000 the collateral would be HKD 1,050,000. When the collateral is cash, the currency exchanged would have been decided at the time of the transaction and the appropriate amount paid by the borrower. If securities are used as collateral, in addition to the over-collateralization amount, there may be a stipulation about the quality rating of the securities used as collateral. This is another level of protection the lender employs to secure their security during the lifecycle of the transaction.

LIFE OF THE LOAN – LENDER ISSUES

While the loan is open and the borrower has possession of the security; there are a number of activities that may have to be addressed. These may have been negotiated at the onset of the transaction but sometimes are deferred to a later date. Each has an impact the lender and borrower.

For instance Lenders, though they don't maintain physical possession of the securities, retain the rights of beneficial ownership. In essence they continue as owners of the securities though someone else has physical possession. The method of ensuring this right is via the collateral. In a 'worst case scenario' if a borrower defaults, for any reason, on their obligation to return the security, the lender is holding collateral of greater value that could be used to repurchase the lent security. The over-

Part III: POST-SETTLEMENT
Chapter 12
Securities Lending

collateralization should be sufficient to cover any commissions or costs related to reacquiring the securities lent.

The right of the lender to recover or replace an asset differ among markets. Some markets permit the lender to take this action upon proper notice to the borrower when the borrower fails to return the securities. Other markets require action within the legal system. The former is the desired course of action as it permits immediate relief to the lender. While the later often requires more time to enact and may result in additional losses due to time delays typical in many legal systems.

Mark to the Market

Marking to the Market means the participants track any appreciation or depreciation in the market price. As the price increases the lender has a proportionate increase in their portfolio reflected by the security loan. The method of ensuring this is to mark the security lent versus the collateral that the lender holds securing the loan transaction. In our example we lent 1,000,000 in HK $ denominated securities lversus collateral of HKD 1,050,000, suppose that the market value of the securities lent increases to HKD 1,500,000. The lender or the tri-party would advise the borrower that additional of HKD 25,000 is required to maintain sufficient excess of 105%. The borrower could also meet this increase by returning a portion of the security borrowed restoring 105% of the excess to the lender. In most circumstances the borrower increases the collateral so that the original loan stays in place.

Conversely if the market value of the security decreases in value, the lender or the tri-party would be obligated to return a proportionate amount of the collateral to the borrower upon request of the borrower or as agreed to by both parties. Mark to the markets are processed on an agreed upon schedule. In some markets and on some products it occurs daily, in other less frequently. Also often there is a minimum mark amount. For example on a security with a market value of HKD 75 mark to the market may only be permitted when the price moves HKD 2.5. Incremental prices movement less than this amount is noted but no change of collateral is required.

Both sides, the borrower and lender, must agree on the incremental market price changes. In markets where closing prices are not readily available the borrower and lender may have different prices resulting in different mark to the markets. This is usually avoided by agreeing on a common source for current market value at the onset of the loan transaction.

Income and Corporate Action Events

Dividends, interest payments and corporate action events that occur while the securities are lent also accrue to the original owner of the security. As such cash dividends become due to the lender on payable date. An increase in shares on loan due to a stock dividend or corporate action event will increase the number of shares on loan on the payment or effective date. Market prices will reflect the post event values as well.

Annual General Meeting

The one privilege of ownership often surrendered by the beneficial owner is the right to vote on matters presented by the board of directors. Unless the securities are recalled in sufficient time for the original lender to become the 'owner of record' the current 'owner' (or borrower) of the shares will vote the shares. This is usually not a major issue unless there's a concern over company management. Most lenders forego the voting privilege for the income earned.

LIFE OF THE LOAN – BORROWER ISSUES

The borrower's main objective is to acquire the use of the security without purchasing the shares. So beyond that, the mark to market and the return of collateral when the value of the borrowed security declines, primary issues are the need to substitute or replace lenders and the right to receive a rebate on the earnings of the lender from their use of the collateral.

The need to replace a lender occurs when the original lender requests that the security be returned before the borrower is ready. This occurs when a lender's client sells the lent security and needs to deliver it to the purchaser. The borrower often is not able to return the security. They may have sold the security short and are not ready to cover their short sale. They may seek to borrow the security from another source. Once a new lender is located and a transaction is negotiated, the borrower returns the securities received to the original lender. As a result their records are updated to reflect a new lender.

Rebates are a share in the revenue that a lender earns from the collateral that the borrower has extended in order to transact the loan. When cash is used the lender usually invests the proceeds and earns revenue during the life of the loan. This rebate is offered to borrowers as an incentive to reward future business to the lender. Rebates may be offered on a graduated scale offering larger rebates as the volume of borrows grow.

Rebates, a major consideration in securities lending, often determines which lender a borrower will use to meet their requirement for shares. Lenders will negotiate different rebate amounts with borrowers based upon their volumes and need for business. Therefore a borrower may have various rebate deals with different lenders. When a borrower is seeking a security, oftentimes the security will be readily available from a number of lenders. The size of the rebate often influences a borrower in the selection of a lender. Of course if the security is difficult to borrow, the rebate on a loan transaction may be reduced or eliminated reflecting that the borrower's sources are limited and that the lender is not inclined to share any revenues earned.

Part III: POST-SETTLEMENT
Chapter 12
Securities Lending

Return of Securities Borrowed and Collateral

The return of borrowed securities transaction process involves the delivery of the security back to the lender or tri-party. Once received the lender returns the collateral to the borrower. As in the start of the loan, the borrower is exposed to the risk of the loss of their asset in this transaction.

OTHER CONSIDERATIONS

Time Limits

In some markets there are limits to the term of a security lending transaction. This may be due to local custom or be tied to civil laws that automatically transfer beneficial ownership to the entity that holds a security. As illustrated in this chapter the lender may change during the life of a security loan. But the original reason for borrowing may also change. For example the original purpose might have been a short sale, but when the sale was covered, the firm that borrowed the security might have a fail to deliver and will use the securities received from the short sale cover to 'clean-up' the fail. So the original borrow transaction is still open, but the reason for the transaction has changed.

In markets that have term limits participants will coordinate the updating of the transactions before the term limit becomes effective. This may seem to 'go around' the law, but in many situations it in the only reasonable response as the physical securities may not be available to permit a return and re-borrow transaction.

This requirement does not exist in the three markets we have been following in this handbook. But this requirement does exist in Japan, Thailand and Malaysia.

Process to Restore Beneficial Ownership

In markets that permit the lender recourse when the securities are not returned a common method of accomplishing this is to reacquire the securities via a buy-in. This is the same practice discussed in Chapter 8 for Fail Control. The major difference is that a procedure is necessary to ensure that the borrower has been notified and has failed to return the securities. Once this notification process has been completed and the borrower has failed to return the security the lender begins the procedure. In most markets the procedure requires that the security loan transaction be converted to a fail to receive transaction. These two transactions are similar as they are both 'receivables'. After the loan transaction has been changed to a fail, the local market custom are followed to execute a buy-in of the securities.

Part III: POST-SETTLEMENT
Chapter 12
Securities Lending

Available Strategies Determine the Need for Loan Activity

Local market practices and procedures dictate the need for and volumes of securities lending. Just a few years ago, short selling was not permitted in many global markets. And in other markets there were no regulations dealing with securities lending practices. As a result, demand for securities lending in these markets were non-existent. The G30 addressed securities lending in their recommendations issued in 1989. They advised that securities lending, at a minimum, should be made legal and be encouraged as a means for reducing or eliminating fails.

Many markets responded to this recommendation and instituted the legal and regulatory changes to incorporate this vital business practice. Today, though many markets may not permit arbitrage or short sales, securities lending is permitted to avoid or clean-up a fail.

Impact of Central Securities Depositories via Intermediation

Many CSDs have responded to pleas by their local market participants to facilitate securities lending activities. The view of participant positions, pending and overdue obligations and general business activities provides CSDs with a unique perspective of many of the need for specific securities of their participants as well as potential sources of these securities. In many instances the CSD could make available many of the securities that would be needed for daily settlement and as a result avoid many of the fails resulting from current processing practices.

The CSD can serve as a 'central clearinghouse' for matching the demand and supply for securities required for fail avoidance or trading strategies. In some cases they would have access to this information without input from the participants from daily trade settlement. In other cases they would need 'wish lists' from participants for needed or available securities based upon their particular situation. And based upon this information the CSD could match the needs with the available resulting in loan transactions.

This is a very sensitive issue as many participants earn substantial revenue from lending activities and CSD are reluctant to disrupt or damage viable business practices. Also in markets with 'investor fully paid for securities' regulations, an interface between the broker and CSD advising which securities were available for loan and which where not would need to be in place.

There are markets where the CSD has addressed this need. For example, Monte Titilo provides list of available securities and affects the loan for the borrower. Although not wide spread CSD will continue to address this need along with their local participants. CSD will play an important role in the evolution of the securities lending business. As in many areas of CSD services, the more active a participant is in global trading and settlement, the more important the role and participation of the a CSD services will

BRAZIL STOCK LOAN PROCESS

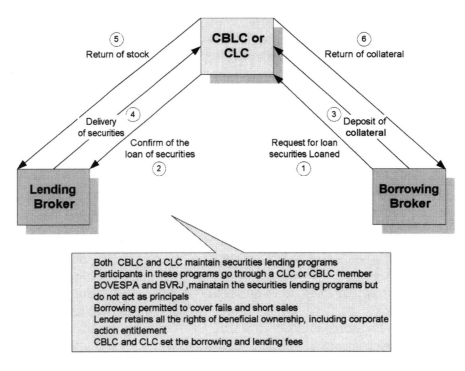

Both CBLC and CLC maintain securities lending programs
Participants in these programs go through a CLC or CBLC member
BOVESPA and BVRJ ,mainatain the securities lending programs but
do not act as principals
Borrowing permitted to cover fails and short sales
Lender retains all the rights of beneficial ownership, including corporate
action entitlement
CBLC and CLC set the borrowing and lending fees

Footnotes	
CBLC	Companhia Brasileira de Liquidacao e Custodia (Clearing House for BOVESPA)
CLC	Camara de Liquidacao e Custodia (Clearing House for BVRJ)
BOVESPA	Bolsa de Valores (Stock Exchange) de Sao Paulo
BVRJ	Bolsa de Valores (Stock Exchange) de RIo de Janeiro

HONG KONG STOCK LOAN PROCESS

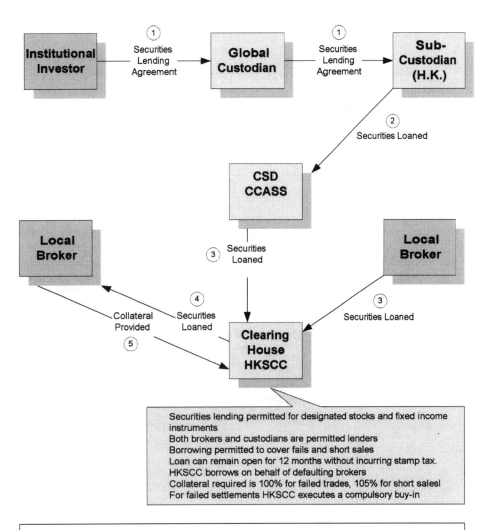

Securities lending permitted for designated stocks and fixed income
instruments
Both brokers and custodians are permitted lenders
Borrowing permitted to cover fails and short sales
Loan can remain open for 12 months without incurring stamp tax.
HKSCC borrows on behalf of defaulting brokers
Collateral required is 100% for failed trades, 105% for short sales!
For failed settlements HKSCC executes a compulsory buy-in

Footnotes
CCASS: Central Clearing and Settlement System
HKSCC: H. K. Securities Clearing Corp.

UNITED KINGDOM STOCK LOAN PROCESS

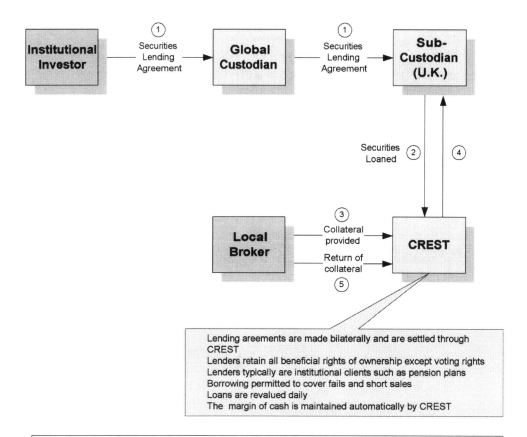

Lending areements are made bilaterally and are settled through CREST
Lenders retain all beneficial rights of ownership except voting rights
Lenders typically are institutional clients such as pension plans
Borrowing permitted to cover fails and short sales
Loans are revalued daily
The margin of cash is maintained automatically by CREST

Footnotes
LSE   London Stock Exchange
SETS   Stock Exchange Trading Service
SEAQ   Stock Exchange Automated Quotations
CREST   Depository for the LSE
LCH   London Clearing House

Part III: POST-SETTLEMENT
Chapter 12
Securities Lending

CHAPTER PROCESS FLOW

The following reflects the flow of internal and external activities required to process a securities lending transaction and maintain accurate records regarding the status of a client's security position. We refer to Investor, Broker and Custodian without specifying which broker or custodian is responsible. This way we hope to reflect the process rather than confuse our readers with 'who' is doing 'what', 'when'

On April 1, 2002
DB, a Broker, identifies the need to borrow
100,000 shares of British Pete for
Client AA that wants to sell the security short

DB Securities Lending area (DB S/L)
attempts to locate 100,000 British Pete

- Review internal inventory to determine if the security is available for loan
  - If available, security will be lent to Client AA
  - If not available internally, DB S/L tries to locate through external sources
- DB S/L contacts other Brokers and Custodians
  - Selection is based upon relationships, costs and projected revenues
- DB S/L determines HSBC has the security available and will lend @ 50BP
- DB S/L advises client that security is available to collateralize the short sale
- Client AA sells 100,000 British Pete short @ 50BP for a total of 5,000,500 which includes a 500BP commission

---

DB S/L pays HSBC
5,200,000 as collateral of 104% for the loan,
HSBC delivers 100,000 British Pete to DB on April 2, 2002

| **DB debits their inventory account, at the CSD or physical inventory, reflecting receipt of 100.000 British Pete** | **DB Credits the Stock Borrow account, reflecting the obligation to return 100,000 British Pete to HSBC** |

- During the life of the loan the following activities may occur
  - HSBC may need their security returned
    - DB would borrow the security from another source and use the security to return the borrowed security to HSBC
  - DB and HSBC will exchange collateral as the market value of British Pete increases or decreases
- Partial or full return of security by DB causing the loan transaction to be closed
  - HSBC would return the cash collateral

Part III

Post-Settlement

Chapter 13
Custody

Part III: POST-SETTLEMENT
Chapter 13
Custody

This chapter addresses the safekeeping, administration and reporting of securities activity for and on behalf of investors, in other words, Custody. The custodian is the investor's representative. As such custodians have a fiduciary responsibility, which means they hold their client's interests first and foremost and ahead of their own. These functions are grouped under the umbrella title of Custody. Investors, the primary beneficiary of custody services, are not the sole users. Investment banks, central securities depositories (CSD) and banks may utilize and or offer custody services.

In this chapter we will explore the following topics:
- Users of custody
- Basic and enhanced custody services
- Roles of Global and Sub-custodians
- Typical interfaces between custodians and their clients

Like so many of the functions addressed in this handbook, Custody is evolving into new forms and services. This ongoing process is driven by many of the same factors as other functions such as the need to speed up the process and the demand by clients for enhanced services and lower costs. In addition many custodians face major technology expenditures in order to update their systems to accommodate new investment instruments and valuation of new instruments. Competition from new sources including brokers and CSD is also placing additional demands on custodians.

Institutional Investors (the BuySide) are the primary clients of custodians. These clients consist of Investment Managers, Pension Funds, Trust Funds, Corporations and high net worth investors. Often the structure of the 'buyside' investor specifies that the entity must maintain the investment products at a separate and independent entity for the protection of the ultimate beneficiaries. The entity that has evolved to provide this service has been Custodians. Banks are the common providers, but custody can be provided by other entity types.

Scope of Services

The role of custodians has changed with the securities industry. In markets without a CSD, the custodian may maintain physical possession of the certificates representing ownership. This critical service is at the very foundation of protecting the investor. In these markets when physical certificates are exchanged the custodian ensures that the delivering party has the legal right to 'transfer' ownership. And at the same time the custodian has to determine that the certificates are valid without any encumbrances attached.

Part III: POST-SETTLEMENT
Chapter 13
Custody

As markets mature and CSD are introduced the maintenance of physical certificates becomes a less important services issue for custodians. But other functions such as pricing assets, collecting income and reporting remained. While other functions grew in importance for the custodians and their clients such as Corporate Action event reporting and collateral management.

Up to the 1980s custody services were usually offered in 'bundled form'. This permitted investor clients to purchase services on a 'whole' basis. The investor paid a per trade fee entitling them to a range of services. There were some enhanced services such as 'contractual settlement' but these were exceptions and usually directed at specific markets.

During the surge in offshore investing, investor clients sought to reduce the costs associated with custody. Bundled pricing was a popular place to start. Investors believed that they often were paying for services they didn't use. Custodians developed a 'cafeteria plan' pricing schedule that listed specific fees for each service. This permitted clients to select the service and understand the cost/benefits. This resulted in two levels of custody services offered: Core, and Custom. Core services were offered at one price per transaction while Custom services were assessed a fee based upon the service delivered. This revenue change impacted the financial viability of many custodians. As a result some custodians chose to discontinue this business. This resulted in some consolidation among service providers.

You will notice that many of the services offered by custodian are the same as or very similar to those offered by brokers. This is due to the custodian performing a similar role for their clients that brokers perform for theirs. For example a client may use a broker for part of their investment needs, order execution for example, and then use a custodian for custody of the asset once the broker is ready to settle the trade with the client. This mirror image of transaction processing also illustrates the blurring of the lines separating the brokerage and custodian businesses due to the need to support client demands and meet internal revenue projections. The custodian's objective is to meet their client's needs as an intermediary and fiduciary in securities transactions. In the future distinctions between brokers, custodians and other service providers will continue to become less distinct or less different, but the basic role of a fiduciary will remain a critical custodial service.

Custody has traditionally been a service provided by Banks. This is due to the geographic distribution of banks, their branch networks and their correspondent bank relationships throughout the world. This positioned banks to offer 'global' custody. In recent year some brokerage firms and CSD have entered this service arena. This trend will continue based upon the ability of these organizations to meet client's requirements.

Part III: POST-SETTLEMENT
Chapter 13
Custody

Core Services provided by custodians fall into four categories. Settlement, Processing Valuation and Reporting. Settlement activities are centered upon the receipt and or delivery of a security versus a corresponding cash transfer payment for securities received or a cash receipt for securities delivered. As outlined in Chapter 6 the custodian is advised of the trade shortly after execution. From that point the custodian prepares to settle the trade. For sales they will ensure that their position for that security at the CSD is sufficient to effect delivery. In markets without a CSD the custodian will locate the securities, ensure that they are in 'good delivery' form and prepare to make delivery to the counterparty on settlement date.

For security purchases the custodian will ensure that sufficient cash will be in the account on settlement date. This may require the custodian to retrieve the required funds from another bank the client may use for cash investments or await receipt of cash from the client directly.

Settlement, for client trades, occurs between the custodian and the broker counterparty. Securities will be delivered to the custodian via their CSD account identifying the underlying account information or through delivery of physical certificates. Identification of the underlying account information appears as' for the account of 'Worldwide Investment Client'. This information alerts the custodian to the name of the beneficial account and is quite helpful when there are multiple settlements of the same security and net settlement monies.

The custodian ensures that the security received is the expected security and that the monies due are correct. Once this is determined, the custodian will initiate the payment process. This process has been discussed in the Settlement, chapter 6.

Other Core services provided by the custodian include the following:

1. **Confirmation/Affirmation**
2. **Safekeeping**
3. **Income Processing & Collection**
4. **Corporate Actions**
5. **Cash Management**
6. **Multi-currency Processing & Reporting**
7. **Verification of Physical Certificates**
8. **Network Management**
9. **Voting Rights & Proxy**

Part III: POST-SETTLEMENT
Chapter 13
Custody

Many core services provided by custodians are addressed, in other chapters of this book. The processes performed by custodians do not differ in practice from those illustrated throughout the book. We address any differences in the appropriate section in this chapter. Activities that are basically identical are found in the following chapters:

> Confirmation/Affirmation in chapter 3
> Safekeeping as Inventory Control in chapter 7
> Income Processing and Collection in chapter 9
> Corporate actions in chapter 10
> Multi-currency Processing & Reporting throughout the book
> Verification of physical certificates in chapter 6
> Voting Rights & Proxy in chapter 10

Custodians, as the client safe guard, are on alert to ensure that clients' assets are validated and 'safekept ' during the investment period. As such core services are vital to their clients. For example in markets where physical certificates are part of the process, it is critical for custodians to verify that the correct certificate has been received and reregistered in their nominee name. Problems, if not identified immediately could arise from counterfeit certificates or the certificate could have been previously reported lost and replaced by another certificate. This protects the client's investment

Network Management, a unique custodial service, refers to the use of local custodians by global custodians. Though global custodians have branches throughout the global markets they may not have a physical presence in every market a client has an investment. To meet this requirement a global custodian will contract with a custodian in that particular market to provide custody services to the global custodian on a 'sub-contractor' basis. That is how these custody providers became known as 'sub-custodians. Another name for sub-custodians, which we use throughout this book, is 'local custodian'. Local custodian is more accurate as they provide expertise and services in local markets on behalf of the global custodian. And, as local custodians, their name is better aligned with global custodians.

A global custodian may employ the use of many local custodians based upon their business reach and their global presence as well as the client's needs. As such the global custodian will have a 'network' of local custodians in-place providing local services on their behalf. This network must be managed from various aspects. Correspondence between the global and local custodians is a critical aspect of the relationship. The normal interaction of instructions between the two custodians as well as well as reporting, problem identification and resolution are other examples of interplay.

Part III: POST-SETTLEMENT
Chapter 13
Custody

Some global custodians have their own proprietary network that facilitates communications between their offices and the local custodians. This is expensive solution and is usually offered by large custodians. The more common method of communication between global and local custodians is SWIFT. Since many already banks use SWIFT for movement of currency transactions it was a natural evolution for custodians. And with the addition of most of the global brokers and many of the global buyside it is a well-known common method of communication.

Network management is an important responsibility of global custodians and is a critical factor that the buyside considers when selecting global custodians. The global custodians client may or may not be aware of the existence of this network. In some cases a client may want to interact with the global custodian solely and have the global custodian interact with the local custodians. While other clients need to interact with the local custodians directly for problem resolution or general inquiries. Either alternative requires the global custodians to be proactive in their supervision of their network to ensure that clients are being properly supported.

Custom Services, those offered at an additional fee, may include the following:

1. **Order Execution**
2. **Tax Withholding Accounting and Reclamation**
3. **Derivatives Processing**
4. **Contractual Processing (Settlement, Income and Corporate Action Events)**
5. **Collateral Management (Securities Lending)**
6. **Risk Management**

Custom services, like the core services, are similar to processes and activities already addressed in this book. One service that is unique is Tax withholding and reclamation which is addressed fully in chapter 11. Activities and processed previously addressed include:

Order Execution in chapter 2
Tax Withholding Accounting and Reclamation in chapter 11
Collateral Management (Securities Lending) in chapter 12
Risk Management in chapter 14

Part III: POST-SETTLEMENT
Chapter 13
Custody

The two activities commonly found in Custom Services provided by custodians are:

> Derivatives Processing
> Contractual Processing (Settlement, Income and Corporate Action events)

The scope of this book and the examples used to track activities are equity focused and as such there are no examples of derivative investment products. Custodians stretch to offer support to clients that hedge or speculate using derivatives. Products defined as derivatives include Option, Futures, Forwards and Swaps.

These products present unique challenges to custodians, brokers and investors alike. Challenges include accurately defining the investment product description, specific characteristics of the investment and asset valuation. When these products are traded on an exchange this information is usually available and the support process, for the custodian, is similar to other investment products such as equities or bonds. And risk management is not a critical service for the custodian as it is addressed through the exchange via margin requirements.

When these products are not traded on an exchange, access to this information becomes more difficult and as a result presents the challenges. Many derivatives are created in the 'OTC' market and as such are transactions specific to trade counterparties. Often there are only two counterparts to the trade, the hedger and the speculator. These investments are custom developed based upon the counterparties requirements and may or may not resemble similar exchange traded products. Custodians assist their clients by tracking the lifecycle of these investments, assign values and attempt to identify and mitigate risks for the investor client.

The term Contractual, when placed before settlement, income and or corporate action events is a service that is quite unique to custody. Most of the services provided as part of custody reflect the investment business and are easy to understand and recognize the client's need. Contractual processing takes over when an event does not occur. In other words contractual processing is performed to maintain a client's books as if every settlement, income or corporate action event, had occurred. For example if the client has purchased 1000 shares of HK Gas on settlement date the client's account would reflect the receipt of the security and payment of cash regardless of whether a delivery had taken place.

Basically contractual processing is the posting of a transaction in the event that it does not occur. Clients prefer this type of processing in order to maintain their records as if the expected event has taken place. Motivations include more 'accurate' reflection of their account when trades fail to settle. Without contractual processing, in that situation, the funds would remain in the account and might, inadvertently, be invested again resulting in the cash balances being used twice. Income and corporate action event processing under the contractual process would reflect the receipt of funds and or new securities in the account on the scheduled payable date instead of days or weeks later.

Part III: POST-SETTLEMENT
Chapter 13
Custody

The business events that create the demand for contractual processing include fails to receive, late dividend, interest and or principal payments as well as the late receipt of a new security as a result of a corporate action. In some markets these issues are of little importance due to local market processing efficiencies, while in other markets there is a great need due to fail rates and or local processing difficulties.

Contractual processing is not available in every market. Each custodian makes a determination on a market-by-market analysis. In markets with high failure rates or delays in processing rates this service may not be available due to the risk to the custodian of this processing.

The transaction flow, of a pending buy trade, in a contractual processing environment would be as follows;

1. Custodian is awaiting delivery of the securities by the local broker and stands ready to pay the monies due

2. Broker fails to deliver the security

3. Custodian enacts contractual processing by reflecting the receipt of the security and charging the client's account the appropriate money

    These entries, are offset by an internal contractual processing account since there was no external activity

    The client will have the position in their account for accounting purposes

4. Broker delivers the security to the custodian, one or more days after settlement date, for the benefit of the client's account

    Custodian processes these external entries versus the internal contractual processing account

Anticipating the next question: What happens if the broker doesn't deliver the securities? Well if the securities or the custodian contractually processed is not received within a pre-determined period of time the transaction will be reversed. But most securities and or cash balances are received before the pre-determined date. But if the securities weren't received in time, the custodian would take away the security position and return the cash balance. The timetable for reversal will be different market to market and perhaps custodian to custodian.

Part III: POST-SETTLEMENT
Chapter 13
Custody

There maybe additional restrictions placed on the asset contractually processed until receipt actually occurs. For example, taking our above same transaction, the client would not be able to borrow the security or might even be unable to sell the asset. This check in the process permits the custodian to ensure that the client is protected.

Contractual processing is extended to include Income and Corporate Action events as well. The process is similar to the illustrated settlement process. The important issue to keep in mind in contractual processing is that it's primary intent is to maintain the 'accuracy' of the investor client's records. This service, as well as other custom services are provided at a per transaction fee.

Conclusion
Custom Services are expected to continue to evolve in the future. How and in which custodians and their client's will determine direction. The services needs, the clients will prompt changes in market practices and the development of new products. As a result some may disappear, while other services will be modified and new services introduced. Custodians will assess the value and internal requirements to offer these services and will price them accordingly.

Custodians are usually under the regulatory supervision of the banking agency in most markets. As such their services and activities are subject to review to ensure that the custodian is performing their function and that their client is not exposed to any undue risk from their custodians activities.

Questions

1) On the London Stock Exchange, ABC Securities sold 10,000 Glaxo Smithkline on behalf of their client. The broker was holding the shares for the client. However, these shares were not available to be delivered on the settlement date. All of the following accurately describes the effect of this fail to deliver, except:
   a) The Broker will credit the sale proceeds to the customer's account
   b) In order to make delivery, the Broker might borrow the shares.
   c) The Broker will incur finance charges
   d) The Broker will receive the sale proceeds from the counter-party on settlement date

2) Of the following, what type of Repo requires no transfer of securities?
   a) Physical
   b) Hold in Custody
   c) Tri-Party
   d) Closing

3) Of the following methods of financing, which one is typically used to finance overnight cash requirements?
   a) Bank Loan
   b) Letter of Credit
   c) An agreement to Pledge
   d) Repurchase agreement

4) In the Global Marketplace, all of the following are examples of the sequence of critical dates when processing dividend income, except:
   a) Trade date occurring before ex-date
   b) Trade date occurring after record date
   c) Ex-date occurring after record date
   d) Settlement date occurring before record date

5) Raffles Ltd announces a stock dividend that will rank pari passu with existing shares. The shareholder is entitled to which of the following?
   a) All entitlements except special dividends
   b) All the entitlements of the existing shares
   c) All future entitlements except the dividends paid within one year
   d) All entitlements except cash dividends

6) Sony, the Japanese company, announces the dividend of JPY10.00 to holders of record March 31. ABC Securities had purchased 10,000 shares for settlement March 28. However, the trade did not settle until April 1. Is ABC Securities entitled to the dividend?
   a) No, because Japan has no procedure for processing dividend claims
   b) Yes, because the shares were owned by the record date
   c) No, because the seller is not legally obligated to honor dividend claims
   d) Yes, if the 15% withholding tax was paid prior to the dividend payment date

7) A shareholder owns 5,000 shares of Raffles Ltd. The company announces a sub-division. Which of the following accurately describes the effect of this corporate event?
   a) The shareholder receives 500 shares of Raffles Hotel, H.K.
   b) Their holdings of 5,000 Raffles Ltd. is exchanged for 500 shares.
   c) The shareholder receives HKD 0.10 dividend per share
   d) Their holdings of 5,000 Raffles Ltd. Is exchanged for 1,000 shares of Straights Trading.

8) On which of the following types of corporate actions, does the ex-date occur on or after the payment date?
   a) All stock dividends
   b) All mergers
   c) A 4 for 1 stock split
   d) A 15% stock dividend

9) Of the following, what is considered an issuance sweetener?
   a) A stock dividend
   b) A subscription right
   c) A spin-off
   d) A warrant

10) A shareholder owns 5,000 H.K. & China Gas. The round lot for H. K. & China Gas is 1000 shares. The company announces a 10% stock dividend with an odd-lot buy-out plan. Which of the following accurately describes an odd-lot buy-out plan?
   a) The company may pay a premium for the 500 shares
   b) The company may offer 500 additional shares at a discount
   c) The shareholder may retain their odd lot of 500 shares
   d) All of the above

11) FEMSA, a Mexican security, has announced a subscription rights issue. All the following accurately describe this corporate action, except:
   a) They normally expire within approximately 15 days
   b) To subscribe, shareholders must produce proof of ownership
   c) Shareholders may either subscribe or sell the rights
   d) The shareholders retain ownership of their original shares

12) Which of the following corporate actions is a Voluntary event?
   a) The call of the following bond: FEMSA 6% of '04
   b) The change of name of British Petroleum to BP Ltd.
   c) The spin-off of Raffles Hotel from Raffles Ltd.
   d) The tender offer of H.K. & China Gas for Asia Gas

13) Siemens, a German company, pays a dividend of EUR 20.00 less 25% tax. The Treaty rate between Germany and the Investor's country is 15%; the Investor submits the documents to reclaim 10% of the tax. What is the deadline for filing this claim?
   a) Immediately after the announcement of the dividend

    b) Before the Dividend's record date
    c) Before the Dividend's payable date
    d) None of the above

14) What is a Franked Dividend?
    a) The dividend amount less corporate tax
    b) The dividend amount less the treaty rate
    c) The dividend amount that requires a reclaim
    d) None of the above

15) A Trader at ABC Securities has sold short 100,000 shares of BP. The Stock Lending area is asked to borrow the securities. The Stock Lending Area will perform all of the following activities, except:
    a) Review their internal inventory for available stock
    b) Contact other Brokers and Custodians to locate stock
    c) Enter a buy order to purchase the stock
    d) Borrow the stock from another Broker

16) The lender of securities tracks the price movement of the loaned securities to determine the stocks current market value vs. the collateral. What is this process called?
    a) Mark to market
    b) Tri-party collateral management
    c) Fail control
    d) Arbitrage

17) The fund manager at a Mutual Fund has sold their 100,000 BP that were loaned to ABC Securities. The Mutual Fund tells ABC Securities they need their stock returned. All of the following describes actions taken by ABC Securities, except:
    a) They return the collateral to the mutual fund
    b) They borrow the stock from another source
    c) They return the stock to the mutual fund
    d) They update their records to reflect the new lender

18) All of the following describe contractual processing, except:
    a) A cash dividend payment, not yet received by the custodian bank, is credited to the client's account on the payment date
    b) The proceeds from the sale of 10,000 Raffles Ltd. are posted on the date that the trade settles.
    c) A purchase of 10,000 BP, due to settle on March 21 but is not received, is posted as settled on March 21.
    d) A purchase of 10,000 BP, posted as settled on March 21 – but still open on March 26, is reversed on March 26

19) Which of the following custody services is considered a 'core' service?
    a) Contractual settlement
    b) Risk management

    c) Tax withholding
    d) Corporate Actions

20) All of the following activities accurately describe the Global Custodian Bank's management of their bank network, except:
    a) The GCB contracts with a local bank to provide custody services
    b) The GCB verifies contractual processing by the local bank
    c) The GCB receives reports on settlement, corporate actions and custody positions from the local bank
    d) The GCB assures that the local bank is supporting their client's requirements

Part IV

Beyond
Settlement

Chapter 14
Risk Management

Part IV: BEYOND SETTLEMENT
Chapter 14
Risk Measurement/Management

Risk is a fundamental aspect of financial services industry. Each facet of investment selection, trading, settlement and custody has its unique risk issues. Some are inherent such as an investment decision and risk of a loss as much as a gain in market value. Others such as settlement risk differ based upon a particular market, regulation and process infrastructure.

But risk in and throughout the global securities transaction lifecycle is ubiquitous. Risks exist in every market. And the risk points must be identified and reasonable indicators and controls to measure and mediate the risk that are appropriate to the exposure and downside must be in place.

In this chapter we will address the following topics:
- Types of Risks
- Importance of Risk Measurement
- Yellow and Red Flag Indicators
- Responses to Risks

Historical Perspective

As with many critical aspects it is helpful to review history and what experiences has taught us from various industry events. Throughout the global marketplace we have a number of events that demonstrate the need for risk management in the trading and settlement process. There's the Barings (United Kingdom) event that demonstrated that control must be dispersed over numerous individuals to provide balance. Barings suffered a devastating loss due to a trader with the authority to commit the firm's capital and the additional authority to deliver the capital to the clearinghouse.

Sumitomo's (Japan) failure to supervise a trader resulted in a loss of $2.6 billion over 10 years in unauthorized copper trading. Inherent in this situation was an absence in dual controls. Kidder Peabody (United States) suffered substantial losses when a trader was able to instruct the operations staff to correct trades. As a result settlement was delayed and therefore the invalidity of the trades was not discovered.

These examples, concentrated in trading, involved the complacency or lack of participation or response of operations. Basically Operations and all the activities described in this handbook are a checkpoint of trading. Many operations areas provide the checks and balances for other operations areas. This 'two-sided' approach permits firms in the securities business to integrate risk controls into the daily operations routine. Thereby the operations process often self-checks the validity of the process and can alert senior management to potential for risk.

Risk is a part of every business, but the securities industry lends itself to many unique risk situations. This is due to the value and volume of trades, many manual steps as well as the multiple internal and external hand-offs associated with the processing cycle.

Part IV: BEYOND SETTLEMENT
Chapter 14
Risk Measurement/Management

Another aspect that contributes to risk is that processing steps differ for bonds, equities, derivatives and other investment products. Each product has their own unique processing cycle that may be similar to or completely different among products in the same market as well as across markets.

This situation presents many challenges to firms involved in securities industry. With profit margins expected to narrow further due to globalization, many firms are focusing on maintaining client relationships and operating efficiently. Extensive risk measurement and management is an ideal first step in securities firms supporting their focus and retaining profits.

Regulators are also turning their attention to risk measurement and management (RM&M) practices. Proper and adequate RM&M is a basic requirement for providing stable financial services to domestic and global investors. The regulators are ensuring that broker and custodians have reasonable controls in-place to ensure timely identification and response to risk situations.

The Bank for International settlement (BIS) has established limits on concentration risks. The Group of Thirty (G30) published 20 best practice price risk management recommendations for dealers and investors. There were four additional recommendations directed to legislators, regulators and self regulatory organizations (SRO)

RM&M must be made consistent with an organization's tolerance for risk. Banks are often more adverse to risk than securities brokers. This relates back to their basic focus, banks were associated with conservative activities, brokers with proprietary trading with quick results. As such the RM&M policies and approach must reflect the organization's philosophy. But the focus must remain appropriate for the business activity. Risk limits should be set for the entire firm's business and further defined for each major business activity.

The foundation of a solid RM&M program is a policy statement outlining the firm's position and general response to risk. Risk should be expressed in terms of risk/reward by business and risk management. Statistically this should define the potential for the worst-case scenario. Senior management must establish a policy that states the type and extent of risk they will accept. Many firms throughout the global financial services community are adopting a value at risk (VAR) model, which calculates the probable risk.

Part IV: BEYOND SETTLEMENT
Chapter 14
Risk Measurement/Management

GENERAL SECURTIES TRADING RISKS

Our focus in this chapter, as it is throughout this book, is operational risk. In addition, there are many risks associated with various activities related to trading and dealing with clients. Some of the most common risks in this category are:

Currency or Foreign Exchange Risk

This is the risk of loss due to exchange rate fluctuations between the national (primary) currency of an organization and the underlying currencies each of its investment positions

➢ Countermeasures

- o Understanding the correlations between the underlying assets, the denominated currencies of the assets, and the treasury currency of the firm

- o Providing cross-currency risk analysis for multi-national instruments

- o Actively managing spot and forward currency contracts and currency futures contracts

Legal and Regulatory Risk

Legal and Regulatory risk is a loss due to a contract that cannot be enforced, including risks arising from insufficient documentation, insufficient capacity or authority of a counterparty, uncertain legality, and unenforceability in bankruptcy. And the risk that compliance and or regulatory requirements are not met.

➢ Countermeasures

- o Establishing clear compliance and regulatory structures

- o Administering a definitive methodology for contracting and conducting business with external parties and employees

Liquidity Risk

Liquidity risk is when an asset cannot be sold or otherwise exchanged for its full market value, causing a failure to meet short-term cash obligations, or to closeout or liquidate positions

➢ Countermeasures

- o Actively matching funding of debt to liquidity of positions, so that appropriate funds are available when required, develop liquidity guidelines to limit exposure in asset classes and instruments

GLOBAL SECURITIES OPERATIONS: The Handbook of

Part IV: BEYOND SETTLEMENT
Chapter 14
Risk Measurement/Management

Market Risk

Market risk causes losses due to changes in position value associated with equity and debt (interest rate) market price movements

➤ Countermeasures

  o Utilizing external transactional information

  o Enforcing trading risk limitations

  o Establishing appropriate policies and procedures and monitoring risk limits

  o Understanding where risk comes from across the firm

  o Providing consistent views of market risk at all decision points across the firm

  o Calculating consistent statistical measures (volatilities, VAR, etc.)

  o Marking to Market derivatives contracts

      ❑ As of December 1998, FASB 133 required companies to record the current market value of their derivatives

      ❑ and the matched underlying asset on their balance sheets

Sovereign Risk

Financial loss risk due to changes in the political climate of the countries in which the firm has an economic dependency and/or investment (direct or indirect)

➤ Countermeasures

  o Insure against risk via World Bank subsidiary or several other entities

  o Establishing prudent political relationships within each country

  o Understanding how to mitigate the risk through cross-national relationships

  o Developing alternative fail-safe communication systems

  o Distributing capital in a systemic manner across borders

Part IV: BEYOND SETTLEMENT
Chapter 14
Risk Measurement/Management

OPERATIONS SPECIFIC RISKS

Operations risk is a topic that processing professionals must focus on to ensure that risk is a consideration when procedures and policies are established, modified and reviewed. Risk indicators must be part of each operations managers view so that they can contribute their expertise to the good health of their firm and their investors.

Trade processing, settlement, custody and portfolio reporting are critical issues that have their own unique risks. And we will present a perspective that will assist you in addressing these risks in your department. They may require some adjustment to accommodate your particular market infrastructure and practices.

Practices are a good place to start because most polices dictate specific practices and procedures. Many innovations evolve from the sharing of procedures that reflect the 'best practices' approach. Simply, best practices are a result of coordinating business, cultural and personal behaviors to meet the desired objectives. In risk this is ensuring that everyone throughout the firm focus on the risk related to various actions. And when a situation arises that presents risks, that action employing a best practice approach is utilized to mitigate or offset the risk.

Credit Risk

Risk that a counterparty, or issuer, fails to meet their obligations. Or the risk that future market moves will create potential contra-party exposures

- ➢ Countermeasures
  - o Utilizing internal and external credit ratings for counterparties, used to limit the amount of exposure the firm has at any one time
  - o Establishing measurement standards that exceed regulatory minimums
  - o Monitoring credit/company exposures relative to limits which should be set by concentrations, and other exposures
  - o Monitoring and periodically resetting Contra-party characteristics and activity levels
  - o Simulating scenarios of market moves, re-pricing derivatives, and quantifying the potential impact on credit exposure

Part IV: BEYOND SETTLEMENT
Chapter 14
Risk Measurement/Management

Operational/Processing Risk

The risk that, due to insufficient internal controls, improper procedures, non-segregation of duties, and inadequate systems, errors (losses) may be introduced into processing business activity

➢ Countermeasures

- o Establish clear and quantifiable performance measurement benchmarks

- o Obtain extensive management information from independent internal audit

- o Establish proper supervision and segregation of duties

- o Minimize human errors with education and proper training

- o Test all systems in a robust and comprehensive manner

- o Establish complete, full loop, reconciliation's between systems (internal and external)

- o Set up redundant and independent environment and operating systems in a back-up facility

Personnel/Staff Risk

The risk that personnel will cause, intentionally or unintentionally, a situation whereby the firm is subjected to the loss of capital or an asset. Nick Leeson activities while employed as a trader at Barings is an example of Personnel/Staff Risk.

➢ Countermeasures
- o Implement Exception processing
- o Transaction processing reports
- o Collect and analyze Background and employment history

Part IV: BEYOND SETTLEMENT
Chapter 14
Risk Measurement/Management

Settlement Risk

The risk that a counterparty to whom the firm has made a delivery of assets or money defaults before the amounts due or assets have been received. A classic example of this is Herrstat case.

➢ Countermeasures

    o Implement netting agreements

    o Increased use of standard practices such as T+1 and Central Counterparty (CCP) and CSD

    o Careful monitoring of contra-party activity and settlement limits

    o Measuring and managing pre-settlement contra-party exposures

    o Developing system architecture plans that facilitate shorter settlement cycles

Technology Risk

The risk that hardware or software fails due to power failure, programming error, faulty information or communication error

➢ Countermeasures

    o Redundant operating sites

    o Duplicate or Uninterrupted power sources

    o Multiple sources of market data information

    o Rigorous testing and upgrade implementation procedures

    o Redundant communications links

Part IV: BEYOND SETTLEMENT
Chapter 14
Risk Measurement/Management

ALTERNATIVE VIEWS OF RISK

Another method of identifying, measuring and managing risk is from the perspective of internal versus external risks. Internal risks can be addressed during best practices, dual controls, and critical indicators and reporting. These risks are considered more addressable because they are internal and in theory can be mitigated directly. But the solution for internal risks is no easier to determine, nor implement than external risks.

Internal Risks

o Credit - client and counterparty exceeds the established business credit limits based upon their capital resources

o Client agreements & instructions – incomplete or inaccurate client profile data that may result in a legal loss to the client or missed and or late deliveries

o Investment Selection/Performance - security investment advice to a client that results in a market loss

o Processing – operations processing and technology disruptions causing a loss of information, transaction or data resulting in missed opportunities and financial losses

o Staffing – ability to staff operations processing activities ensuring adequate staffing, redundancy and capacity to support current and project volumes

External Risks

o Custody/Safekeeping – inaccurate processing and reporting provided by Custodian

o Inaccurate balances or positions – faulty processing and reporting by any external agent resulting in insufficient or late payments, late or inaccurate corporate action data or reporting of activity and financial losses

o Legal – effective and fair laws protecting domestic and global participants that do not permit pursuit of legal resolution through the legal system in a fair, just and timely manner

Part IV: BEYOND SETTLEMENT
Chapter 14
Risk Measurement/Management

- o Market & Operations Infrastructure – local market entities that can not support current and projected business volume, oversight of participants and enforced guidelines

- o Regulators – government representative inability to uphold the interests of domestic and global investors, enforcing market regulations fairly and consistently

- o Securities Lending – inadequate protection to the borrower and lender

- o Trading – trading environment unable to support current and projected volumes in an automated manner reducing disputed or questioned trades, settlement delays and potential market losses

- o Settlement – environment that us unable to protect both counterparties and encourage timely and accurate settlement

TYPICAL RISK COUNTER MEASURES

- o Contractual agreements – with clients and counterparties specifying the expected performance of each participant

- o Credit limits – business limits established and updated to reflect a client or counterparty's ability to perform based upon their capitalization

- o Exception reporting – reports identifying transaction or event failures requiring additional analysis or process activity in order to complete the transaction

- o Fail Analysis – rapid identification of failed settlements and their causes so that resolution can be completed in a timely and efficient manner

- o Internal controls – split responsibilities that results in multiple staff/areas participating or over-sighting processing and reconciliation function insuring accurate records, reports that separate data presentation highlighting critical issues requiring management response or involvement

- o Multiple sources of market data information – to ensure adequate and accurate information for pricing, processing and reporting to client and firm positions

- o Periodic stress tests – to validate the integrity and capacity of market systems, operations staff and industry infrastructure to ensure ability to process during peak times o   Prompt claims on third parties – for dividends and corporate actions to ensure receipt of entitlement of cash and securities

o   Redundant communications – between and among brokers, industry utilities and other participants to ensure the processing capabilities in the event of a local power or building outage

o   Risk indicators – critical indicators reflecting the state of the market and processing activities status

o   Secure and redundant data processing facilities – ensuring the ability to continue normal business activities during local power or building outages and disruptions

o   Standardized electronic exchange of data – encouraging automated interfaces among and between industry participants for information such as indications of interest, orders, notice of execution and settlement instructions

o   Systems designed for peak volumes – scalable information technology to support continued growth in trade, settlement, reporting and other related volumes

o   Testing and back up procedures – operations and technology involvement to ensure that systems and procedural changes are tested and confirmed before implementation, should include redundant sites for operations and technology staff in the event that the main facility is unavailable

o   Timely reconciliation – between internal records and external sources such as custodians or agents for security positions and cash balances, ideal environment would be electronically, should be completed as close to daily as possible

Part IV

Beyond
Settlement

Chapter 15
Industry
Organizations

Part IV: BEYOND SETTLEMENT
Chapter 15
Industry Organizations

There are many organizations that have been formed to study and improve the trading and settlement of global securities. They range from organizations formed by Investment Managers, Brokers and Custodian Banks to organizations formed by Stock Exchanges and Depositories.

In this chapter, we will examine the history and focus of a few of the (too numerous to cover here) industry organizations that are instrumental in improving global operations.

Central Depository Associations
Many of the world's local depositories have formed organizations to examine settlement and risk within their region. When securities began to trade in more than their home market, the depositories began to explore how best to settle these trades. Historically, a security only settled in the depository of the issuer's country. Now, as depositories establish links between one another, the security can settle in through the depository of the investor's country (i.e., the security is still held in the country of issuance, but held for the account of another depository). As the number of links increase and as the quantity of cross-border trade increase, depositories are examining how best to accept collateral in and for a security or currency held in another depository.

The Central Depository Associations are

- Americas' Central Securities Depositories Association (ACSDA)
    o Web address www.acsda.org
    o The members of the ACSDA are depositories and clearinghouses from Argentina, Brazil, Canada, Colombia, Costa Rica, Chile, El Salvador, Nicaragua, Panama, Peru, United States and Uruguay.
    o Their mission is to share information, collaborate on regional issues and facilitate cooperation and integration of members Three working committees have been set up to examine trends and challenges facing the ASCDA, current risk assessment methodology and ways to integrate all CSDs of the Americas into the association
    o Recent workshops and Seminars have focused on Cross Border Linkages and achievements made by the ACSDA member countries and Best Achievements of ACSDA members. The processes the members discuss are Entitlement Processing and Corporate Actions, processes and models for Dematerialization, Beneficial Owner Account Structure, Securities Lending practices, Participant Standards for Collective Risk

Management, Approaches to true DVP, Cross Border Linkages and Market Integration and the T+1 settlement cycle.
Source: Americas' Central Securities Depositories Association and Mr. Javier Jara Traub of Chile's Depósito Central de Valores S. A.

- Asia Pacific Central Depositories Group (ACG)
  - Web address: n/a
  - The members of the ACG are Australia, China, Indonesia, India, Japan, Korea, Malaysia, New Zealand, Pakistan, Philippines, Singapore, Taiwan and Thailand

- Central and Eastern European Securities Depositories and Clearing Houses Association (CEECSDA)
  - Web address: n/a
  - The members of the CEECSDA are Bulgaria, Croatia, Czech Republic, Estonia, Hungary, Latvia, Lithuania, Poland, Romania, Slovak Republic and Slovenia

- European Central Securities Depositories Association (ECSDA)
  - Web address www.escda.com
  - The members of the ECSDA are Austria, Belgium, Denmark, Finland, France, Germany, Greece, Italy, Ireland, Netherlands, Norway, Portugal, Spain, Sweden, Switzerland and the United Kingdom
  - Founded in 1996, their work has focused on the delivery of secure and efficient DVP cross border settlement. Amongst other accomplishments, they have developed standards for cross-border settlement against payment of securities transactions and for the automated support of corporate actions. They have developed standards that are used when building the links between the depositories. These standards have resulted in substantial implementation savings (e.g., the cost of development has been reduced form EUR 2 million to EUR 130,000).
  - Working Groups include the Technical Group (working on a common CSD Interface), the Legal Group (analyzing the legal aspects of the DVP model and common agreement framework), the Clearing and Settlement Group (developing a model for DVP, relayed links and modeling the influence of CCP to settlement) and the Corporate Actions Group (working on Tax Reclaim and Relief At Source processes and Electronic Voting). The recent report from the Corporate Actions Working Group, entitled Cross Border Corporate Actions and Event Processing,

shows the flow of messages to and from the CSD of the Investor's settlement system to the CSD of the issuing country. As depositories develop links to settle multi-listed securities (i.e., the trade can settle in the investor's CSD if they have a link with the issuing CSD), it is crucial to develop an automated function to process the ensuing corporate actions. Details on the various working groups and documentation on the reports issued can be found on their web site.
Source: European Central Securities Depositories Association.

Stock Exchange Associations

- CCP12
  - Web address: n/a
  - Created by major Securities Clearing Houses, the association is made up of representatives from Australia, Brazil, Canada, France, Germany, Hong Kong, Japan, Mexico, Singapore, U.K. and the U.S.
  - Their purpose is to improve global clearing, netting and central counterparty (CCP) services. The group is working on a broad range of issues including improved information sharing, enhanced collateral usage, development of collaborative opportunities and identifying minimum standards for risk management practices

- Federation Internationale des Bourses de Valeurs (International Federation of Stock Exchanges) (FIBV)
  - Web address: www.fibv.com
  - The FIBV's membership is comprised of 55 regulated exchanges representing all regions of the world.
  - Their purpose is to provide guidance as to the minimum level of organization, regulation and supervision a securities market needs to have in order to qualify as an organized market. Their recommendations include requirements for market participants; Regulatory infrastructure should include rules on trading, listing, market participation, discipline and sanctions, clearing and settlement and recourse procedures; sufficient capacity in exchange systems to ensure the operation of an orderly market.
Source: Fédération Internationale des Bourses de Valeurs
Note: For those interested, their web site contains a tremendous amount of statistics – e.g., new listings, market capitalization, trading volume, etc.

Part IV: BEYOND SETTLEMENT
Chapter 15
Industry Organizations

Market Associations and Agencies
- Association of National Numbering Agencies
  - Web address: www.anna-web.com
  - Their objective is to make available an international securities identification number (ISIN) in a uniform structure for use in any securities trading and administration application.
  One of the nine recommendations of the Group of 30 (see below) was for each market to adopt the ISIN numbering system for securities. To implement the recommendation, ANNA was formed. In 1995, ANNA was approved as maintenance agency and registration authority by the International Standards Organization (ISO). ANNA sponsored GIAM (the Global ISIN Access Mechanism). GIAM primary objective is to support the National numbering agencies in carrying out their role of allocating and maintaining ISIN numbers in their country. As of this writing, 50 countries have established a national numbering agency
  Note: The ISIN code is a 12 digit number beginning with two alfa characters of the country of issuance. The next nine characters are the local security number. Where national numbers consist of fewer than nine characters, zeros are inserted in front of the local number. The last character is a check digit. For example, the ISIN code for Hong Kong & China Gas is HK0003000038.
  In 2000, ANNA formed the ANNA Service Bureau with Standard & Poors and Telekurs. The Service Bureau offers access to a database of ISIN numbers from more than 70 countries. The new annaservice@standardandpoors.com has replaced GIAM.
  Source: Association of National Numbering Agencies

- EMTA (formerly known as Emerging Markets Traders Association)
  - Web address: www.emta.org
  - Formed in 1990, EMTA's membership are financial institutions actively engaged in the trading of Emerging Market Instruments – Broker Dealers, Banks and other financial institutions.
  - In collaboration with other industry trade groups, including The Bond Market Association (TBMA), the International Swaps and Derivatives Association (ISDA) and the International Securities Market Association (ISMA), EMTA works to develop an orderly marketplace and to facilitate Emerging Market trading activity.
  - From September 1994 to September 2000, EMTA regularly operated the Multilateral Netting facility to net and settle outstanding trades of Russian loans. In 1996 and 1997, EMTA operated a Multilateral Netting Facility for the netting and cash

settlement of matched transactions relating to past due interest claims in Argentina.

- o In 1995, EMTA, prompted by a risk management report to its board, created a study group composed of global dealers, brokers and clearing agents to evaluate the existing clearing process for emerging market debt. The result was Em-clear, or as it now know, EMCC. EMCC was developed by EMTA and a unit of the U.S.'s National Securities Clearing Corp. EMCC receives trade data from its members, forwards matched transactions to Risk Management and is interposed as the counterparty. EMCC creates settlement instructions for eligible trades and transmits them to Euroclear or Clearstream (per client settlement agent). Finally, EMCC receives and processes settlement reports (pending, fail, settlement) from Euroclear or Clearstream.

Source: EMTA and Emerging Markets Clearing Corporation

- Financial Information Exchange (FIX) Protocol Committee
  - o Web address: www.fixprotocol.org
  - o The Fix protocol was initiated in 1992 by a group of institutions and brokers interested in streamlining their trading processes. FIX is an open message standard controlled by no single entity, that can be structured to match the business requirements of each firm. The FIX website serves as the central repository and authority for all specification documents, committee calendars and training presentations. The FIX protocol specification is maintained by the FIX Technical Committee. They have Steering Committees in Europe, Hong Kong, Japan and the U.S.
  - o The types of messages have increased from the initial quote request, order entry and allocation and settlement instructions to the current types of instructions which number more than 40 messages. The messages have replaced the old practice of an Institutional Client (the Buy-Side) receiving calls from their Brokers (the Sell-Side) informing them of news updates, soliciting orders to buy or sell a security or notifying them of an executed order. Now, with an electronic message, an Indication of Interest message can be sent, the Buy-Side can send orders to the Sell-Side (eliminating many errors) and instantaneously. Brokers can up-date their clients with progress reports on the status of an order. Orders can be entered to Stock Exchanges (e.g., London's Sets system), ECNs and matching systems. Many other steps are automated using the dozens of

standardized messages. Check the web site for the many messages that have been developed to automate the process from alerting the customer to news on a potential order to settlement instructions on the executed order.
Source: The Financial Information eXchange (FIX) Protocol. The FIX specification is provided free of charge and copyrighted by FIX Protocol Limited.

- Global Straight Through Processing Association (GSTPA)
  - Web address: www.gstpa.org
                   www.axion4.com
  - The GSTPA is an industry association open to all Investment Managers, Broker/Dealers and Global Custodians involved in the processing of cross-border and domestic institutional trades. Their goal was to find a solution to the problems encountered in institutional trade processing (including manual procedures, multiple service providers, incompatible databases, lack of standardization and relatively high error rates). The GSTPA wants to enable cross-border trade activity to interface with domestic market settlement processes as efficiently as possible. To make this happen, they evaluated several firms and selected a consortium composed of SIS SegaInteresttle AG, TKS-Teknosoft SA, and SWIFT. The three companies founded a new company named axion4gstpa Ltd. They have developed, and will operate, a central matching facility called the Transaction Flow Monitor as well as a set of complementary utility services (e.g., customer support and implementation, training and finance).

Source: The Global Straight Though Processing Association and Axion4gstpa Ltd.
Note: For further information on the Transaction Flow Monitor and Omgeo's Central Trade Manager see Chapter 3.

- Group of 30 (G30)
  - Web address: www.group30.org
  - Established in 1978, G30 is a private, non-profit, international organization. It's membership of 30 representatives currently include representatives from the International Monetary Fund, Argentina, Brazil, Canada, France, Germany, Japan, Mexico, Poland the U.K. and the U.S.
  - Among its many accomplishments, in 1989 the Group of 30 published the now famous nine (9) Recommendations (see Exhibit 17-1) to address settlement risk in the securities

markets. Originally designed as recommendations for developed markets to improve their settlement systems, many of the new and emerging markets have also adopted the recommendations.

Part IV: BEYOND SETTLEMENT
Chapter 15
Industry Organizations

Exhibit 15 – 1

GROUP OF 30 RECOMMENDATIONS   *(1995 Revisions in italics)*

1) By 1990, all comparisons of trades between direct market participants (i.e., brokers, broker/dealers, and other exchange members) should be accomplished by T+1. *(by T+0 and matched trades linked to the settlement system)*

2) Indirect market participants (institutional investors, or trading counter-parties which are not broker/dealers) should, by 1992, be members of a trade comparison system which achieves positive affirmation of trade details. *(by T+1)*

3) Each country should have an effective and fully developed central securities depository, organized and managed to encourage the broadest possible industry participation (directly or indirectly) in place by 1992. *(The range of depository eligible instruments should be as wide as possible. Immobilization or dematerialization of financial instruments should be achieved to the utmost extent possible. If several CSDs exist in the same market, they should operate under compatible rules and practices, with the aim of reducing settlement risk and enabling efficient use of funds and available cross-collateral.)*

4) Each country should study its market volumes and participation to determine whether a trade netting system would be beneficial in terms of reducing risk and promoting efficiency. If a netting system would be appropriate, it should be implemented by 1992. *(a trade netting system that fully meets the Lamfalussy-recommendations or Real Time Gross Settlement)*

5) Delivery versus payment (DVP) should be employed as the method for settling all securities transactions. A DVP system should be in place by 1992. *(DVP is defined as the Simultaneous, final, irrevocable and immediately available exchange of securities and cash on a continuous basis throughout the day.)*

6) Payments associated with the settlement of securities transactions and the servicing of securities portfolios should be made consistent across all instruments and markets by adopting the same day funds convention.

7) A rolling settlement system should be adopted by all markets. Final settlement should occur on T+3 by 1992. As an interim target, final settlement should occur on T+5 by 1990 at the latest, save only where it hinders the achievement of T+3 by 1992. *(Final settlement should occur no later than T+3)*

8) Securities lending and borrowing should be encouraged as a method of expediting the settlement of securities transactions. Existing regulatory and taxation barriers that inhibit the practice of lending securities should be removed by 1990.

9) Each country should adopt the standard for securities messages developed by the International Organization for Standardization (ISO Standard 7775). In particular, countries should adopt the **ISIN** numbering system for securities issues as defined in the ISO Standard 6166, at least for cross border transactions. These standards should be universally applied by 1992.

Source: International Securities Services Association and the Group of 30

Part IV: BEYOND SETTLEMENT
Chapter 15
Industry Organizations

- International Organization of Securities Commissions (IOSCO)
  - Web address: www.iosco.org
  - Want to know what the regulators are planning? IOSCO is the primary international cooperative forum for securities regulators in the World. It's membership consists of government securities regulators from more than 100 jurisdictions.
  - IOSCO's mission is to promote, through cooperation, high standards of regulation, to exchange information on the respective experiences of its members in order to promote the development of markets, to establish an effective surveillance of international securities transactions and to provide mutual assistance to promote integrity in the marketplace.
  - To address the important changes taking place in today's global marketplace, IOSCO is tackling key regulatory issues. The list of IOSCO's public reports can be found on its web page. Most reports can be readily downloaded.
  - ISOCO offers its members that are regulating emerging securities markets an On-the-Job Training Program and a Seminar Training Program to address key regulatory issues.
  - IOSCO maintains important consultative and cooperative links with the industry and with other international organizations. All the major stock exchanges of the world are affiliate members of IOSCO. The IMF (the International Monetary Fund), the World Bank, the OECD (Organization for Economic Cooperation and Development) and most regional development banks are also affiliate members of IOSCO.
  - IOSCO has created, with the banking and insurance supervisors (the Basle Committee and the International Association of Insurance Supervisors - the IAIS), the Joint Forum to look into the technical aspects of common regulatory issues.
  - IOSCO is a member of the Financial Stability Forum.
  - Source: International Organization of Securities Commissions

- International Securities Market Association (ISMA)
  - Web address: www.isma.org
  - ISMA is the self-regulatory organization and trade association for the internal securities market. Established in 1969, and formerly known as the Association of International Bond Dealers (AIBD), the Association's membership currently numbers some 570 organizations, based in almost 50 countries.
  - ISMA works closely with governments and domestic authorities to ensure that regulation does not undermine or adversely affects its independent, self-regulatory status or have a

damaging effect on market participants and their trading activities. ISMA's board and committees are comprised of elected professionals who work in the market. Their involvement enables ISMA's rules and recommendations to correspond closely to the market's changing needs.

o Since 1989, ISMA has owned and operated TRAX, its post-trade matching and regulatory reporting system. ISMA sponsored COREDEAL, an electronic exchange for debt instruments.

o ISMA distributes market data via isma.info. This on-line service provides the latest prices for more than 8,000 straights, convertibles, FRNs and MTNs. Since thee 1970s, ISMA has offered a series of courses and seminars for market practitioners.

- International Securities Services Association (ISSA)
  o Web address: www.issanet.org
  o Founded in 1979, the ISSA is represented by 92 members in 43 countries.
  o The focus of the ISSA is to collect and disseminate information on developments in the international securities markets and to provide open discussion platforms for securities market practitioners, to tackle industry-overarching problems in a collegiate manner. The ISSA sponsors a bi-annual Symposium and Regional Meetings. They also publish the ISSA Handbook, a collection of trading and settlement rules and regulations covering around 60 markets. The ISSA has published numerous series of recommendations. The most widely known ones included, in 1995, an update of the recommendations of the Group of 30 (See Exhibit 15-1). In 2000, they published recommendations to address securities systems' governance, technology, technical standards, market practice, settlement risk, market linkages, investor protection and legal infrastructure. (see Exhibit 15-2)

Source: International Securities Services Association

Exhibit 15-2

ISSA 2000 Recommendations
Note: The term `Securities Systems' includes depositories, settlement and clearing systems

1)   Securities Systems have a primary responsibility to their users and other stakeholders. They must provide effective low cost processing. Services should be priced equitably.

2) Securities Systems must allow the option of network access on an interactive basis. They should cope with peak capacity without any service degradation, and have sufficient standby capability to recover operations in a reasonably short period within each processing day.

3) The industry world-wide must satisfy the need for efficient, fast settlement by full adherence to the International Securities Numbering process (ISO 6166) and uniform usage of ISO 15022 standards for all securities messages. The industry should seek to introduce a global client and counterparty identification methodology (BIC – ISO 9362) to further facilitate straight through processing. Applications and programs should be structured in such a way as to facilitate open inter-action between all parties.

4) Each market much have clear rules assuring investors protection by safe-guarding participants from the financial risks of failed settlement and ensuring that listed companies are required to follow sound policies on corporate governance, transfer of economic benefits and shareholder rights.

5) The major risks in Securities Systems should be mitigated by five key measures, namely:
♦ The implementation of real delivery versus payment
♦ The adoption of a trade date plus one settlement cycle in a form that does not increase operational risk
♦ The minimization of funding and liquidity constraints by enabling stock lending and borrowing, broad based cross collateralization, the use of repos and netting as appropriate
♦ The enforcement of scrip-less settlement
♦ The establishment of mandatory trade matching and settlement performance measures

6) Convergence of Securities Systems, both within countries and across borders, should be encouraged where this eliminates operational risk, reduces cost and enhances market efficiency.

7) Investor compliance with the laws and regulations in the home countries of their investments should be part of their regulators' due diligence process. Investors, in turn, should be treated equitably in the home country of their investments especially in respect to their rights to shareholder benefits and concessionary arrangements under double tax agreements.

8) Local laws and regulations should ensure that there is segregation of client assets from the principal assets of their custodian. And no possible claim on client assets in the event of custodian bankruptcy or a similar event. Regulators and markets, to further improve investor protection, should work:
♦ To ensure clarity on the applicable law on cross border transactions
♦ To seek international agreement on a legally enforceable definition of finality in a securities transaction
♦ To ensure that local law fully protects the rights of beneficial owners
♦ To strengthen securities laws both to secure the rights of the pledge and the protection accorded to client assets held in Securities systems.

- International Swaps and Derivatives Association (ISDA)
  - Web address: www. isda.org
  - ISDA was chartered in 1985 and has over 500 members from 41 countries.

o ISDA's focus is to identify and reduce the sources of risk in the derivatives and risk management business. They have developed the ISDA Master Agreement, produced legal opinions on the enforceability of netting and promoted sound risk management practices. To support its members, ISDA has offices in Hong Kong, London, New York, Singapore and Tokyo.

Industry Utilities

Perhaps the most universally known organizations in the global securities industry are Clearstream, DTCC, Euroclear and SWIFT. SWIFT is best known for their development of standardized messages that are used, not only by SWIFT users but also vendors, to enable interoperability between their systems and SWIFT.

Clearstream International and Euroclear are the two International Central Securities Depositories. They have often discussed a merger, though strong individual identities, fierce competition and the timing never being quite right have kept them apart. Clearstream was formed by the merger of Cedel Bank and the Deutsche Bourse Clearing (formerly the Kassenverein) in 1999. On December 7, 2001, Clearstream's Board of Directors recommended discussions with Deutsche Borse AG to reach an agreement for the total acquisition of Clearstream International - by the time you read this, it may have happened. To develop market share, each has designed a strategic program to merge with other major CSDs with the hopes of becoming the single pan-European settlement provider for bonds, equities and funds. Euroclear has become the settlement facility for the Euronext markets. (Euronext was formed with the merger of the Brussels, Paris and Amsterdam Exchanges and is likely to expand further to include other European markets.) France's Depository SICOVAM merged with Euroclear to form Euroclear France. Euroclear has also merged with the Netherlands's NECIGEF; is the settlement facility for Ireland's Government Bonds, is the CSD for Belgium (excluding physical securities transactions) and also has a stake in Clearnet, the clearing house for the Euronext market.

As the saga continues between Clearstream and Euroclear, the industry as a whole is asking, what do the banks, brokers and investors want? Globally and universally, they want more and better service at the lowest price. Competition encourages each entity to prove its value, refine and increase services and always attract newcomers to build its customer base. Clearstream and Euroclear, as competing ICSDs, are highly regarded in the industry as offering quality service and products. Has competition between these two entities encouraged them to expand their services? Competition in the European CSD and clearing agencies has fostered CSDs to lower prices and offer additional services to an expanded client base. But as the U.S.'s DTC has shown, a combined depository can offer services at lower cost and reduce settlement risk. A combined CSD would standardize processing which would reduce operating costs. A Central Counterparty would reduce operating costs as well as improve risk management practices, which would reduce settlement risk. Would one CSD in Europe or Asia offer brokers and investors settlement with lower fees? A recent published report from the Center for European Policy Studies (CEPS) argues that the centralization of all national CSDs into one European settlement agency, similar to DTCC, would not result in greater cost savings (although this is being disputed both in Europe and elsewhere). Major banks and broker/dealers in the U.S. would argue that the study did not factor in the benefits of netting, which reduces financial obligations by 97%. The study argues that the increased costs of cross-border settlement are not created by securities processing institutions, but result from national governments tax, legal and regulatory barriers. As the discussion continues, one conclusion is clear. Cross border trading will continue to increase. As Brokers and Investors struggle with multiple and distinct settlement mechanisms, the industry is in desperate need of an efficient and cost effective settlement environment. Is the answer a merger of clearinghouses and depositories intra-country and inter-country?

The merger of the U. S. clearinghouses and the depository may have an influence on the future global infrastructure. The Depository Trust & Clearing Corporation (DTCC) is the holding company for six subsidiary businesses - five clearinghouses and the depository (DTC). DTCC is, by volume and dollar value, the largest financial services post-trade infrastructure organization in the world. It is the leading clearinghouse for mutual funds and insurance products providing custody and asset servicing form more than two million securities from the U. S. and 65 other countries, worth more than $22 trillion. Their growing list of services includes Tax withholding Information products and, through their joint venture with Thomson Financial Services Group (called Omgeo), they developed the central matching facility called the Central Trade Manager.

Follows an overview of these organizations.

- Clearstream International
    - Web address: www.clearstream.com
    - Cedel International was established in 1970 by 66 financial institutions from 11 countries with the charter to reduce the costs and risks of settling securities in the Eurobond market. In 1999 Cedel announced their merger with Deutsche Borse Clearing (DBC) creating Clearstream.
    - Clearstream International has three divisions - - Clearstream Banking Frankfurt, Clearstream Banking Luxembourg and Clearstream Services.

- Clearstream Banking contains the core clearing and settlement business.
- Clearstream Services provides securities processing services to the Clearstream Banking units and the industry. Clearstream Services, in responding to increasing market demand for centralized securities processing, is using a single IT system for clearing, settlement and custody based on the system called Creation.
  - They have 41 sub-depositories (23 Europe, 11 Asia and 7 Americas/South Africa) in 39 countries (23 Europe, 8 Asia, 8 Americas/South Africa) They are:

Argentina	Hong Kong	Portugal
Australia	Hungary	Singapore
Austria	Indonesia	Slovak Republic
Belgium	Ireland	South Africa
Canada	Italy	South Korea
China	Japan	Spain
Czech Republic	Luxembourg	Sweden
Denmark	Malaysia	Switzerland
Estonia	Mexico	Thailand
Finland	Netherlands	Turkey
France	New Zealand	United Kingdom
Germany	Norway	United States
Greece	Poland	Uruguay

  - The services they offer are:
    - Reports including reports of settled and unsettled trades
    - Communications via their own system, CEDCOM or via SWIFT
    - Cash management and Long or short-term financing
    - Automated Securities Lending (ASL) a fails prevention lending and borrowing service
    - Multi-currency repo transactions including Tri-partite repo service
  - Via Cedcom Direct, a participant can fully automate the sending of instructions to Clearstream and retrieve reports.
  - Participants of Clearstream, enter instructions (via SWIFT or Cedcom); Clearstream then matches the instruction with the counterparty. Matched Instructions are forwarded to the next step which is to verify the seller has the securities for delivery (or has authorized a Securities Borrow) and that the buyer has issued a payment advise. Electronic transfer then takes place

between the participant's accounts.(or via the bridge with a
Euroclear participant – or a settlement with a non-participant).
The securities are held in the depository of the country via their
agent-bank network or, if not depository eligible, in book-entry
form or at their agent bank. This is a simplified overview of the
process. To view all the steps in the process I suggest you
access their web site.
Source Clearstream International

- CLS Group Holdings Ltd (Incorporated as CLS Services Ltd).
  - o web address: www.cls-services.com
  - o Due to go live in 2002, CLStm (Continuous Linked Settlement)
    is a real-time system that enables simultaneous settlement of
    multi currency transactions irrespective of time zones.
  - o As of October 2001, CLS Group had 70 shareholder banks from
    Australia, Belgium, Canada, Denmark, France, Germany, Italy,
    Japan, Luxembourg, Netherlands, Norway, Singapore, Spain,
    Sweden, Switzerland, United Kingdom and United States.
  - o CLS Group is the holding company for CLS Bank International,
    which provides the settlement service and is regulated by the
    Federal Reserve. Shareholders will become members of CLS
    Bank. CLS Services is the Group's operations company
    providing the technical, logistical and operational support.
  - o CLS Bank will be a multi-currency bank with accounts at
    relevant Central Banks. Through these accounts, CLS Bank has
    agreed in principle to process payment instructions from the
    Settlement Members in 11 currencies, Australian Dollar,
    Canadian Dollar, Danish Kroner, Euro, Great Britain's Pound
    Sterling, Japanese Yen, Norwegian Krone, Singapore dollar,
    Swedish Krona, Swiss Franc and the U. S. Dollar. More
    currencies may be added later.
  - o Historically, F/X deals settle during the hours of the country's
    payment system. For example, a payment of Japanese Yen (vs.
    receipt of U.S. Dollars) is made during Japan's banking hours,
    before the United States' regular banking hours. The time risk
    inherent in the payment of Yen leg of the transaction before the
    Dollar leg can settle is eliminated by CLS. The central banks
    involved have extended RTGS operating hours into a new five-
    hour window that overlaps the USA, Europe and Asia. The CLS
    system, utilizing the five-hour timeframe, will simultaneously
    settle the two legs of the currency transaction. It provides real
    time information on matched and settled transactions. For more

information on the day in the life of multi-currency transaction, see their web site.
Source: CLS Group. CLS is a trademark of CLS Group (Incorporated as CLS Services Ltd.)

- Depository Trust & Clearing (DTCC)
  - Web address: www.dtcc.com
  - The DTCC is a holding company owned by its principal users, leading banks and brokers as well as the New York Stock Exchange and National Association of Securities Dealers (NASD). It is made up of six subsidiaries, the National Securities Clearing Corporation (NSCC), the Government Securities Clearing Corporation (GSCC), MBS Clearing Corporation (MBSCC), Emerging Markets Clearing Corporation (EMCC), European Central Counterparty Ltd. (EuroCCP) and the Depository Trust Company (DTC). They have been involved in many global industry-wide initiatives including:
    - In October 2000, they sponsored a global conference to explore global issues that will impact the development of Central Counterparties (CCP).
    - The publication of the White Paper, Year 001: *Central Counterparties: Development, Cooperation and Consolidation* in which it identified issues that require discussion and encouraged coordination, cooperation and consolidation among CCPs to reduce operating costs and settlement risk. (see CCP12 and ECSDA earlier in this chapter).
    - The launch of the European Central Counterparty Ltd. (EuroCCP) to clear and settle trades for Nasdaq Europe and other European markets.
    - With Euroclear and Clearstream International, they developed the European Pre-Issuance Messaging (EPIM) service. EPIM is a central messaging hub linking all parties, including banks, dealers, numbering agencies, issuing and paying agents, ICSD and CSDs, involved in the issuance of euro-denominated commercial paper.
    - With Thomson Financial ESG, a unit of the Thomson Corporation, they created the joint venture Omgeo, to provide products that enable STP (including the Central Trade manager discussed in Chapter 3).
    - They developed global tax products, including Taxinfo and DALI, that are available to DTC members and non-members. Taxinfo is a tax information database

providing information on withholding rates for international securities held at DTC. DALI (Data Analytics & Link for Intermediaries) helps financial institutions meet new U. S. withholding tax regulations.
Source: The Depository Trust & Clearing Corporation

- Euroclear
  - Web address: www.euroclear.com
  - Euroclear was founded in 1968 by Morgan Guaranty. Located in Brussels, Belgium, Euroclear is the world's largest settlement system for domestic and international securities transactions. In 1972 Morgan Guaranty sold its interest in Euroclear to its users. In 1986, Euroclear Clearance System Société Cooperative was formed. Shares in the Cooperative were offered to all participants and more than 1,400 are now shareholders. Morgan Guaranty Brussels was contracted by the Euroclear Board to operate Euroclear until 2001, when Euroclear Bank was created to take over Morgan Guaranty's role. Euroclear has about 2,00 participants worldwide (see above for recent merger events).
  - Euroclear settles trades in 180,000 different securities, including international securities such as eurobonds, funds and bonds/equities from 32 countries, which are:

Argentina	Indonesia	Portugal
Australia	Ireland	Russia
Austria	Italy	Singapore
Belgium	Japan	South Africa
Canada	Luxembourg	Spain
Denmark	Malaysia	Sweden
Finland	Mexico	Switzerland
France	The Netherlands	Thailand
Germany	New Zealand	United Kingdom
Greece	Norway	United States
Hong Kong	The Philippines	

  - The services they offer are
    - Securities transaction settlement (either real-time or in an overnight batch settlement process)
    - Money transfer in more than 40 currencies
    - Wholesale custody
    - Securities lending and borrowing
    - Collateral management
  - The bridge between Euroclear and Clearstream was automated in the 1980s

- o The methods used to communicate with Euroclear are their proprietary communication channel, Euclid, SWIFT or Telex
Source: Euroclear

- Society for Worldwide Inter-bank Financial Telecommunication (SWIFT)
  - o Web address: www.swift.com
  - o In 1977 a consortium of banks (239 of them from 15 countries) set up SWIFT to replace the cumbersome paper-based transaction processes that existed in the payment instruction procedures. In 1987, the membership voted to permit Securities firms as participants followed by Investment Managers in 1992. By 2000, SWIFT had over 7,000 users from 192 countries.
  - o SWIFT is an industry owned co-operative supplying security messaging services and interface software
  - o Developed by banks to automate currency payment processes, in 1990, SWIFT expanded into the securities markets. As a result, Banks, Brokers and Institutional Investors now can exchange confirmations and send their trade instructions via SWIFT. Although used primarily in the `back office,' the Category 5 messages range from the MT502 (order to buy) through clearing and settlement instructions (see Chapter 3) and Corporate Actions and income advises. In 1998, SWIFT introduced a series of messages based on the ISO 15022 standard to replace the ISO 7775 messages. The ISO 15022 standard is a more structured, business-oriented message protocol which largely eliminates the free format data fields, common in ISO 7775 messages, that made straight through processing (STP) difficult, if not impossible.
Source: SWIFT

Answers

Answers

1) Of the countries listed, Chile requires an investor to be an institutional investor

2) Why does the investor's broker forward the order to an overseas broker?
   a) No, this is incorrect. They do not have to be a member of the clearing house to execute an order; they can outsource this to an agent or broker who provides clearance services
   b) No, this is incorrect. They do not have to be a member of the settlement facility to execute an order, they can outsource this to an agent or broker who provides settlement services
   c) Yes, you are correct.
   d) No, this is incorrect. Although this might present a challenge, usually a common language can be found.

3) Regulations of the overseas exchange include all of the following except:
   a) Yes, you are correct.
   b) No, this is incorrect. Since some exchanges require approval of a new account before investing, this requirement must be verified.
   c) No, this is incorrect. Exceeding the maximum number of shares that may be purchased by a foreign investor can cause legal and monetary difficulty; this requirement should be determined before investing.
   d) No, this is incorrect. Not following the regulations for selling short may result in possible fines and suspension from future investment.

4) All of the following describe a price-driven execution system except:
   a) No, this is incorrect. Brokers advertise their bid and ask price in the price-driven market
   b) No, this is incorrect. The ability to negotiate the execution price with a broker is one of the factors in a price-driven market
   c) Yes, you are correct.
   d) No, this is incorrect. Market Makers work large orders (i.e., provide special handling of a difficult order) in the price-driven market

5) What is the type of execution when a broker sells from their trading account?
   a) No, this is incorrect. A Stock Exchange execution usually refers to orders executed on the exchange.
   b) Yes, you are correct.
   c) No, this is incorrect. The broker, as the agent, executes an agency order with another party.
   d) No, this is incorrect. A Price-driven execution is the term used to describe an execution by a market-maker versus their trading account.

6) What action does the Investor take when they disagree with the trade details?
   a) Yes, you are correct..

    b) No, this is incorrect. The affirmation is the agreement to the trade.
    c) No, this is incorrect. Settlement instructions do not include the trade details.
    d) No, this is incorrect. Please tell me you didn't select this answer.

7) What is the process of splitting a trade execution to multiple accounts called?
    a) No, this is incorrect. The confirmation is the notification of the completed trade details.
    a) Yes, you are correct.
    b) No, this is incorrect. The affirmation is the agreement to the trade details.
    c) No, this is incorrect. The matching process is the comparison of the trade details.

8) If the round lot is 2000 shares, what is the quantity of 10,000 shares that should be allocated to 4 accounts?
    a) No, this is incorrect. In Hong Kong, only the round lot is transferable. If the round lot is 2000 shares, the allocation must be in multiples of 2000.
    b) No, this is incorrect. In Hong Kong, only the round lot is transferable. If the round lot is 2000 shares, the allocation must be in multiples of 2000.
    c) Yes, you are correct.
    d) No, this is incorrect. In Hong Kong, only the round lot is transferable. If the round lot is 2000 shares, the allocation must be in multiples of 2000.

9) What information is not contained in the Investor's SSI?
    a) No, this is incorrect. The account number of where the securities will be received is required to effect settlement.
    b) No, this is incorrect. The Global custodian Bank's settlement information is required.
    c) No, this is incorrect. The Sub-custodian Bank's settlement information is required.
    d) Yes, you are correct.

10) Of the following, what is a trade matching function?
    a) No, this is incorrect. By matching the input from both parties, the affirmation process is eliminated.
    b) No, this is incorrect. The trade matching system compares allocated trades.
    c) Yes, you are correct.
    d) No, this is incorrect. By matching the input from both parties, the affirmation process is eliminated. Also, in a confirmation / affirmation system, it is the broker's confirmation that is affirmed, not the broker's NOE.

11) Which type of trade best describes the `market-side' of the trade?
    a) No, this is incorrect. Market-side is a trade executed by brokers in the market.
    b) Yes, you are correct.
    c) No, this is incorrect. Market-side is a trade executed by brokers in the market
    d) No, this is incorrect. Market-side is a trade executed by brokers in the market

12) What is not a benefit of a locked-in trade?
    a) No, this is incorrect. As the trade data matches at execution, locked-in trades do not require a comparison

    b) No, this is incorrect. A report of a locked-in trade is immediately available to the broker

    c) Yes, this is correct.

    d) No, this is incorrect. Because of the automation in the locked-in environment, STP is possible.

13) Which execution system results in a locked-in trade?

    a) Yes, you are correct.

    b) No, this is incorrect. Trades executed via Hong Kong's Internal Telephone System (ITS) are verbal executions that require booking to the AMS system.

    c) No, this is incorrect. Trades executed via London's Stock Exchange Automated Quote System (SEAQ) are verbal executions that require entry to the system.

    d) No, this is incorrect. Trades executed by London's Market Makers are verbal executions that require entry to the system.

14) On which report will the following trade appear: Broker knows a purchase of a security at a price different from the counter-party?

    a) No, this is incorrect. Only the counter-party's information appears on the advisory report.

    b) No, this is incorrect. Only the broker's information appears on the unmatched report.

    c) Yes, you are correct.

    d) No, this is incorrect. Since it has not yet been determined who is correct, the information appears on both the unmatched and advisory report.

15) What is not the role of the Central Counter-Party (CCP)?

    a) No, this is incorrect. As the trade is reassigned to the CCP, the exposure to the counter-party is assumed by the CCP.

    b) Yes, this is correct.

    c) No, this is incorrect. The CCP performs the risk management through monitoring brokers activity and collecting 'guarantee funds' from brokers

    d) No, this is incorrect. The CCP becomes the counter-party to all compared executed trades.

16) Which party does not participate in the clearance process?

    a) No, this is incorrect. The Clearance entity is the main player.

    b) No, this is incorrect. The Clearance entity processes the trades of the brokers

    c) No, this is incorrect. The Clearance entity processes the trades of the brokers

    d) Yes, you are correct.

17) What is the reason for a Trade Guarantee Fund?

    a) Yes, you are correct.

    b) No, this is incorrect. The Guarantee fund does not protect against price depreciation.

    c) No, this is incorrect. The Fund will only compensate for failed trades if executed by a defaulting broker

    d) No, this is incorrect. It is the obligation of brokers have controls in place that monitor and protect themselves against counter-party credit risk.

18) What is the primary reason a market has not implemented a trade guarantee mechanism?
   a) Yes, you are correct.
   b) No, this is incorrect. Well capitalized brokers have been known to default.
   c) No, this is incorrect. Broker's trading volume, stable or unstable, will benefit from a Guarantee Fund
   d) No, this is incorrect. The regulators broker review is practiced in all well regulated markets but does not negate the need for a guarantee fund.

19) A trade guarantee mechanism based on the broker's current volume does not include:
   a) No, this is incorrect. To determine the broker's current volume, the mechanism tracks current volume
   b) Yes, you are correct.
   c) No, this is incorrect. The contribution amount varies with the broker's current volume
   d) No, this is incorrect. Uncompared trades are not included in the daily computation.

20) What statement does not accurately describe a CNS system?
   a) No, this is incorrect. Typically only very liquid securities are eligible
   b) No, this is incorrect. Only compared (or locked-in) trades are included in any netting system
   c) No, this is incorrect. The major difference between CNS and other netting systems is the ability to include failed trades in the CNS process.
   d) Yes, you are correct.

Answers

1) All of the following statements accurately describe an efficient settlement process except:
   a) No, this is incorrect. An efficient process will move securities and cash.
   b) No, this is incorrect. DVP is an efficient settlement process
   c) Yes, you are correct.
   d) No, this is incorrect. An efficient process will verify the funds have been paid.

2) Which of the following statements accurately describe 'true' DVP?
   a) No, this is incorrect. Payment of funds prior to the securities is not true DVP
   b) Yes, you are correct.
   c) No, this is incorrect. Transfer of the securities prior to payment is not true DVP
   d) No, this is incorrect. Since both the certificate and check require clearing / verification, this is not true DVP

3) Which settlement occurred in the book-entry environment?
   a) No, this is incorrect. This is not part of settlement; the name of the new shareholder can only be recorded on the books of the registrar after settlement has taken place.
   b) No, this is incorrect. Certificates do not exist in the book-entry environment.
   c) No, this is incorrect. Securities held in a vault are in physical form – not part of the book-entry environment.
   d) Yes, you are correct.

4) All of the following statements accurately describe dematerialized settlement except:
   a) Yes, you are incorrect.
   b) No, this is incorrect A dematerialized depository is sometimes called a Central Registry.
   c) No, this is incorrect. Positions in a dematerialized environment are maintained in an automated record at the CSD.
   d) No, this is incorrect. Settlement in a dematerialized environment is recorded via a computerized transfer.

5) If paid through a payment netting system, when are the funds due?
   a) No, this is incorrect. Instructions may be sent the day before settlement date, but the funds are only due when the system reports the net debit or credit for each participant.
   b) No, this is incorrect. Payment may be made in the morning, but the funds are not due until the system determines the net debit or credit for each participant.
   c) No, this is incorrect. Funds are due when the system advises the participant of the net debit or credit due/receivable.
   d) Yes, you are correct.

6) Which system offers the simultaneous transfer of securities and funds?
   a) Yes, you are correct.
   b) No, this is incorrect. A Payment netting system does not transfer securities.
   c) No, this is incorrect. An Electronic Funs Transfer system does not transfer securities.
   d) No, this is incorrect. Payment via check is separate from the transfer of the securities.

7) In Hong Kong, what is the most like result of a fail to deliver?
   a) No, this is incorrect. Although permitted by H. K. law, the broker's suspension occurs only after repeated offenses.
   b) No, this is incorrect. Some countries require the failing broker to deposit a percentage of the trade value pending settlement; in Hong Kong brokers do not have this option.
   c) Yes, you are correct.
   d) No, this is incorrect. There are very strict procedures for failed trades in Hong Kong.

8) All of the following statements accurately describe securities with multiple listings except
   a) No, this is incorrect. Dual or multiple listed shares do trade in more than one marketplace.
   b) No, this is incorrect. Dual or multiple listed shares may settle in either the currency of issuance or the currency of the country where traded.
   c) No, this is incorrect. Dual or multiple listed shares may settle in the CSD where traded if the CSD has established a link with the CSD of issuance.
   d) Yes, you are correct.

9) What is the effect of a partial delivery on settlement date?
   a) No, this is incorrect. Part of the trade will settle vs. the pro-rated funds, but this is only part of the answer.
   b) No, this is incorrect. The settlement instructions, reflecting the remaining shares, are required; but this is only part of the answer.
   c) No, this is incorrect. The shares not delivered will fail; but this is only part of the answer.
   d) Yes, you are correct.

10) What is the Broker's deadline for settlement instructions on a U. K. trade?
   a) No, this is incorrect. The client's Custodian Bank does not determine the deadline for the Broker trade.
   b) Yes, you are correct.
   c) No, this is incorrect. The Broker's Clearing Agent may require the instructions prior to CHAPs deadline.
   d) No, this is incorrect. The Broker's Clearing Agent may require the instructions prior to the CREST deadline.

Answers

1) All of the following describe the effect of a fail to deliver except:
   a) No, this is incorrect. Since the Broker is holding the customer's shares, they will credit the customer's account.
   b) No, this is incorrect. Since the Broker appears to be having some problem delivering the shares, they might borrow the shares to make delivery.
   c) No, this is incorrect. Since the Broker will credit the customer's account with funds they have not received from the buyer or borrow the shares to make delivery, they will incur finance charges
   d) Yes, you are correct.

2) What type of Repo requires no transfer of securities?
   a) No, this is incorrect. A physical repo requires the physical exchange of the security
   b) Yes, you are correct.
   c) No, this is incorrect. A tri-party repo utilizes the services of an agent which may either hold in the securities in custody or transfer the securities
   d) No, this is incorrect. The term closing refers to the return of the securities and funds at the completion of the deal.

3) What is the method of financing most often used to finance overnight cash requirements?
   a) No, this is incorrect. Because of the higher borrowing costs and amount of securities needed to collateralize a bank loan, this is not the first choice for overnight financing.
   b) No, this is incorrect. Not the least expensive financing alternative.
   c) No, this is incorrect. A mechanism only available to brokers with the highest credit rating.
   d) Yes, you are correct.

4) All of the following are examples of the sequence of dividend income dates, except:
   a) No, this is incorrect. In markets that process trades in a trade-date based environment, the trade date occurs before ex-date
   b) Yes, you are correct.
   c) No, this is incorrect. Ex-date after record date is common practice in Europe
   d) No, this is incorrect. In markets that process trades in a settlement-date based environment, the settlement date occurs before record date

5) Shares that rank pari passu are entitled to which of the following?
   a) No, this is incorrect. Pari Passu shares are equal to existing shares
   b) Yes, you are correct.
   c) No, this is incorrect. Pari Passu shares are equal to existing shares
   d) No, this is incorrect. Pari Passu shares are equal to existing shares

6) Do regulations in the Japanese market entitle unsettled trades to dividend payments?
   a) No, this is incorrect. Claims are processed in the Japanese market; however, the holder of record is not legally obligated to honor the claim.
   b) No, this is incorrect. Because the shares were owned by the record date, a claim may be processed; however, in the Japanese market the holder of record is not legally obligated to honor the claim.
   c) Yes, you are correct.
   d) No, this is incorrect. In Japan, the withholding tax is withheld at source

7) Which of the following describes the corporate action known as a sub-division?
   a) Yes, you are correct.
   b) No, this is incorrect. A sub-division is a spin off of a subsidiary through the issuance of new shares. A share exchange from 5000 to 500 shares is called a reverse split
   c) No, this is incorrect. A sub-division is a spin off of a subsidiary through the issuance of new shares. A cash payment of HKD 0.10 is a cash dividend
   d) No, this is incorrect. A sub-division is a spin off of a subsidiary through the issuance of new shares. An exchange of the target company's shares for shares of the surviving company is called a takeover or tender.

8) When does the ex-date occur on or after the payment date?
   a) No, this is incorrect. The ex-date occurs after the payment date when the event reflects a substantial change in the corporate structure.
   b) No, this is incorrect. The purpose of the ex-date is to show the reduction in market price due to a dividend distribution
   c) Yes, you are correct.
   d) No, this is incorrect. The ex-date occurs after the payment date when the event reflects a substantial change (25% or more) in the corporate structure

9) What is an issuance sweetener?
   a) No, this is incorrect. Although a stock dividend `sweetens' the investment of the shareholder, it is not distributed at the time of the security's issuance
   b) No, this is incorrect. Although a rights issue may `sweeten' the investment of the shareholder, it is not distributed at the time of the security's issuance
   c) No, this is incorrect. Although a spin off may `sweeten' the investment of the shareholder, it is not distributed at the time of the security's issuance
   d) Yes, you are correct.

10) Which accurately describes an odd-lot buy-out plan?
   a) No, this is incorrect. It is only part of the answer.
   b) No, this is incorrect. It is only part of the answer.
   c) No, this is incorrect. It is only part of the answer.
   d) Yes, you are correct.

11) All of the following describe a subscription rights issue, except:
  a) No, this is incorrect. 15 days is the average life cycle of a rights issue
  b) No, this is incorrect. Shareholders (or their agent/SCB) must produce proof of ownership
  c) Yes, you are correct. (Markets and/or the prospectus might restrict the subscription and/or sale of rights)
  d) No, this is incorrect. A rights issue does not impact the right to own the original shares.

12) Which of the following is a voluntary corporate action?
  a) No, this is incorrect. A called bond is a mandatory event
  b) No, this is incorrect. A name change is a mandatory event
  c) No, this is incorrect. A spin-off is a mandatory event
  d) Yes, you are correct.

13) What is the deadline for filing a tax reclaim?
  a) No, this is incorrect. Most markets permit filing from 1 to 7 years after the event.
  b) No, this is incorrect. Most markets permit filing from 1 to 7 years after the event.
  c) No, this is incorrect. Markets with at-source withholding require filing before the payable date; most markets permit filing for tax reclaim from 1 to 7 years after the event
  d) Yes, you are correct.

14) What is a Franked Dividend?
  a) Yes, you are correct.
  b) No, this is incorrect. A franked dividend is the amount paid less the corporate tax
  c) No, this is incorrect. A franked dividend may require a reclaim, but it is the amount paid less the corporate tax
  d) No, this is incorrect. A franked dividend is the amount paid less the corporate tax

15) All of thee following activities are performed by the Stock Lending Area, except:
  a) No, this is incorrect. This is the first step in the process
  b) No, this is incorrect. If the securities are not available internally, they will contact external sources
  c) Yes, you are correct.
  d) No, this is incorrect. The Stock Lending Area borrows from other Brokers or Custodians

16) What is the process of revaluing securities based on the current market value called?
  a) Yes, you are correct
  b) No, this is incorrect. Although included in the collateral management function, it is not what the process is called.
  c) No, this is incorrect. Fail control is the prevention of unsettled trades.
  d) No, this is incorrect. Arbitrage is the buying of one security and selling a related security / or the same security in another market (hopefully for a profit)

17) All of the following actions are taken when closing out a loan, except:
   a) Yes, you are correct.
   b) No, this is incorrect. If the borrowed security is not yet available, the securities are borrowed from another source.
   c) No, this is incorrect. The stock (either the original or stock borrowed from another source) is returned to the lender.
   d) No, this is incorrect. If replacement stock was borrowed from another source, their records are updated to reflect the new lender.

18) All of the following describe contractual processing, except:
   a) No, this is incorrect. Contractual processing is the posting of income regardless of when it is actually received.
   b) Yes, you are correct.
   c) No, this is incorrect. Contractual processing is the posting of securities regardless of when they are actually received
   d) No, this is incorrect. Trades, marked as settled on the settlement date, are reversed if the trade does not actually settle after a stipulated period of time.

19) Which of the following custody services is considered a `core' service?
   a) No, this is incorrect. Contractual settlement is a value added service offered by only some custodian banks.
   b) No, this is incorrect. Risk management is a value added service offered by most custodian banks
   c) No, this is incorrect. Tax withholding is a value added service offered by most custodian banks
   d) Yes, you are correct.

20) Network Management includes all of the following except:
   a) No, this is incorrect. The first step in the process is to contract with the local banks in the country of settlement.
   b) Yes, you are correct.
   c) No, this is incorrect. Reporting, via an internal network or via SWIFT, is a main responsibility of the local bank
   d) No, this is incorrect. Local banks that do not provide adequate support of the GCB's client's requirements will eventually be replaced!

APPENDIX A

A VMU's Customer Value Proposition to Investment Managers

The value that a VMU brings to its users will vary by constituency, but is largely predicated on providing an infrastructure that facilitates STP (Straight Through Processing) not only within the given firm, but between that firm and its trade counterparties, agents and the agents of its counterparties.

This section will provide an overview of the so-called Customer Value Proposition that a VMU offers to Investment Managers, with a focus on the problems typically faced by that constituency in terms of:

- the various business, operational/administrative and systems problems related to trade
  comparison and settlement
- the short-, medium- and long-term needs that arise from those problems, and
- the potential solutions and benefits that a VMU can offer to that constituency.

A. Problems faced by Investment Managers

A.1. Business (trade cycle)

1. Manual processing and duplication of information input and maintenance predominates throughout the transaction cycle for many Investment Managers, which is costly to manage and precludes exception-based processing.
2. The fragmented nature of the trade comparison processes introduces difficulty in monitoring transaction status after a trade has been allocated by the Investment Manager
3. The increasing complexity involved with global investment strategies requires a greater focus on the business, rather than the administration, of the trades, and capital and resources within Investment Management firms are often dedicated to the management of the portfolio and trading processes, as opposed to the operational and administrative handling of these transactions.
4. Difficulties entering new markets with new procedures and processes cause problems as these activities are incorporated into existing Investment Management organizations.
5. Additional (uncontrolled) operational costs also degrade the performance/return of the fund for end investors – thereby introducing a potential loss of competitive edge for the Investment Manager against its peers.

A.2. Operational/Administrative

1. After trade execution and allocation, the Investment Manager tends to act as an intermediary or middleman between the Broker/Dealer (B/D) and the Global Custodian (GC) prior to the settlement instructions being submitted to the local market for matching. This results in two roles for the Investment Manager that they prefer not to maintain – the delivery of the GC's standing settlement instructions to the B/D via Third Party standing settlement instruction databases, and the delivery of settlement instructions to the GC containing the

B/D settlement details. Both of these processes are often un-automated, are subject to massive data input errors, and are therefore often the source of the settlement failures that characterize cross-border trading.

2. Matching occurs late (if at all) at domestic market level prior to presentation of instructions for settlement and may not occur at all between B/D and GC prior to submission of instructions to their respective domestic Agents.

3. Problems in the timely processing of transactions occur as a result of the continued reduction of settlement cycles in the worlds major securities markets as noted in the Industry Background section of this Foreword. This is exacerbated by timezone constraints for cross-border business.

4. Operational problems also result from high costs arising from a historical reluctance to automate within the industry and a tradition of paper based procedures supported by stand alone IT solutions. Analysis of SWIFT securities message traffic and institutional processes across a variety of industry players and markets has revealed that up to 50% of settlement costs are related to not achieving STP, such as (duplication of) manual input or transaction repair. These resultant costs have the potential to spiral if firms reach their processing capacity, with transaction costs and temporary/additional staffing costs increasing. These high costs will ultimately impact the investment performance of the Investment Manager.

5. The lack of standards in communicating with counterparties also inhibits the process by creating breaks that require manual processing and repair. Due to lack of in-house automation and the late entrance of Investment Managers into the SWIFT network, the use of ISIN codes as security identifiers and BIC codes as organizational identifiers is also not universally accepted. Standardized identification schemes for client account numbers within GCs is an industry issue that also needs to be addressed.

A.3. Systems

1. Multiple systems/platforms/databases are typically used, respectively, in the Front, Middle and Back offices of Investment Managers, leading to an environment that systematically makes it difficult to achieve STP. Middleware can sometimes be used to bridge these disparate legacy systems, but often at a high capital and maintenance cost to the Investment Manager.

2. The high end-to-end cost of maintaining piecemeal proprietary solutions/channels, multiple databases and legacy systems further undermines the goal of achieving STP. The difficulty in upgrading systems to accommodate new products and differentiate performance also constrains the ability of Investment Managers in achieving this goal.

3. The current Electronic Trade Confirmation (ETC) products for cross-border trade confirmation do not integrate the global custodian into the trade matching process – therefore there is an overhead (clerical) cost to process this element of the trade cycle for Investment Managers.

4. High variable costs are required to facilitate repair queues/reconciliation/investigations of trade breaks.

5. Globalization, and the increasing complexity within the securities industry, requires Investment Managers to communicate with an ever-expanding group of B/Ds and GCs. These communications, by necessity, have be fully electronic and processable by the all parties in order to achieve external STP – and this

implies use of an industry standard communication protocols that are still not universally employed by Investment Managers.

A.4. Other

1. The inability of Investment Managers to receive and adhere to standard business Service Level Agreements (SLAs) from B/Ds and GCs for operational activities results in the fragmentation of the information exchange process.
2. The inability of Investment Managers to perform a consistent evaluation and ranking of the performance of service suppliers (B/Ds and GCs) using a commonly-recognized benchmarking method, inhibits their ability to monitor these service suppliers in a transparent and objective manner.

B. Needs of Investment Managers

B.1. Short term

1. Investment Managers need to control and reduce unit costs per trade and fixed overheads associated with the business, particularly as margins shrink and the size of assets under management is threatened by both market and competitive forces.
2. Investment Managers need an ability to seamlessly integrate new business/investment opportunities with minimal disruption and cost.
3. Investment Managers need an operational infrastructure which helps minimize their sensitivity to volume and peak business conditions from an operational standpoint, which providing a foundation for systems scalability. They need to be able to process increasing trading volumes generated both through both business growth and market volatility, with minimal impact on systems, procedures and organizational resources.
4. Investment Managers need access to information at the soonest possible time through effective distribution to all business areas within the firm.
5. Investment Managers require effective security facilities provided through the use of industry-strength systems with proven security features and controls that are appropriate to the high-value transactions being handled.
6. Investment Managers need the ability to receive a competitive and standard business SLA from B/Ds and GCs.
7. Investment Managers need the ability to link securities and FX transactions together.

B.2. Medium term

1. Investment Managers need the ability to minimize internal operational risks through effective use of information and improved automation
2. Investment Managers need the ability to meet the trend for shorter settlement cycles, already mandated for US, GB and Japan and expected across numerous other markets in the medium term.
3. Investment Managers need the ability to meet industry working practices and standards convergence plans (ISO15022, XML, FIX) and to integrate fully

electronic messaging systems into their in-house systems architecture to enable usage of common industry-standard formats when transferring information both internally and externally with agents and trade counterparties.

4. Investment Managers need the ability to meet increasing regulatory requirements and an ability to efficiently and cheaply produce appropriate data for the regulators (often in a number of jurisdictions where the Investment Manager is a global player).

5. Investment Managers need the ability to undertake effective and consistent benchmarking of the performance of suppliers (B/Ds and GCs).

6. Investment Managers need the ability to be able to integrate new products into the trade processing regime at minimal cost.

B.3. Long term

1. Investment Managers need the ability to consolidate and integrate systems, linking the front order (global) Order Management Systems to middle-office trade comparison processing and (centralized) back office accounting/reporting systems which provide global support of the business.

2. Investment Managers need the ability to be able to adopt and integrate changes to market practices and standards without undue effect/cost on the ongoing business.

3. Investment Managers need the ability to outsource back office and IT functions, where this route is chosen for business and technical reasons by Management as an alternative to maintaining these functions and resources on an in-house basis.

C. Solutions and Benefits offered by VMUs to Investment Managers

C.1. Business (trade cycle)

1. The VMU will perform much of the trade matching processing centrally, therefore operational bottlenecks and paper will be reduced, as will manual intervention required for exception management. Also, interaction with the VMU will require a systematic approach to managing data and information within the Investment Manager, as opposed to a myriad of connections, standards and procedures required by the current model for trade comparison and settlement.

2. The status of a trade will always be available in real-time from the VMU. Status updates arising from subsequent enrichment and changes performed by the GC and B/D will be broadcast to the Investment Manager to ensure that the status is up to date within that their internal systems.

3. The VMU acts as a central processor and repository of information regarding transaction processing and trade/allocation status. Given appropriate in-house systems to consolidate this information, less resource is required at the administrative end of the business, allowing the focus of the Investment Manager to be on the business behind, and not the administration of, the trade.

4. Most operational implications of entering a new securities market will be transferred completely to the GC with their early involvement in the process, because the VMU should be independent of end market (note: this does not

remove appropriate due diligence and risk management needs from the Investment Manager).

5. Effective management of costs can be undertaken, with the knowledge that the VMU can support volume peaks and market volatility (assuming that appropriate internal systems are implemented to interface to the VMU).

C.2. Operational/Administrative

1. The need to act as an intermediary between B/D and GC disappears as the VMU will route all allocation information to the GC as soon as it is identified by the Investment Manager. Additionally, the B/D will be advised of the GC associated with each allocation, allowing them to better prepare for settlement on their end.

2. The VMU ensures that the B/D and GC are in a position to match instructions **_before_** they are released to the domestic market. Hence, after matching in the VMU, there is no reason why the trade should fail to match domestically, assuming that the B/D has the appropriate credit/inventory positions and the GC is prepared on its end for both the cash and securities movements implied by the trade.

3. VMU typically will work in a just-in-time environment. Assuming appropriate internal systems are operational within the Investment Manager, the post-trade/pre-settlement activities should all be completed on trade date allowing all T+1 markets (and beyond) to be effectively supported.

4. Automation and scalability within the VMU will ensure that volume increases (whether predicted or otherwise) will be manageable within the existing operational framework. Therefore, with initial investment in appropriate in-house solutions to interface with the VMU, management of costs related to increasing volumes should be achievable.

5. Communication with all participants using the VMU will be through the industry-standard message formats and best market practice guidelines. The work required to interface with the VMU allows the Investment Manager and/or their third- party vendors to standardize the internal systems architecture and applications with minimal need for translation and conversion overheads. The initial take-on/conversion expense will lead to improved efficiencies and reduced costs in the longer term.

C.3. Systems

1. The internal systems architecture deployed in the Investment Manager presents issues that are wider in scope than just interfacing with a VMU; however, if the Investment Manager is serious in addressing the fundamental issues raised by implementing STP within their institution, a strategy and plan needs to be implemented that, at minimum, will lead to in-house integration with a VMU.

2. The processing flows required by a VMU enable IT solutions to be implemented using industry standards and components (from vendors). Such solutions will introduce standardization in available third-party products which, with shared developments costs spread over a number of users, will enable a reduction in individual firm's maintenance overheads and an improvement in their ability to upgrade systems in the future.

3. The VMU fully integrates the GC into the trade flow and removes the need for Investment Managers to maintain overheads to support the information required to complete settlement instruction processing.
4. The VMU should reduce the repair overhead as numerous matching processes (block, allocation, proceeds and settlement instructions) will ensure that data is validated at the soonest opportunity, reducing the likelihood of failure later in the cycle. In addition, the data added to the transaction during the trade lifecycle is sourced by the underlying data owner. Transaction repairs that are required on an exception basis will be managed through the VMU through advice of errors, warnings etc during the course of processing.
5. The VMU is built to facilitate high volume cross-border trade flows through the use of a set of industry-standard message formats. The work required to interface with the VMU allows the Investment Manager to redesign and standardize its internal systems architecture and applications with minimal need for translation and conversion overheads.

C.4   Other

1. Automation delivered by the VMU will allow for a standard SLA to be agreed with GCs and B/Ds.
2. The VMU will give the Investment Manager the ability, through MIS and other benchmarking, to pro-actively monitor the performance of B/Ds and GCs in a consistent manner, providing a fair and independent evaluation of performance.

APPENDIX B

A VMU's Customer Value Proposition to Broker/Dealers

The value that a VMU brings to its users will vary by constituency, but is largely predicated on providing an infrastructure that facilitates STP (Straight Through Processing) not only within the given firm, but between that firm and its trade counterparties, agents and the agents of its counterparties.

This section will provide an overview of the so-called Customer Value Proposition that a VMU offers to Broker / Dealers, with a focus on the problems typically faced by that constituency in terms of:

- the various business, operational/administrative and systems problems related to trade
  comparison and settlement
- the short-, medium- and long-term needs that arise from those problems, and
- the potential solutions and benefits that a VMU can offer to that constituency.

A.   Problems faced by Broker/Dealers

A.1. Business (trade cycle)

1. No standard, universally-accepted method exists for the matching and comparison of block trades between Broker/Dealers and Investment Managers (IMs). Widespread use of fax/phone/telex and/or third-party ETC systems with high levels of manual intervention are the norm for most Broker/Dealers involved in institutional trading. Broker/Dealers are at risk during parts of the trade life cycle in which the fundamental details of the block trade remain unmatched.
2. No standard, universally-accepted method exists among Broker/Dealers for receiving and enriching allocation details from IMs in order to communicate net proceeds and settlement details. Information is typically received through numerous channels, including fax/phone/telex and/or third party systems. Furthermore, Broker/Dealers often have to resort to the manual input of IMs' allocation details into their trade position-keeping systems, which gives rise to an administrative overhead and is a potential source of delay and error.
3. Regarding the generation of and matching of settlement instructions for underlying local domestic market settlement, Broker/Dealers often suffer from delays in the matching of settlement instructions with the IMs' global custodian (GC). Currently, settlement instructions are often not matched prior to their transmission to the local domestic market. Broker/Dealers' dialogue regarding settlement is undertaken through the IM, rather than directly with the GC, which is responsible for settling the trade on behalf of the IM. As a result, a Broker/Dealer's exposure to trade failure increases the later that the GC is involved in the process as there is less time to react to trade matching problems (especially for cross border trades with timezone implications).
4. Cash / securities management within the Broker/Dealer is also negatively impacted by delays in matching settlement details, because this implies less time for the accurate projection of cash and securities financing requirements. The lack of timely

information also impairs the Broker/Dealer's ability to execute optimal financing arrangements to accurately reflect resultant trading positions (cash borrowing, repo, FX etc.)

5. Trade failures occur in over 20% of cross border trades, and as a result, Broker/Dealers face unplanned, unprovisioned and expensive financing required to cover trade fails. Additional market and counterparty risk is being incurred by Broker/Dealers during the fail period.

A.2. Operational/Administrative

1. The operational requirements associated with trade comparison and matching require that Broker/Dealers staff be allocated to process all operational aspects of the business, rather than for managing the exceptions. This increases operational overhead that can't be scaled as easily as systematic infrastructure.
2. Operational bottlenecks arise within Broker/Dealers because of the accumulation of, and delays associated with, receiving paper-based information.
3. Many Broker/Dealers encounter an inability to cope with volume increases due to business growth and market volatility.
4. To retain and win institutional trade execution business Broker/Dealers often resort to implementing and resourcing client- specific procedures, rather than utilizing standardized means of supporting Investment Managers through such facilities as Service Level Agreements, Performance Benchmarking monitoring systems and electronic communication protocols.

A.3. Systems

1. Broker/Dealers typically suffer from a lack of integrated internal systems/databases that can efficiently manage the data generated by the institutional trade execution business.
2. Broker/Dealers have to rely on extensive suite of data translation, message formatting and external communication facilities in order to cope with the myriad of non-standard information exchanges that take place with IMs.

A.4. Other

1. The lack of common industry-wide standards in producing messages associated with the trade execution, confirmation and pre-settlement processes inhibits the ability of Broker/Dealers to integrate the Front Office with Middle Office and Back Office functions.
2. The inability of Broker/Dealers to create and adhere to standard business Service Level Agreements (SLAs) with IMs for operational activities results in the fragmentation of the information exchange process.
3. The inability of Broker/Dealers to perform a consistent evaluation and ranking of the performance for/by IM clients, using a commonly-recognized benchmarking method, inhibits their ability to monitor and manage these operational activities in a transparent and objective manner.

B. Needs of Broker/Dealers

B.1. Short term

1. Broker/Dealers need to control and reduce the unit cost per trade and fixed overheads associated with the trade execution business.
2. Broker/Dealers need the ability to seamlessly integrate new business/clients with minimal disruption and cost
3. Broker/Dealers need to actively manage stock inventory to minimize financing costs and capital allocation requirements.
4. Broker/Dealers need to reduce their exposure to external risks (counterparty, market, systemic) through the effective management and control of trading and depot positions.
5. Broker/Dealers need to access to information at the soonest possible time through the effective distribution to all business areas
6. Broker/Dealers need to minimize internal operational risks through the effective use of information and by an improvement in the automation of operational activities.
7. Broker/Dealers require effective security facilities provided through the use of industry-strength systems with proven security features and controls that are appropriate to the high-value transactions being handled.

B.2. Medium term

1. Broker/Dealers need to actively monitor and manage the trade execution and comparison performance by use of MIS and performance metrics that enable them to identify problem areas before they become a client problem
2. Broker/Dealers need to be able to process increasing trading volumes generated both through institutional business growth and market volatility, with minimal impact on systems, procedures and organization.
3. Broker/Dealers need to be able to integrate new products into the trade-processing regime at minimal cost.
4. Broker/Dealers need the ability to produce and manage a competitive and standard business SLA for clients.

B.3. Long term

1. Broker/Dealers need to consolidate and integrate systems to provide global support of the institutional trade execution, comparison and settlement business.
2. Broker/Dealers need to be able to adopt and integrate changes to market practices and standards without undue effect and/or cost on their ongoing business.

C. Solutions and Benefits offered by VMUs to Broker/Dealers

C.1. Business (trade cycle)

1. Broker/Dealers will be able to perform full block trade matching and confirmation on VMUs, which will match their Notice of Execution with a Block Order Notification from the IM. The Broker/Dealers' period of risk will be minimized if matching can be effected in real-time within the VMU.

2. The receipt of trade allocation and the subsequent enrichment (net proceeds and counterparty settlement instructions) by the Broker/Dealer will occur through the VMU, which will provide standard format messages advising allocation and enrichment details. The Broker/Dealers will be able to retrieve the details from the VMU and automatically split/allocate the block trade and enrich with other details without the need for any manual intervention
3. The generation and matching of settlement instructions for underlying local market settlement by Broker/Dealers will be facilitated by the VMU, which allows the IM's global custodian to receive advice of the allocation at the same time as the Broker/Dealer. As such, the GC it is positioned to match settlement instructions earlier in the trade cycle than in today's processing model. The Broker/Dealer is also given early advice of which agent the IM is using (this is especially if the settlement is not in line with standing instructions held on the Broker/Dealer database). Matching instructions in the VMU there minimizes the risk of settlement failure in the domestic market.
4. Cash / securities management within the Broker/Dealer is also improved by a heightened ability to match trades (on a same-day basis) which will significantly improve the ability of the Broker/Dealer to effectively forecast and manage its inventory and financing requirements.
5. Trade Failure for Broker/Dealers will be reduced as a compacted and best market practice timeframe for trade comparison is enforced by the VMU. The matching of each allocation in the VMU will reduce the likelihood of trade failure on the client side and the early involvement of the GC in the trade comparison process will reduce the likelihood of trade failure on the agent side.

C.2. Operational/Administrative

1. The VMU will reduce manual intervention while facilitating a move to exception management.
2. The VMU will perform much of the trade comparison processing; therefore operational bottlenecks and paper will be reduced.
3. Automation and scalability within the VMU will ensure that volume increases (whether predicted or otherwise) will be manageable within the Broker/Dealers' existing operational framework.
4. The VMU creates a standard platform giving a common standard approach to processing the trade comparison business. Consequently, the need for specific processing solutions for each new client is minimized.

C.3. Systems

1. The VMU provides a single common technical platform for trade comparison and matching, where all data is stored centrally in a standard format. This data is available to all authorized parties to the trade for integration into internal systems and databases.
2. Communication is through an industry-standard suite of messages, which can be accommodated within Broker/Dealer systems. The work required to interface with the VMU allows the Broker/Dealer to redesign and standardize its internal systems architecture and applications with minimal need for translation and conversion overheads.

3. The VMU (and the associated access modules) are built to accommodate the industry-accepted security features of a Virtual Private Network, using commonly-employed Internet Protocol (IP) technologies.

C.4   Other

1. Automation delivered by the VMU will allow for a standard SLA to be agreed with IMs and GCs.
2. The VMU will give the Broker/Dealer the ability, through MIS and other benchmarking, to pro-actively monitor the performance of IMs and GCs in a consistent manner, providing a fair and independent evaluation of performance.

APPENDIX C

A VMU's Customer Value Proposition to Custodian Banks

The value that a VMU brings to its users will vary by constituency, but is largely predicated on providing an infrastructure that facilitates STP (Straight Through Processing) not only within the given firm, but between that firm and its trade counterparties, agents and the agents of its counterparties.

This section will provide an overview of the so-called Customer Value Proposition that a VMU offers to Custodian Banks, with a focus on the problems typically faced by that constituency in terms of:

- the various business, operational/administrative and systems problems related to trade
comparison and settlement
- the short-, medium- and long-term needs that arise from those problems, and
- the potential solutions and benefits that a VMU can offer to that constituency.

A. Problems faced by Custodian Banks

A.1. Business (trade cycle)

1. The actuality of the market settlement experience makes delivering contractual settlement (a service the Custodian Bank provides to its client) difficult to achieve in a cost-effective way. Necessary account funding and securities financing requirements associated with contractual settlement are complex operations that are compromised by actual settlement failures.
2. Different procedures per market and per country and/or financial instrument are often required. The way this information is provided to the Custodian Bank is not streamlined or standardized and is often very different for each Investment Manager (IM) agent of the Custodian Bank's underlying customer.

A.2 Operational/Administrative

1. Bottlenecks and manual overheads are incurred in receiving the IMs' settlement instructions. The IMs' information arrives via a number of different methods (phone, fax, telex and e-mail) depending on the client.
2. The settlement instructions typically arrive late at the Custodian Banks (mostly T+1, T+2, later or even too late for settlement on actual settlement date). This is problematic since the Custodian Banks have to ensure the availability of the securities (which could be out on loan) and need to turn around the instructions to the local market on time. In general under today's processing arrangements, Custodian Banks are involved too late in the settlement instruction process which

jeopardizes their ability to match the instruction from the broker's clearing agent and hence to settle on time in the local market.

3. Since there is still excessive manual processing involved in the basic settlement process, Custodian Banks have to employ an often-sizeable staff of operations people. For Global Custodians, this also results from having to service different time zones and needing a sufficient buffer to reduce volume-sensitivity across markets. The result is the need for more operations staff as the underlying custody business grows.

A.3. Systems

1. Many different IT systems are employed by Custodian Banks for client input (multiple interface products), and these often are not integrated. This also makes maintenance and support costs very high.

2. Current information channels available to Custodian Banks do not cater for different information capture requirements. The clients of the Custodian Banks often have special requirements in terms of servicing needs from the custodian (e.g., pure clearing and custody versus special accounting needs). This requires capturing different pieces of information from the different clients. Once this information is captured, it also needs to be routed to separate systems for different product types. This is problematic since the automatic communication link is often only built for one product line, requiring additional input through (most likely) manual channels.

3. The information that is provided by clients to the Custodian Bank is often of a) poor quality, b) not consistent and c) sometimes even wrong (e.g., counterparty is given, not clearing agent).

A.4. Other

1. A lack of standards used by the Investment Manager clients make STP investments very costly and hard to maintain for Custodian Banks. A mixture of ISITC formats, proprietary formats, bilaterally-agreed formats and pure SWIFT standards are being sent to the Custodian Banks and this makes streamlining the information flow very difficult and costly.

2. Bad settlement information is often communicated to the Broker/Dealer by the Investment Manager on behalf of the Custodian Banks in today's processing model. Moreover, the Custodian Bank is typically unaware of any information that is communicated to the Broker/Dealer counterparty of its Investment Manager client.

3. Non-matched information finds its way to the Custodian Bank in circuitous ways and this often causes huge settlement delays in the local market. The IM and the B/D have not always agreed on the net amounts that will be paid at the local market. This will cause unmatched instructions in the local market, requiring the agents to go back to their clients and causing a delay in the settlement process.

B. Needs of Custodian Banks

B.1. Short-term

1. Custodian Banks need to control and subsequently reduce unit cost per trade settlement and any fixed overheads associated with the business.

2. Custodian Banks need to have ready access to all information at the soonest possible time through effective distribution to all business areas.
3. Custodian Banks need to be able to process increasing settlement volumes generated both through both business growth and market volatility, with minimal impact on systems, procedures and organization.
4. Custodian Banks need to actively manage stock and cash inventory to minimize financing costs and capital allocation requirements.
5. Custodian Banks need to reduce exposure to external risks (counterparty, market) by effective management and control on trading positions and transactions management.
6. Custodian Banks need the ability to produce a competitive and standard business SLA for the IM client. This includes to ability to proactively monitor performance internally.

B.2. Medium term

1. Custodian Banks need to quickly integrate new business (i.e., new clients) with minimal disruption and cost.
2. Custodian Banks need to actively monitor and manage the business performance (in 'real-time') by use of MIS and performance metrics thus being able to identify problem areas before they become a client problem.
3. Custodian Banks need to be able to create and integrate new products and business lines very quickly and at a minimal cost.
4. Custodian Banks need to minimize internal operational risks through effective use of information and automation. Goal is to find one single standardized automated interface reducing the manual input and repair to an absolute minimum.

B.3. Long term

1) Custodian Banks need to consolidate and integrate systems to provide global support of the business.
2) Custodian Banks need to be able to integrate changes to market practices without undue effect/cost on the ongoing business.
3) Custodian Banks need to reduce market and counterparty risk through reduction of settlement cycles.

C. Solutions and Benefits offered by VMUs to Custodian Banks

C.1. Business (trade cycle)

1. VMUs will harmonize the input across markets and products for Custodian Banks. VMS's will form a common denominator across markets/countries and instrument types. The problem of having different procedures will be reduced. The need to reduce integration of market practices without excessive cost will be achieved.
2. VMS's will feed the information much faster into the Custodian Bank. Also, the accuracy of the information will be much higher (match net proceeds, settlement info directly from counterparty, etc.). And, potentially, the settlement instructions from

global VMS's can be forwarded to the local market to effect settlement. This will make settlement efficiency much higher and the contractual settlement problem will be much smaller. Several needs of Custodian Banks will be addressed as a result: The early information will allow Custodian Banks to actively manage stock and financing needs; the exposure to external risks can be better managed through better control of positions), and better client SLAs can be put place.

3. VMUs will provide Custodian Banks a channel for communicating trade-relevant as well as accounting-relevant information. It will funnel all the information that is required for a specific service through one electronic gateway, allowing the Custodian Bank to create one platform on which they can develop the different product types. This addresses the problem of current trade communication channels not being equipped to support the different information capture requirements. This will also address the need for Custodian Banks to be able to integrate new products into the trade-processing regime at minimal cost.

4. Costs for Custodian Banks are reduced through the use of a VMU, as follows:
   - The funding cost for exposures and financing will be reduced through higher settlement efficiency, reduction of failed trades and a concomitant reduction of credit needs.
   - The operational cost will be reduced through the use of one standard, one electronic fully-STP compliant interface, and a reduction of repairs, cancellations and corrections of settlement instructions.
   - The resources required to handle the same volume will be reduced as well. The automatic handling of transactions will significantly reduce the Custodian Bank's administrative needs.

5. Risk is reduced for Custodian Banks through the use of a VMU, as follows:
   - Market risk is reduced by agreeing on all trade details at the earliest opportunity. Problems are identified before the settlement goes forward. This facilitates the move to shorter settlement cycles.
   - Operational risk is reduced by automation and the use of a common central VMU – used by all parties to the transaction. The subsequent ability to centralize operations and reduce manual intervention and paper / e-mail flows will be significant. Capacity constraints are also relieved with more automation.
   - Counterparty risk can be alleviated by ensuring prompt settlement (i.e. reduced fails), thereby minimizing the exposure to a counterparty on any one trade to the minimum period allowed by the market in question.
   - Systemic risk is minimized by using a proven, secure, reliable network and central 'industry strength' software.

6. Because operations can happen in a more automatic manner and the quality of operational information will be much higher, there will be an opportunity for the Custodian Bank to increase the reconciliation possibilities for its IM clients. Time can be spent on problem solving for the client.

7. The VMU will create new product opportunities for the Custodian Banks. Faster and better information input allows the Custodian Banks to create real-time performance and compliance measurement services. The availability of higher lending pools (through the more effective settlement) will create a potential revenue stream for both the IM client and the Custodian Banks.

8. If the commoditized settlement business is automated, it will be much easier to add new markets and instrument types for Custodian Banks. When the IM client demands settlement in new areas, the Custodian Bank will be able to roll this out in a shorter cycle than under today's processing model.

C.2. Operational/Administrative

1. A Custodian Bank's staff-needs can be reduced and manual bottlenecks can be minimized or eliminated as a result of the automation opportunities afforded by a VMU. Again, the need to reduce overhead costs per trade can be met and the need to minimize internal operational risks can be reached. Also, Custodian Banks will be able to cater for increased trading volumes with minimal impact on the internal systems.
2. VMUs will potentially be the only input mechanism for cross-border, as well as domestic, institutional trades. VMUs will reduce the wide variety of input mechanisms currently employed by Custodian Banks.
3. VMUs will match trades and will solve all discrepancies before releasing the instructions for local market settlement. This will reduce mismatch delays currently suffered by Custodian Banks and hence, will allow for improved transaction management. This will help Custodian Banks to increase operational efficiency, while reducing operational risk.

C.3. Systems

1. The Custodian Bank's system requirements can be rationalized by increased integration onto one platform can be attained through the use of a VMU. Consolidation of internal databases with financial instrument information and transaction records can be merged.
2. VMUs will provide an electronic communication platform for Custodian Banks. A set of electronic messages can be accepted, processed and distributed internally within custodial systems, thereby reducing input bottlenecks and manual overhead problems. This also addresses the Custodian Bank's need to have one single standardized interface to IM clients.
3. VMUs will work in a real-time fashion. Through the VMU, all participants will have to reorganize their processing in order to enforce a real-time communication flow. The Custodian Bank's need for real-time performance measuring and more effective management and control on trading positions and transactions management will be catered for.
4. The information that a VMU will feed into the Custodian Bank will be automatically verified. This information will have to come in a standard computer-readable way and will be of high quality. As a result, the Custodian Bank's problem of having bad or non-consistent and poor quality information will be minimized.
5. A Custodian Bank's volatility dependence will be reduced through the use of a VMU, as they will be better able to absorb transaction volume increases resulting from both business expansion (new products lines (markets/securities) and business growth (new clients).

C.4. Other

1. Through the real-time availability of information afforded by a VMU, MIS systems can be created by Custodian Banks to follow up very closely the day-to-day operations, and the emphasis can go to exception processing and problem solving.
2. A VMU will require the Custodian Bank to feed settlement information for its side of the settlement chain. In this way, the Custodian Bank is sure that the B/D knows

where to deliver/receive the securities. The Custodian Bank no longer needs to rely on its IM client to forward this information to the B/D.

3. Automation delivered by the VMU will allow for a standard SLA to be agreed with IMs and B/Ds.

4. The VMU will give the Custodian Bank the ability, through MIS and other benchmarking, to pro-actively monitor the performance of IMs and B/Ds in a consistent manner, providing a fair and independent evaluation of performance.

GLOSSARY

Term	Description
Account	The client or entity owning a portfolio of securities.
Accrued Interest	The amount of interest due the seller from the buyer upon settlement of a bond trade. Prorated interest due since the last interest payment date. Commonly used methods of calculating interest are 30/360, Actual/365 day (366 in leap year) and Actual/Actual day
Active Box	A physical location where securities are held awaiting action.
Actual Settlement Date	This is the date the trade or transaction actually settles (it may not be the same as the contractual settlement date.)
Ad Valorum	The Latin term meaning according to value refers to a way of assessing tax. An Ad Valorum tax or duty is based on the value of an item rather than its quantity.
Affirmation	The custodian or investor's assent to settlement terms that have already been agreed and ratified by the buying and selling brokers.
After Hours Trading	Trading based on rules and terms of equity, futures or terminal market after the official close of the market.
Aftermarket	A market for a security either over the counter or on an exchange after an initial public offering has been made. A term also used to describe trading in securities after the official close of the market.
Aged Fail	An incomplete contract between two broker/dealers. A contract becomes an aged fail if it remains unsettled after 30 days from the time that delivery and payment should have been completed.
Agent Bank	Bank appointed by an Institution, Broker or Bank as their representative for execution, clearance, settlement and custody of securities. See Global Custodian Bank and Sub-Custodian Bank.
Agents of Change	Associations that promote change to reduce risk, enhance processing, or provide better functionality to the financial services industry.
Amendment Date	A company amends the date a corporate action. There can be multiple occurrences of Amendment Dates
American Depository Receipt (ADR)	A security that represents shares of foreign stock or bonds. A negotiable receipt for foreign securities held by the foreign correspondent bank of an American Depository Bank. ADR are usually denominated in a ratio to the overseas stock, where one overseas share equals a multiple denomination of ADR.
And Interest	A bond transaction in which the buyer pays the seller a contract price plus interest accrued since the corporation's last interest payment.

319

GLOSSARY

Term	Description
Announcement Date	Public disclosure by an entity of an upcoming event such as a dividend payable, rights offerings, stock split, or exercising a call on a bond.
Annual Report	A formal statement issued yearly by a corporation to its shareowners. It shows assets, liabilities, equity, revenues, expenses, and so forth. It is a reflection of the corporation's condition at the close of the business year and the results of operations for that year.
As Agent	The role of a broker/dealer firm when it acts as an intermediary, or broker, between its customer and another customer, a market maker, or a contra-broker. For this service the firm receives a stated commission or fee. May also be referred to as an agency transaction. See As Principal.
As Principal	The role of a broker/dealer firm when it buys and sells for its own account. In a typical transaction, it buys from a market maker or contra-broker and sells to a customer at a fair and reasonable markup; if it buys from a customer and sells to the market maker at a higher price, the trade includes a markdown. See As Agent.
Asset Backed Security	A security that is backed by a specific type of asset, i.e., mortgages, car loans, credit card loans, or commodities.
Auction Marketplace	A term used to describe an organized exchange where transactions are held in the open and any exchange member present may join in.
Audit	Independent review of business, operational, and financial processes, procedures, and controls to ensure that they are adequate and are operating in a satisfactory manner.
Back Office	An industry expression used to describe non-sales departments of a brokerage firm:
Back Valued Trades	Taking money for a past period to largely offset a funding error cost incurred as a result of a failed trade or failure to make a payment.
Bad Delivery	A delivery of securities that does not fulfill the requirements.
Base Currency	Currency against which exchange rates are normally quoted in a given currency or country, e.g., the Argentine Peso or Great Britian's Pound Sterling.
Bear Market	A securities market characterized by declining prices. See Bull Market.

GLOSSARY

Term	Description
Bearer Form	Securities issued in such a form as not to allow for the owner's name to be imprinted on the security. The bearer of the security is presumed to be the owner who collects interest by clipping and depositing coupons semiannually. Income is usually payable upon coupon presentation.
Beneficial Owner	The entity, which receives the benefits of ownership (such as income) and exercises ultimate control over the asset's holding or disposal. Often used to refer to an investor whose name is registered on the face of securities, books of the issuer, or security account at a central depository or central bank. Depending on local regulations, the registered beneficial owner could be the principal custodian or investment manager of the portfolio or plan. (See Registration and Nominee).
BIC Code	The Bank Identification Code used to identify the Settlement Agent and Bank
Big Bang	The term applied to the date when major changes occur in a market place. E.g., when markets abandon fixed commission in favor of negotiated commissions.
Bilateral Netting	When all trades executed on the same day in the same security are netted between two counter-parties at the end of the day and one movement of securities and cash is made.
Bill	A short-term, discounted debt obligation with three-month to one-year terms to maturity.
Blotter	A book or individual unit used as a record of original entry to record transactions as they occur. It covers purchases, sales, cash receipts and disbursements, and securities received and delivered.
Board Lot	The standard unit of shares commonly traded in the market. Share amounts that are fractions of a board lot are referred to as odd lots, and may not be readily negotiable. Certificates are also sometimes issued in multiples of a board lot, particularly where taxes or transaction charges vary with the number of certificates. These can be called jumbo lots and, like odd lots, may be less liquid than standard board lots. Also called "round lots" or unit of trading
Bond	A certificate representing credit in a corporation and issued by the corporation to raise capital as an alternative to issuing equity. To the company, it represents debt to the investor. The company pays interest on a bond issue at specified dates and eventually redeems it at maturity, paying principal plus interest due. Bonds issued in some countries have nicknames, i.e., Bulldog (UK), Shogun and Samurai (Japan).

GLOSSARY

Term	Description
Bonus issue	Issue by a company of shares to existing shareholders and for which cash payment is not required.
Book Closure Date	Most often used in the context of entitlements and voting privileges, it is the day by which a change of registration must be submitted to the company registrar in order for the new registrant to receive an upcoming entitlement or corporate action directly from the issuer, or issuer's agent. Failed delivery of a security traded cum-entitlement after book closure does not change the buyer's right to the entitlement, but it does normally mean that the buyer must make a separate claim for value lost against the broker who failed to deliver in time or the last registered shareholder.
Book Entry	A certificate-less environment whereby positions are held by an entity rather than issuing a physical certificate.
Bourse	Term used for Securities exchange, grain exchange, or exchange dealing in other commodities.
Broker	An agent, often a member of a stock exchange firm or the head of a member firm, who executes public orders to buy and sell securities and commodities, for which service a commission is charged..
Bull Market	A securities market characterized by rising prices. See Bear Market.
Buy In	The action taken by the buying broker or the stock exchange to acquire on the open market the securities which the selling broker failed to deliver on time. Buy-ins can happen as early as the end of contractual settlement day, or any time thereafter. Although most markets have established buy-in procedures, some markets invoke them more stringently than others. As a rule, the party at fault must bear all costs, e.g., commissions, fees, penalties, and rise in prices, but is not entitled to any price differential in its own favor. Buy-ins usually settle on the cash market, if one exists, with a shorter settlement time frame than normal settlements. A buy-in is a severe consequence of trade failure. (See Sell-Out for a definition of the reverse action).
Buy Side	Institutional investors who purchase and sell securities for their client portfolios. The term is used to describe those firms that are trading securities through broker/dealers, the "sell side".
Capital Markets	The markets in which corporate securities (equity and debt) are traded, as opposed to money markets in which short-term debt instruments are traded.

GLOSSARY

Term	Description
Cash Dividend	Any payment made to a corporation's shareholders in cash from current earnings or accumulated profits. Cash dividends are usually subject to tax
Cash Trade	A transaction involving specific securities, in which the settlement date is the same as the trade date.
Central Securities Depository CSD	A facility for holding physical or dematerialized securities to effect transfers between accounts, typically by book-entry. Most securities depositories operate clearing systems among their participants and have some means to move cash in parallel to the securities. A depository may also provide pre-settlement matching, and often distributes income and entitlements. In registered markets, the depository generally serves as central common nominee. In bearer markets it is the largest (or sole) holder of securities.
Certificate	A paper document attesting to the holder's ownership of an issuer's stock or debt obligation. It is required for settlement and often also for collection of income. A certificate may be bearer or registered. Depending on the country, a certificate may indicate the name of the issuer, specific type of the share/debt, serial number, interest rate (if debt), quantity (number of shares or par value of debt), name and address of shareholder, paying agent, and tax-related information such as country of domicile of beneficial owner. Coupons, if any, are normally attached to the certificate but may also be issued separately.
Clearance	Preparation for settlement of a trade, arranging for shares and funds required for settlement. May also include guarantee funds and netting.
Clearing Bank	A bank that provides services for their custodial accounts, such as holding inventory positions, receiving and delivering securities, and disbursing funds.
Clearing Broker	A broker who clears and settles trades on behalf of an executing broker.
Clearing House	The central location for comparing and matching security transactions of members to determine quantities to be received or delivered.
Clearing Price	Daily price at which a clearinghouse clears all trades and settles all contracts between members for each contract month.
Collateral	Securities or Funds that are pledged to guarantee trade settlement and other financial obligations

GLOSSARY

Term	Description
Confirmation	An announcement of transaction terms and conditions and other pertinent information that is prepared for customer trade activities. It serves as a bill for customer purchases and as an advisory notice for sales.
Contra-broker (Contra Side)	A term used to describe the broker with whom a trade was made.
Contractual Settlement Date	The date a trade or transaction is contracted to settle (may not be the same as actual settlement date.)
Corporate Actions	Restructuring the ownership of the company generally through an action such a stock split or conversion.
Counterparty	One party to a trade legally bound to make a good delivery or a good payment.
Country Risk	Risk of lending funds to or making an investment in a particular country
Coupon	The interest payment on a debt instrument. Generally occurring annually or semi-annually.
Credit Rating	Quantification or classification of a borrower's ability to come up with future payments of interest and repayment of principal on a particular debt (debt service), based on a "credit analysis". Also used loosely to describe a company's general creditworthiness.
Credit Risk	The risk that a party will default on its settlement obligation for either full or partial value.
Cross Border Trading	Trading which takes place between persons or entities from different countries.
Cross Currency Settlement Risk	Currency risk associated with a cross-border transaction due to the timing difference between foreign exchange settlements.
Cross Rate	The exchange rate between two foreign currencies. The U.S. dollar is used in determining the cross rate. For example, to exchange Japanese Yen for Singapore Dollars, you would sell Yen against the US dollar and the buy Singapore dollars versus US Dollars..
Cum Capitalization (Cum New)	The share price including free shares issued to shareholders under a capitalization issue.
Cum Coupon	The situation where the purchaser of a bond is entitled to receive the next interest payment.
Cum Dividend	A term applied to stock at a time when the purchaser will be entitled to a forthcoming dividend.
Cum Rights	A term applied to a stock trading in the marketplace with subscription rights attached, which is reflected in the price of that security.

GLOSSARY

Term	Description
Custodian	A person or institution legally charged with the responsibility of safeguarding the property of another. See Global and Sub-Custodian.
Custody	Safekeeping of securities for institutions and individuals generally including settlement of trades, collection of income, and processing of corporate actions
Dated Date	With regard to bonds and other debt instruments, the date from which interest is determined to accrue, upon the sale of the security. The buyer pays the amount equal to the interest accrued from the dated date to the settlement date and is reimbursed with the first interest payment on the security.
Dealer	An individual or firm in the securities business acting as a principal rather than as an agent. See As Agent; As Principal.
Delivery Date	The day delivery of securities is made, which may be on or subsequent to settlement date.
Delivery Instructions	Delivery information for a trade, used in settlement that indicates where securities should be delivered or received.
Delivery Versus Payment	The purchase of securities in a cash account with instructions that payment will be made simultaneously upon the delivery of the securities, sometimes to the contra broker but usually to an agent bank.
Dematerialization	The elimination of physical documents as evidence of ownership for securities, so that records exist only as electronic data. This environment is also referred to as paperless or scriptless.
Denomination	The smallest unit that can be bought or sold of a debt instrument.
Depositary Receipt	Receipt for the shares of a foreign-based issue held in a local country and marketed to investors instead of the underlying stocks. All related transactions are in the local currency.
Derivatives	Financial contracts whose value is determined by the market price of the underlying instrument, which could be a bond issue, a company's shares, a currency, an index figure, an interest rate, a commodity, etc.
Dividend	Distributions to stockholders declared by the corporate Board of Directors. There are several special conditions for dividends, some of which are country specific.
Dividend Payable	A current liability showing the amount due to stockholders for dividends declared but not yet paid.
Dividend Payout	The percentage of dividends distributed in terms of what is available out of current net income.

GLOSSARY

Term	Description
DK	A slang expression for Don't Know, as applied to a securities transaction on which transactional data are missing when the brokers exchange comparison sheets.
Double Tax Treaty	An agreement between two countries to off-set the tax paid on income. The treaty stipulates the maximum amount of tax (called the reduced treaty rate) that should be paid on dividend or interest income. See withholding tax
DVP	See Delivery Versus Payment.
Electronic Settlement Database	An electronic database that contains Broker Delivery Instructions and Standard Settlement Instructions. The Instructions are used by the parties to the trade in the settlement of the trade.
End Date	Last day of a period, i.e., interest payment period, last day a corporate action may be taken or the maturity date for a bond..
Eurobond	Bonds issued outside the country of the borrower and denominated in a currency that is generally not that of the issuer's country. Normally sold on international markets by groups or syndicates in units equivalent to one thousand US dollars. Custody and settlements take place through the international clearing systems (Euroclear and Clearstream). The market is regulated by the ISMA (Interactive Securities Markets Association) in Zurich, Switzerland.
Ex Div	Ex dividend, excluding the right to the current dividend on a share. The opposite is cum dividend.
Ex-Distribution	The security is trading so that the buyer will not be entitled to a distribution that is to be made to holder.
Executing Broker	The broker executing a trade on his or her own behalf (as principal) or on the behalf of a client (as agent).
Execution	Synonym for a transaction or trade between a buyer and seller.
Execution Report	A report that confirms the details of a trade and that is generated after a match is made (trader vs. contra side) and systematically routed to the originating branch.
Expiration Date	The date an option contract becomes void. The expiration date for some listed stock options is the Saturday after the third Friday of the expiration month. All holders of options who wish to exercise must indicate their desire to do so by this date.
Ex-Rights	A term applied to stocks trading in the marketplace for which the value of the subscription privilege has already been deducted and which therefore no longer bears such a right; it is literally trading rights off.

GLOSSARY

Term	Description
Ex-Warrants	The security is trading so that the buyer will not be entitled to warrants that are to be distributed to holders.
Fail	A security transaction, which does not settle per its contract terms because of a failure by one of the counter parties to meet their obligation.
Fail to Deliver	A situation in which the selling broker/dealer does not receive securities from the client in time to make delivery with the buying broker/dealer.
Fail to Receive	A situation in which the buying broker/dealer has not received the securities from the selling firm.
Failed Trade	A securities transaction that does not settle on contracted settlement date because one of the settlement parties does not meet the settlement conditions. A failed trade may have negative consequences for the party at fault, including buy-ins, sell-outs and penalties.
Financial Information Exchange (FIX)	Financial Information Exchange, a proposed standard for communicating order and trade information between investors and brokers.
Foreign Currency	The currencies of individual countries other than the local currency.
Foreign Exchange (FX) Rates?	Foreign exchange rates refer to the number of units of one currency needed to buy another
Foreign Exchange (FX):	The exchange of one currency for another at an agreed upon price and value date. See Forward Rate and Spot Rate.
Forward Rate	A commitment to buy or sell a currency at a specific price to settle on a date greater than two business days after the trade date.
Gilts	British and Irish government securities, as well as other British authorities. In the secondary market, gilts may trade on the London Stock Exchange.
Global Custodian Bank	The agent bank designated by Institutions, Brokers and other Banks to clear and settle trades and hold securities in custody via their global network of affiliates or agents. See Sub-Custodian Bank and Custody
Global Custody	Providing custody services on an international basis. Generally, it involves setting up an agent bank (sub-custodian) network in many countries.
Group of Thirty	An international economic consortium, which studies worldwide economic situations and makes recommendations to benefit the world economy.

GLOSSARY

Term	Description
IMF	International Monetary Fund. A specialized agency of the UN .It provides funds to member countries under certain conditions of need and commitments of policy. The Bretton Woods Agreement on a system of differential quota subscriptions representing drawing rights and voting power established the fund.
Immobilization	The practice of using physical certificates as evidence of total ownership, while recording the specific investors' proportional holding by book-entry. Immobilization may be based on fungible certificates (which can sometimes be withdrawn for physical holding) or on jumbo certificates.
Indication of Interest	An expression of consideration by an underwriter's circle of customers for investment in a new security expected to be offered soon. It is not a binding commitment on the customer or the underwriter.
Institution	A large organization engaged in investing in securities, such as a bank, insurance company, mutual fund, or pension fund. An institutional broker buys and sells securities for any of the above dealing in large volumes and charging a lower-than-usual per unit commission. An institutional investor is any of the institutions above who buy and sell securities. An institutional house is any brokerage firm dealing with such institutions. Institutional sales are sales of any type of securities by such institutions.
Institutional Investor	Investor of large holdings of collective assets (pension funds, insurance companies, investment funds, etc.) or of corporate assets.
International Central Securities Depository ISCD	A transnational depository that provides financial institutions with a book-entry settlement and depository system for internationally traded securities. It may also provide domestic clearing and depository services as Clearstream does for the Luxembourg Stock Exchange.
ISDA	International Swap Dealers Association.
ISIN	International Securities Identification Numbering system designed by the International Organization for Standardization (ISO) and advocated by the Group of 30; increasingly accepted by worldwide securities markets as international industry standard for cross-border transactions. The ISIN code is a 12-character code that includes an ISO country code, the local code of the national numbering agency (such as CUSIP in the U.S. and Canada), and a check digit.
ISMA	International Securities Market Association Eurobond rule-making association.

GLOSSARY

Term	Description
Issuer	A corporation, trust, or governmental agency engaged in the distribution of its securities. Also known as originator.
Locked-in Trade	A trade that is matched at the point of execution and does not require further comparison of the trade details
Markdown	The fee charged by a broker/dealer acting as a dealer when he or she buys a security from a customer and sells it at a higher price to a market maker. The fee, or markdown, is included in the sale price and is not itemized separately in the confirmation.
Market Data Vendors	Providers of security indicative data, prices, income and corporate action event information, general and financial market news; local market trading and settlement practices.
Market Maker	An exchange member who trades for their own account and risk. This member is charged with the responsibility of trading so as to maintain a fair, orderly, and competitive market. They may not act as agent. A firm actively making bids and offers in the listed or OTC market.
Market Order	An order to be executed immediately at the best available price.
Markup	The fee charged by a broker/dealer acting as a dealer when he or she buys a security from a market maker and sells it to a customer at a higher price. The fee, or markup, is included in the sale price and is not itemized separately in the confirmation.
Maturity Date	The date on which a loan, bond, debenture, or other debt security comes due; both principal and accrued interest due must be paid at this time.
Merger	The friendly and voluntary union of two corporations.
Multicurrency	A loan or bond issue involving several currencies. A bond issue may be made in a specific currency but repayable in several. A rollover credit may be available in different currencies to suit the borrower.
Multi-currency Accounting	Systems that tracks global securities and cash investments. May include tax-lot accounting permitting sell versus, income tracking and local tax reporting. System maintains individual denominations of securities and currencies but also converts to user's base currency for information and reporting purposes.
Multilateral Netting	A netting agreement involving more than two counterparties, which may imply a joint, and several guaranty as a member of a multilateral netting organization, such as a clearinghouse.

GLOSSARY

Term	Description
Netting	An automated clearing process whereby sequences of transactions in a single issue of securities are consolidated and then reduced into a small number of delivery obligations. The CNS (Continuous Net Settlement) system allows the netting of transactions for a given settlement date against all open positions from prior settlement dates, as well as the automated transmission of instructions for the book-entry delivery.
Nominee Name	The name of a legal entity (a depository, bank or broker) that is used to register securities. This type of registration eliminates the need to re-register a certificate each time it is traded or transferred.
Odd Lot	Amount of a security held or traded that is less than the normal trading unit.
Ordinary Dividend	Part of the profit accruing to the ordinary capital, which is distributed to its holders.
Ordinary Shares	see stock
Organization of Petroleum Exporting Countries (OPEC)	Formed in 1960, its members are Algeria, Ecuador, Gabon, Indonesia, Iran, Iraq, Kuwait, Libya, Kuwait, Libya, Nigeria, Qatar, Saudi Arabia, United Arab Emirates, and Venezuela. It controls around half of the world's oil trade and sets an official price for crude oil, which may dictate world price levels.
Original Maturity	Time to maturity of a security at the date on which it was issued.
Over-the-Counter Market	The market for securities transactions conducted through a communications network connecting dealers in stocks and bonds.
Over-the-Counter Option (OTC)	A market, conducted mainly over the telephone, for securities made up of dealers who may or may not be members of a securities exchange. Thousands of companies have insufficient shares outstanding, stockholders, or earnings to warrant listing on a national exchange. Securities of these companies are therefore traded in the over-the-counter market between dealers who act neither as agents for their customers or as principals. The over-the-counter market is the principal market for U.S. government and municipal bonds and for stocks of banks and insurance companies. A market for options traded directly between buyer and seller, unlike a listed stock option. These options have no secondary market and no standardization of striking prices and expiration dates.
Pari Passu	Latin for on par, the designation signifies that new shares rank the same as old shares in all respects. The precise status of new shares relative to existing shares may be determined by the company or by regulatory practice. A new issue's entitlement status is almost always described in detail in the prospectus or offering statement.

GLOSSARY

Term	Description
Prime Brokerage	Prime brokerage accounts are used by hedge funds, funds of funds managers, professional traders, and high net worth individuals. This service allows for clients to execute trades through several different broker/dealers and settle and centralize their assets all in one place.
Principal Trade	Any transaction in which the dealer or dealer bank affecting the trade takes over ownership of the securities.
Proprietary	A term applied to the assets of a brokerage firm and those of its principals that have been specifically pledged as their capital contribution to the organization.
Proprietary Trading	Generally used to describe risk positions for an institution's own account as principal and distinct from client business.
Proxy	Written authority to act or speak for an absent shareholder at shareholder meetings. Depending on the regulations of the market, the party acting on behalf of the shareholder may be a nominee, custodian, lawyer, broker, or local representative.
Rating	As assessment of the ability and willingness of a borrower to pay. Prepared by specialized "rating agencies" (such as Standard & Poor's and Moody's) based on a credit investigation of a borrower's ability to service and repay a specific issue.
Rating Agency	Organization that assigns a quality rating to companies and or governments that issues securities (debt or equity); investors to determine the risk of an investment use this data. The most often cited are Moody's Investor's Service and Standard & Poor's Corporation.
Receive Versus Payment (RVP)	The long sale of securities in a cash account with the instructions to pay the seller upon the delivery of the securities to the broker/dealer.
Reclamation	The privilege of a seller in a transaction to recover his or her certificates and return the contract money, or of a buyer to recover his or her contract money and return the certificates, should any irregularity be discovered upon delivery and settlement of the contract.

GLOSSARY

Term	Description
Reclamation / Reclaim	The process by which a non-resident investor obtains a refund of taxes previously withheld from income when the taxes were withheld in error, or the investor is qualified for local tax reduction under the provisions of a double-taxation treaty. Some tax authorities require individual reclamation filing for each dividend and after each payment, while others allow for yearly filing for the aggregate reclamation amount. Some markets do not allow for reclamation. These markets make the benefits of double taxation agreements available only by reduced withholding, which must be requested prior to the income payment. See Double Tax Treaty and Withholding Tax
Record Date	The date named by an issuer for the purpose of determining investor entitlements. In general, shareholders or bondholders officially recorded on the registrar's or depository's books on record date will receive the next scheduled entitlement, or in the case of voting shareholders, will be allowed to vote. The record date may, or may not, coincide with the book closure date. Record date need not be a business date, and may fall on a weekend or national holiday.
Redemption Provision	There are a number of conditions or provisions, which could impact redemption, i.e., Borrower (issuer) in default, Redemption linked to an economic or other index, debt repurchased based on contingency clause.
Refunding (Refinancing)	The issuance of a new debt security, using the proceeds to redeem either older bonds at maturity or outstanding bonds issued under less favorable terms and conditions.
Registered Bond	A bond registered in the owner's name on the books of the issuing corporation. To transfer ownership, the registered owner or representative must endorse the bond.
Registered Form	A term applied to securities that are issued in a form allowing the owner's name to be imprinted on the certificate and that allow the issuer to maintain records as to the identity of the owners. Opposite of bearer form.
Registrar	The registrar is responsible for keeping track of the owners and issuance of stocks and bonds. Working with the Transfer agent, the registrar keeps current files of the owners of issued securities. The registrar verifies that no more than the authorized amount of stock is in circulation and certifies that a bond is a government's/ corporation's genuine debt obligation.

GLOSSARY

Term	Description
Registration	The recording of ownership of securities by the issuer's registrar or transfer agent, or a central depository. Actual registration may take the form of stamping on the certificates or, in a market with a central depository; registration may be defined as the name of the account at the depository. Registration attests to ownership and all shareholder entitlements, which are generally protected upon timely receipt of shares by the registration authority, provided that the eventual registration can be successfully completed. Registration applications can be rejected because of defective shares, incorrect share identification, non compliance with the registration procedures, etc., as well as unavailability of foreign ownership allocation in companies subject to ownership restrictions. In many countries, foreign investors must declare their identity, although the same may not be required of local residents. Local regulations and conditions determine the length and cost of registration. In most markets, physical securities in the registration process cannot be sold. (See Nominee).
Regular Way Contract (Delivery)	The most frequently used delivery contract. For stocks and corporate and municipal bonds, this type of contract calls for delivery on the third business day after the trade.
Rejection	The privilege of the purchaser in a transaction to refuse a delivery lacking in negotiability or presented in the wrong denominations, without prejudice to his or her rights in the transaction.
Reorganization Department	The department in a brokerage firm responsible for effecting the conversion of securities, as well as completing the execution of rights and warrants, tender offers, and other types of conversions. For example, when a customer who owns convertible bonds wishes to convert them and use them to fulfill a sale of the underlying common stocks, the reorganization department would accomplish the conversion.
Repurchase Agreement (Repo)	An arrangement in which a dealer contracts to purchase a government or agency security at a fixed price, with provision for its resale at the same price at a rate of interest determined competitively. Used by dealers in government and corporate securities to reduce carrying costs. A method of financing inventory positions by sale to a non-bank institution with the agreement to buy the position back.
Retail Investor	Individuals investing in the securities generally through a broker.
Reverse Repurchase Agreement (Repo)	A transaction by which a broker/dealer provides funds to customers by means of purchasing a security with a contract to resell it at the same price plus interest.

GLOSSARY

Term	Description
Rights	The opportunity given a shareholder by a company to buy additional shares at a discounted price for a limited time. Rights may, or may not, be transferable or negotiable. In some countries, companies cannot honor all subscription requests and the eventual exercise of rights may be subject to the company's allotment. Rights differ from warrants in that they must be exercised within a relatively short time frame.
Risk	The variability of value. In investing, risk can be credit risk, principal risk, inflation risk or interest rate risk, to name a few. The type of risk incurred by a shareholder varies from financial instrument to financial instrument.
RTGS	Acronym for Real Time Gross Settlement. RTGS is the immediate processing of DVP trade instructions on the settlement date.
Samurai Bond	A bond denominated in Japanese YEN and issued in the Japanese capital market by a foreign borrower.
Security	A transferable instrument evidencing ownership or creditor-ship, such as a note, stock or bond, evidence of debt, interest or participation in a profit-sharing agreement, investment contract, voting trust certificate, fractional undivided interest in oil, gas, or other mineral rights, or any warrant to subscribe to, or purchase, any of the foregoing or other similar instruments.
Security Identification Code	Securities are identified by coding schemes specific to countries, i.e., U.K. seven character Tradable Instrument Display Mnemonic (SEDOL), Belgium uses up to 6 alphanumeric characters, Canada uses up to 8 alphabetic characters, Japan uses 9 alphanumeric characters, one character security type, five character issuer code, and 3 character issue code (QUICK).
SEDOL	The local numbering system used on the London Stock Exchange to identify securities on the Stock Exchange Daily.
Segregate	To keep customer securities physically separate from those owned by the broker/dealers.
Sell Out	The action taken by the broker or the exchange when the buying broker has not paid for the trade by a determined number of days after settlement. The bought securities are sold and any money difference is charged back to the buyer. See Buy-in for the reverse action
Sell Short	To sell securities that one does not own. Typically, the seller's brokerage firm arranges to borrow stock to make delivery to the buyer, until the seller closes the position by purchasing stock and turning it over to the brokerage firm.

GLOSSARY

Term	Description
Sell Side	The sell side is used to describe broker/dealers. They buy and sell securities for their clients. Their clients are typically retail investors and institutional investors. Institutional Investors are the "buy side".
Settlement	The exchange of value. In a securities trade it represents the delivery of the securities and the purchase payment amount
Settlement Date	Date on which securities and payment are exchanged and credited to proper accounts. If securities are debited from the seller's account one or more days prior to being credited to the buyer's account, or if securities and cash move at different times, the date on which securities are received by the buyer, which in most cases is also the value date of the payment, is commonly perceived as the settlement date. In general, the term refers to the contracted settlement date. The actual settlement date, as opposed to the contracted settlement date, may be delayed in the settlement process.
Share	A stock certificate-a unit of measurement of the equity ownership of a corporation.
Shareholder	An investor; the owner of shares of a mutual fund or the owner of shares of corporate stock.
Short Position	The number of shares in a given security sold short and not covered as of a particular date. A term used to denote the writer of an option.
Society for Worldwide Interbank Telecommunications (SWIFT)	An electronic funds transfer (EFT) network that sends payment instructions between financial institutions around the world. SWIFT employs an elaborate message formatting protocol, which allows its user to explicitly define the details of a message in a standardized manner, i.e., delivery terms, security terms, payment terms.
Sovereign Risk	Risk of lending too much results in banks normally observing limits on the amount of lending they will make to any single government or organization whose borrowing is guaranteed by that government. Such a sovereign risk is, however, more acceptable than one incurred on a loan not subject to a government guarantee.
Spin Off	A distribution of stock in a company that is owned by another corporation and that is being allocated to the holders of the latter institution.

GLOSSARY

Term	Description
Split	A corporate action giving a stockowner more shares of stock at a lower price. A division of outstanding shares of a corporation into a large number of shares, by which each outstanding share entitles its owner to a fixed number of new shares. Individual shareholders' overall equity remains the same, but they own more stock, since the total value of the shares remains the same. For example, in a two-for-one split, the owner of 100 shares, each worth HK100, would be given 200 shares, each worth HK50.
Spot Rate	A commitment to buy or sell a currency at a specific price at a maximum of two business days after the currency trade date.
Start Date	Start date applies to a number of security specifications. The wording may be specific to the type of specification, i.e., interest rate periods start on "accrual" start dates, and "start date" is used for a corporate action such as a merger/takeover.
Stock borrowing and lending/Securities Lending	Transaction where securities are lent versus receipt of collateral. Institutions such as fund managers with large holdings in stock can earn an additional return on their portfolios by lending stock to market makers temporarily short of stock. Although considered risk free, there is a credit risk associated with this activity. Should the stock borrower face bankruptcy the lender is exposed to the full value of the stock.
Stock Dividend	Payment of income to stockholders in the form of shares of stock.
Stock Exchange	Organized trading floor for stock and share transactions.
Stocks	Certificates representing ownership in a corporation and a claim on the firm's earnings and assets; they may yield dividends and can appreciate or decline in value. See Authorized Stock; Common Stock; Issued-and-Outstanding Stock; Preferred Stock; Treasury Stock; Un-issued Stock. Generally a synonym for shares, but in the U.K., Ireland, Australia and New Zealand, can refer to debt instruments as well.
Sub-Custodian Bank	A local bank in the country of the security's issuance designated by a Global Custodian Bank to clear and settle trades and hold securities in custody in that country. Also called the Local-Custodian Bank. See Global Custodian Bank and Custody
Tender	An offer to purchase outstanding shares from current shareholders of a company at a specified price. The offer may originate from the company itself, a subsidiary or another company.

GLOSSARY

Term	Description
The Euro	The European Currency introduced on Dec 31, 1999 (for financial transactions) and Dec 31, 2001 (for all transactions). The original countries were Austria, Belgium, Finland, France, Germany, Ireland, Italy, Luxembourg, Netherlands, Portugal and Spain
The European Union	Formed in 1957 with the `Treaty of Rome,' it included the following countries: Austria, Belgium, Denmark, Finland, France, Germany, Greece, Ireland, Italy, Luxembourg, Netherlands, Portugal, Spain, Sweden and the United Kingdom.
Trading Lot	Defines the minimum, and or the maximum amount of a security traded. Usually one share for stocks. For debt securities, it is usually stated as a currency amount.
Value Date	A date attached to a particular entry of funds posted to a bank account, and intended to reflect the date on which such funds are deemed to cease to be available to the bank in the case of a debit entry, or to become available to the bank in the case of a credit entry. A value date can be different, backward or forward, from the date on which the relevant entry is posted to the account. Customarily (variances exits), where a bank serves credit interest or charges debit interest on an account, the balance of funds examined for calculating such interest is determined by compiling debit and credit entries based on their respective value dates, to determine value-dated balances. Value-dated balances may differ from book balances, including the possibility that, for example, on any day an account may simultaneously carry a negative value-dated balance (and be subject to payment of debit interest) and a positive book balance. Assignment of value dates can be driven by a variety of factors such as bank policy, market practices, adjustments of errors, and regulatory mandates.
VAT	Value Added Tax. System of taxing products on the amount of value added at each stage of their production and exchange.
Vault	A safely guarded and secure place within a bank or brokerage firm where client assets are kept.
Virtual Matching Utility	The VMU is an infrastructure for comparing and matching trade date between brokers, and brokers / Investors and transmitting the trade instructions to their respective agents and custodians. Also called central trade matching facilities

GLOSSARY

Term	Description
Warrant	A security attached to a company's debt or equity issue, or in certain cases on a stand-alone basis. Each warrant unit allows the holder to purchase a pre-determined number of the company's common stock/bond at a pre-determined price at, or within, a certain time frame (usually less than 15 years). Warrants may be detached and trade as discrete securities after separation date or they may be recalled on recall date. Warrants are like options in that they have exercise prices and dates. Warrant statistics include the issue price, the amounts issued, recalled, and outstanding, an indicator if the exercise may be for more than one security and amendment date(s) for changes to warrant terms.
Withholding Tax	Tax that is deducted from income by the country's tax authority. See Double Tax Treaty and Reclamation.
World Bank	Another name for the International Bank for Reconstruction and Development.
Yankee Bond	A dollar-denominated, foreign issued bond that is registered for sale in the U.S.

TRADERS PRESS, INC.®
PO BOX 6206
GREENVILLE, SC 29606

Publishers of:

A Complete Guide to Trading Profits (Paris)
A Professional Look at S&P Day Trading (Trivette)
A Treasury of Wall Street Wisdom (Editors: Schultz & Coslow)
Ask Mr. EasyLanguage (Tennis)
Beginner's Guide to Computer Assisted Trading (Alexander)
Channels and Cycles: A Tribute to J.M. Hurst (Millard)
Chart Reading for Professional Traders (Jenkins)
Commodity Spreads: Analysis, Selection and Trading Techniques (Smith)
Comparison of Twelve Technical Trading Systems (Lukac, Brorsen, & Irwin)
Complete Stock Market Trading and Forecasting Course (Jenkins)
Cyclic Analysis (J.M. Hurst)
Dynamic Trading (Miner)
Exceptional Trading: The Mind Game (Roosevelt)
Fibonacci Ratios with Pattern Recognition (Pesavento)
Futures Spread Trading: The Complete Guide (Smith)
Geometry of Markets (Gilmore)
Geometry of Stock Market Profits (Jenkins)
Harmonic Vibrations (Pesavento)
How to Trade in Stocks (Livermore & Smitten)
Hurst Cycles Course (J.M. Hurst)
Investing by the Stars (Weingarten)
It's Your Option (Zelkin)
Magic of Moving Averages (Lowry)
Market Rap: The Odyssey of a Still-Struggling Commodity Trader (Collins)
Pit Trading: Do You Have the Right Stuff? (Hoffman)
Planetary Harmonics of Speculative Markets (Pesavento)
Point & Figure Charting (Aby)
Point & Figure Charting: Commodity and Stock Trading Techniques (Zieg)
Private Thoughts From a Trader's Diary (Pesavento & MacKay)
Profitable Grain Trading (Ainsworth)
Profitable Patterns for Stock Trading (Pesavento)
RoadMap to the Markets (Busby)
Short-Term Trading with Price Patterns (Harris)
Single Stock Futures: The Complete Guide (Greenberg)
Stock Patterns for Day Trading (2 volumes) (Rudd)
Stock Trading Based on Price Patterns (Harris)
Study Helps in Point & Figure Techniques (Wheelan)
Technically Speaking (Wilkinson)
Technical Trading Systems for Commodities and Stocks (Patel)
The Amazing Life of Jesse Livermore: World's Greatest Stock Trader (Smitten)
The Handbook of: Global Securities Operations (O'Connell & Steiniger)
The Opening Price Principle: The Best Kept Secret on Wall Street (Pesavento & MacKay)
The Professional Commodity Trader (Kroll)
The Taylor Trading Technique (Taylor)
The Trading Rule That Can Make You Rich* (Dobson)
Top Traders Under Fire (Collins)
Trading Secrets of the Inner Circle (Goodwin)
Trading S&P Futures and Options (Lloyd)
Twelve Habitudes of Highly Successful Traders (Roosevelt)
Understanding Bollinger Bands (Dobson)
Understanding Fibonacci Numbers (Dobson)
Viewpoints of a Commodity Trader (Longstreet)
Wall Street Ventures & Adventures Through Forty Years (Wyckoff)
Winning Edge 4 (Toghraie)
Winning Market Systems (Appel)

**Please contact Traders Press to receive our current catalog describing these and
many other books and gifts of interest to investors and traders.** 800-927-8222 ~ 864-298-0222
fax 864-298-0221 ~ traderspress.com ~ customerservice@traderspress.com